T0366385

Reparative Universities

CRITICAL UNIVERSITY STUDIES
Jeffrey J. Williams and Christopher Newfield, Series Editors

Reparative Universities

Why Diversity Alone Won't Solve
Racism in Higher Ed

Ariana González Stokas

JOHNS HOPKINS UNIVERSITY PRESS   BALTIMORE

© 2023 Johns Hopkins University Press
All rights reserved. Published 2023
Printed in the United States of America on acid-free paper
9 8 7 6 5 4 3 2 1

Johns Hopkins University Press
2715 North Charles Street
Baltimore, Maryland 21218
www.press.jhu.edu

Cataloging-in-Publication Data is available from the Library of
Congress.
A catalog record for this book is available from the British Library.

ISBN: 978-1-4214-4560-1 (hardcover)
ISBN: 978-1-4214-4561-8 (ebook)

*Special discounts are available for bulk purchases of this book. For more
information, please contact Special Sales at specialsales@jh.edu.*

For my mother, Dahlia,
who refused taxonomies

In short, American colleges were not innocent or passive beneficiaries of conquest and colonial slavery. The European invasion of the Americas and the modern slave trade pulled peoples throughout the Atlantic world into each others' lives, and colleges were among the colonial institutions that braided their histories and rendered their fates dependent and antagonistic. The academy never stood apart from American slavery—in fact, it stood beside church and state as the third pillar of a civilization built on bondage. —Craig Wilder

For capitalism to die, we must actively participate in the construction of Indigenous alternatives to it.—Glen Coulthard

Capitalism cannot include and diversify its way out of white supremacy. —Sandy Grande

In the face of these conditions one can only sneak into the university and steal what one can. —Fred Moten and Stefano Harney

Contents

Prelude

As I began this project, finding the words to adequately capture what is occurring across the United States and in many other countries in response to the lynching of George Floyd by officers of the Minneapolis police in the midst of a global pandemic felt impossible. The impact of the murder on higher education in the United States has yet to fully emerge; the pandemic, the Capitol insurrection, and the antiracist movements are already leaving it forever changed. This period in history poses questions that must be answered collectively: What society lies beyond this violence? Where can we turn to develop the knowledge we need to move into a future that is radically caring and transformative of hate and oppression? Where can we dream and co-create new possibilities that are centered on care, anti-oppression, and the dismantling of systems that facilitate racism?

Colleges and universities are increasingly turning to their diversity officers to manage the impact of these events on their institutions. They are asking what to say and how to say it in order to ensure that they won't be perceived as racist. They hashtag BlackLivesMatter while retaining persistently white leadership and faculty, and they perpetuate the logic of racial capitalism. They look for the right words to signal their commitment to diversity and antiracism, yet they are reluctant to take radical, concrete actions that generate the new systems and new imaginaries that are necessary for a society in which racist systems are abolished.

Simple tinkering will not shake loose many of the oppressive legacies that corrupt higher education's systems and practices. Words like *reparation, abolition, decolonization,* and *anti-capitalism* are unimaginable as holding promise to situate institutions of higher education as locations of radical hope and social transformation. In fact, these concepts pose the risk of unraveling institutions that depend on racial capitalism for their survival. So many of our institutions do not say *yes* to the elimination of debt, to the return of land, to taking power away from persistently racist faculty. They do not say *yes* to redistributing ownership of the institutions to the workers who sustain them, nor do they say *yes* to boards of trustees composed of students, community members, staff, and faculty rather than titans of industry directly responsible for the perpetuation of racial and economic forms of exploitation.

The presidents and administrators of some institutions are making courageous moves to give space to transformative justice work in order to enact radical equity for their students. They have issued statements unprecedented in their transparency, intimacy, and rage at the murderous behavior of police in the United States. Some are, as evidenced by their statements and actions, edging toward transformative leadership, yet they are hamstrung by their boards, by students who want initiatives rather than systemic changes, and by trustees who are ultimately more concerned with brand, endowments, and reputation than with transformative social change. This moment offers colleges and universities an invitation to undertake profound transformation—transformation that requires letting go of the many privileges that the most elite among them hoard; transformation that reckons with the reality of a dying system, one that, in its efforts to survive, is once again, through the pandemic, revealing the depth of its dependence on the extraction of life in exchange for economic survival. But what can rise from all this, if we say *yes* to the workings of reparation—to the promise of its poetic endeavors—is something that I hope we all are willing to risk.

This book is an invitation to say *yes*. It is a critique of diversity work, but it is a critique offered not with contempt but with love for all of those who are struggling in this work. It is an invitation to collectively unsettle ways of knowing and existing that cannot serve the aims of building societies of nonviolence, openness, and caring. It is an offering of what reparative activity has to show us about the possibilities of educational transformation.

Introduction

Knowledge production and creation shouldn't be attributed to the efforts of one individual. I cannot take much credit for the ideas presented in this book, as they are the culmination of my own reflections on a vast collective effort to clarify coloniality, decolonization, reparations, justice work, and healing in education. I must confess upfront that I am tired of the supreme value placed on individual creation that the academy breeds and rewards. This book reveals the isolation of the administrative diversity worker concerned with exerting unsettlement, often unable to speak honestly. Isolation is always a problem and one that I have, likely, unsuccessfully navigated. I have done my best to cite all that has informed this work, yet the enormity of how everything, when one is working to create something, collaborates to help is impossible to accurately capture. To cite the world, as Edouard Glissant reminds us, is perilous, as it threatens the very opacity that, for those of us interested in a world beyond coloniality, has a right to be upheld. This book is an effort to add to the collective voices and actions seeking to contend with what to do with higher education as a colonial construction—one characterized by settler colonial logics—and as a social organism entangled with slavery.

As Sandy Grande writes in *Refusing the University*, when we theorize the academy as an arm of the settler colonial state, we can understand that at the core of its function is the reconstitution of logics such as elimination, capital accumulation, and dispossession (Grande 2018). How to unravel this reconstitution is what interests me. In the pages that follow I describe universities in North American contexts in particular as entities that have refined the reproduction of ways of knowing and existing that facilitate ongoing capitalist exploitation and the coloniality of power in the form of extraction, racial hierarchies, productivity, and disciplining. Indigenous scholars such as Grande, Eve Tuck, Glenn Coulthard, and Audra Simpson have been discussing, examining, and highlighting this character of settler societies and their educational systems for more than a decade. The publication of Robin D. G. Kelly's *Black Study, Black Struggle* in 2018 supported my belief that it was possible, albeit deeply risky to my own personal financial and career prospects, to turn to work within higher educational institutions in order to subvert neoliberal aims; to support the struggles of students, faculty, and staff by ensuring that they were well informed and educated in the tactics of neoliberal diversity management. I would suggest to readers of this book unfamiliar with their work and the works of the Black radical tradition (Frantz Fanon, Amílcar Cabral, W. E. B Du Bois, Steve Biko, Ida B. Wells, the Black Panther Party, and Audre Lorde to name but a few) to take time to familiarize themselves with this body of literature. These collective theories are critical groundings for understanding the educational institutions that we have inherited. These traditions undergird the ideas of this book, and it is because of these scholarly communities that it was even possible to imagine it. They have been an abiding community for me, sustaining voices while I occupied administrative roles that often left me feeling, as many diversity workers do, very alone in choosing to even attempt reparative, abolitionist, or decolonizing efforts. It is my hope that I have contributed something that is helpful to furthering the collective questioning as to what higher education is, the perilous ground of diversity work, and what is needed if we are to transform higher education, whether within the existing institutions or through the creation of ancillary spaces.

I do not refuse the possible redemption of higher education, nor do I argue for its complete abandonment. I cannot predict what comes. I do view reparative work as "undoing work," work that cuts against the heart of higher education's capitalist dependencies. Abolitionist work, as I understand it, looks at what we need to say *yes* to and what we need to put to rest forever, what to assist through the dying process. It is not utterly deconstructive work but, rather, radically creative and generative. The prison abolitionist work of Mariame Kaba, though importantly different from reparative efforts in the space of universities, stands as a critical and ongoing source for learning methods to unravel or undo aspects of higher education. I think of this as an effort to figure out the critical role of the past in the future of higher education. This is not an argument for reform. If this book comes across as that, then it should be taken as a failed project. Tinkering with systems, as I have learned doing diversity work, that are the means to uphold racial and class hierarchies doesn't result in very much. I am interested in offering a picture of how to start to pull at the strings that unravel all the knots. Slightly altering admissions criteria or financial aid packages, for example, doesn't remove the critical issue of indebtedness, both materially and epistemically, as a criterion for participation in learning. All the while, fundraising offices tell students to wait, and the government's disinvestment in higher education in exchange for unabated investment in surveillance and war continues. What aspects of social efforts to educate do we need to keep in order to achieve a better present? I do not deny that higher education has made a material difference in the lives of many, myself included. The economic precariousness of so many of my past and present students is material, and to ignore the power of higher education to intervene, albeit in increments and with significant indebtedness, in cycles of poverty would be a decadent position. But what is gained for so many BIPOC (Black, Indigenous, and people of color) and low-income people who are admitted to the miniscule number of slots in elite colleges or for those who find their way through the labyrinth of community college to four-year college to graduate school, often on their own, exerts a psychological toll and provides a powerful socializing mechanism into the values of productivity, indebtedness, competition, and extraction on which neoliberal society depends. The toll comes for some when they sense that society has conspired to use them, their bodies, and their identities as capital. Or when, as a former student told me, he realized that all the friends he left behind were no different than him in their ability to succeed in college; they didn't have anyone to guide them through the sorting devices of college access. The realization that higher education is a continued reproduction of dispossession and enslavement behaviors is confusing for many students I have worked with; they ask why it matters and how it should matter. The toll arises for some when the realization comes that you were not brought into these elite spaces to learn much about who your community is, was, and could be other than as objects of study by persistently white faculty and students, but rather to fascinate, educate, and ensure that the white majority is reassured that society has moved on from the harms of the past.

What this book seeks to do is to examine diversity work at its conceptual root in order to better understand that it has been offered as a good, as a value that will lead us to social justice, though the evidence increasingly shows that its aims have stagnated in spite of commitments. I seek to question whether diversity is indeed the conceptual category, the socially imagined good, that can lead to racial justice or decolonization in higher education, and I explore reparative practices and poetics as an approach to creating antiracist institutions. I seek to reveal that diversity was never a self-determined way of knowing and existing for racialized and other excluded people.

Throughout this book, I use the terms *settler colonialism, coloniality, decolonization, social justice,* and *racial justice.* These terms are not intended to be interchangeable: their aims are not the same, and since they concern different identities, geographies and political histories, they carry conceptual tensions. Often, the choice to engage in decolonization, which I understand to mean the return of land, territory, and decision-making around land, water, and other forms of life to the stewardship and care of the Indigenous communities that were dispossessed, gets collapsed with social justice. They are not the same kinds of efforts. Social justice or antiracist work does not necessarily attempt to fundamentally shift social order. While I disagree with scholars who describe such actions as inattentive to changing the structure of the present world, social justice efforts often seek to distribute existing power to those groups that have been excluded from it. Antiracist work seeks to provide privileges, as Ibram X. Kendi explains in *How to Be an Anti-Racist,* in an effort to achieve equity due to existing racist systems. Antiracist work is driven by the belief that we can enact policies to correct or remedy existing systems, institutions, and beliefs; it maintains that such systems can be reconciled to no longer function to uphold white supremacist values, attitudes, and beliefs. This work takes its cue from how reparation—understood not only as financial compensation for abuse and injury but also as a way of knowing and existing—provides a set of life behaviors that upend and unsettle the order of our social world. Reparation, as I explore it, assists in the processes to abolish those systems, orders, values, and attitudes that are fundamentally dedicated to settler colonial values of white supremacy, extractivism, exclusion, and accumulation. In the end I hope that my arguments support a vision of the co-resistances of those concerned with decolonization, social justice, or antiracism as holding many values in common I am also aware that for people outside these areas of study and conversation, these distinctions and terms can feel exclusionary. Universities are, in my thinking, social organisms in which the intertwining logics of settler colonialism and slavery's continued impact on Black and Indigenous people are acutely detected.

I understand settler colonialism through the framework offered by Patrick Wolfe's logic of elimination: as a form of existence that produced white supremacy as a justification for the genocide of Native peoples and systematic enslavement of Black people in North America in particular. I seek to identify universities as sites in which the intertwined oppressions of dispossession, extraction, erasure, accumulation, racism, and racial capital can be detected. As early as Bartolome de las Casas's *Defense of the Indies,* published in 1552, Native people's "humanity," as defined through forced participation in religion, tribute, rape, and removals, was offered in exchange for the groundwork of justifying the use of Black people as slaves to replace the lost labor source. This practice of establishing the criteria of humanness, survival, and mode of participation in existence reveals something of how white supremacy and Eurocentrism worked to establish boundaries of existence between Indigenous and the forcibly de-territorialized Indigenous African person. The production of "Blackness" erases the individual, the particular, and the cultural identities of the enslaved person.

Wolfe offers settler colonialism as an uninterrupted system of erasure and dispossession of Native peoples that was in turn used to eliminate the identities—the distinct cultural, ethnic, and linguistic attributes—of forcibly removed and en-slaved Black people. This logic of elimination, according to Wolfe, removes Indigenous people from land and uses multi-culturalism as a moral justification for its continuance. If we are multicultural in the United States and Canada, for in-stance, this diversity is a good that obscures the continued erasures and eliminations of Native people. This logic strips individuality, self-determination, and agency from the con-struction of Black identity as well; to be Black in the United States is to be homogeneous without the possibility of differ-ence or individualism, and individualism, for those shaped by Enlightenment values, is the highest expression of what it means to be human.

Diversity emerged as an epistemology of difference during the historical period of settlement and conquest of the Amer-icas. It is used today as a value and a method to assert that universities are inclusive places because of the presence of dif-ference, of multiculturalism as a concealment device for the responsibility to redress historical injustices. Decolonization rarely, if ever, enters administrative conversations with racial justice, and anti-Blackness arises only slightly more often. Af-firmative action has lost its gleam in the United States as an equity-seeking effort, one that, in its original legislation, sought redress for systematic exclusion of Black people from higher education. It has been replaced with diversity. This effort to understand how universities can participate in the reproduction of reparative knowing and being, in spite of their legacies, oper-ates from the position that forms of recognition, such as rec-onciliation or apology, will never exert what decolonization or racial justice asks; only the fundamental reconstitution of power and control over the university as a resource will. This also calls into question how profound any antiracist or abolitionist efforts in universities can be. For this project, the intertwined root is that the future of what universities will be can only be figured out through the self-determined actions of the people and cultures that have been oppressed through its history, its present, and the logics that it reproduces. We should not mistake the renaming of buildings, the removal of statues, and the placement of plaques as sufficient to achieve the aims of racial justice or decolonization in higher education.

Decoloniality—a concept not interchangeable with ending settler colonialism, though the two are interrelated—is frequently used in calls to decolonize the university. As evidenced in recent protest movements outlined in Achille Mbembe's *Decolonizing the University* and Roderick A. Ferguson's *We Demand: The University and Student Protests,* this undertaking often focuses on decentering European hegemony and white male heteropatriarchy within curriculum and institutional practices. Calls to "decolonize a syllabus" most often mean to include intellectuals, creative works, and other types of epistemic resources besides written texts. Calls to "decolonize the university" in many instances can mean, to be simplistic, to take down statues that honor white supremacy, rename buildings, and recognize the institutional entanglements with slavery and dispossession. As Eve Tuck and K. Wayne Yang (2012) helpfully note, decolonization should not be a metaphor for other things. Decolonization cannot take place without the rematriation of land and the relinquishing of power and resources to Indigenous people and lifeways. Decoloniality is common discourse across Latin America and the Caribbean. The struggle for a decolonized education is a struggle for the right to determine the criteria of participation in universities; it is not the struggle for inclusion according to existing criteria. It is fundamentally a struggle over territory, space, and ultimately land. According to Nelson Maldonado-Torres in his "Outline of Ten

Theses on Coloniality and Decoloniality," decoloniality refers to efforts "at rehumanizing the world, to breaking down hierarchies of difference that dehumanize subjects and communities that destroy nature, and to the production of counter-discourses, counter-knowledges, counter-creative acts, and counter-practices that seek to dismantle coloniality and to open up multiple other forms of being in the world."

Maldonado-Torres explains in his second thesis that coloniality is distinct from colonialism and that decoloniality is different from decolonization. For Maldonado-Torres, colonialism and decoloniality are concepts that are often thought of as static, located somewhere within the past. This is distinct from Wolfe's explanation of settler colonialism as a continued set of epistemic behaviors that societies are socialized to reproduce. These logics of "elimination," as Wolfe calls them, and "coloniality," as Maldonado-Torres explains it, are concerned with the persistence of a set of modes of being, beliefs, attitudes, and understandings as society continues socializing subsequent generations into a system of exploitation, domination, erasure, and extermination of Indigenous and Black people and cultures.

These strands of inquiry—settler colonial studies, decolonization, decoloniality, and the post-colonial—have important distinctions in their approaches, geographies, and concerns. Where they often overlap is in the centrality of how societies descended from varying forms of colonization practices maintain systems that are dependent on the exploitation, erasure, and accumulation of non-white and low-income people for the benefit of the few. For a number of theorists studying within these interlocking areas, the university is suspect. I seek to contribute to these discourses by locating the university as a settler colonial creation, one that must be understood as actively reproducing logics of coloniality and settlerism by circumscribing the production of knowledge with criteria of inclusion determined by the elites. I seek to examine what happens to universities when reparative knowing and being are unleashed.

In part I, I examine how our present notion of diversity was birthed from ways of defining difference that arose from the violent settlement of the "Americas," which in turn helped birth the transatlantic system of chattel slavery. I explore how this epistemology of difference is manifested through behaviors toward BIPOC people and cultures that institutions still engage in. This epistemology of difference, or what I believe we now describe as "diversity" (though its morphology has shifted over time), can be detected in the behaviors and artifacts of the work of higher education. Indeed, higher education was created in settler colonial societies from the fabric of this epistemology of difference. I examine these ways of knowing by examining a set of behaviors and practices. I explore the university and an epistemology of difference as sprung from the *Wunderkammern*, or curiosity cabinets, of Europe, a practice of collecting and organizing difference which contributed to the development of academic disciplines (Menakem 2017) within university spaces and through the behaviors of accumulation, colorblindness, partitioning, and dispossession. Part I approaches this examination through a series of artifacts, one of many, that compose what we may use to examine the genealogy of diversity.

The second part of the book engages with reparation as a constellation of activities and ways of knowing that are connected to the activation of collective energy. A central concern is how societies might take up seriously reparative actions and the role of higher education in this undertaking. I propose that the reparative, as a mode of existence, must be examined through the social imaginary of a given society to understand why, particularly in the case of the United States, it has not gained traction in many institutions and policy settings as part of the pursuit of equity, justice, or decolonization for Black and Indigenous communities. Or, if reparation has gained traction, as in the case of Georgetown University, it has not connected its efforts at recompense to the way the institution teaches, learns, or adjudicates the harms of its past. I focus on offering a definition of reparation that places its epistemic and ontological character at the center: how we are socialized to relate to the injustices and harms of the past and exist as if they have little bearing on the current violence, inequality, and injustice inflicted on Black, Indigenous, and Latinx people, cultures, and countries. I argue that it is possible for societies to shift their collective understanding of how the past persists into the present through socialization into taking responsibility and creating epistemic resources necessary for shifting ways of knowing and acting. I locate education, specifically *higher* education, as a key socialization mechanism for exercising what I call *epistemic reparation*, or ways of knowing that develop a sensibility for how one's present society is understood through the lens of the continued harms exerted by racism. Epistemic reparation, as I attempt to outline, is socio-historical: it is an effort to shift, through affective and poetic interventions, ways of knowing and being in the present in order to perceive and atone for the persistence of the past.

The final part of the book undertakes a discussion of counterspace as a poetics of refusal and identifies this as an action that BIPOC communities call upon to intervene in the dominant regimes bequeathed to us by settler colonialism and the coloniality of power. It attempts to explore this as a mechanism for reparation, as a way to understand reparative measures beyond something administered to "victims" but rather as self-determined creative action by communities that have sought methods to resist oppressive conditions. These moves are ways to enact refusals and redressals and invent a present that cares for their communities. I examine specific examples of counterspace through a discussion of the spatial politics used by the Black Panthers, Young Lords, and the American Indian movement in an effort to connect these social movements to how Black, Latinx, and Indigenous groups have used spatial politics in universities to create counter-spaces that enact self-determined existence. This enactment of a self-determined existence is, I argue, a pedagogic for reparative existence. Efforts to amend, heal, or atone for the persistence of harmful history, to enact justice in the present, should be determined by those who have been impacted materially. Reparative environments, ones that provide for the needs of marginalized groups through self-determination, do not have to wait for the sanction of administrative or governmental edicts.

PART I

A Cabinet of Diversity

Working as a chief diversity officer (CDO) or diversity, equity, and inclusion (DEI) administrator was not part of my plans when I began a PhD program in philosophy and education. While discrimination, cultural marginalization, and inequities had characterized my own life experience and what I had observed throughout my time in higher education, the professional field of what is now called Diversity, Equity, and Inclusion, or DEI, was only emerging in the early 2000s, manifested in multicultural affairs departments and equal opportunity employment offices. The microaggressions and microinequities that I had experienced as a young Puerto Rican woman studying philosophy made me feel either overlooked, not smart enough, or the object of sexual harassment. I never felt as if I belonged or had power in the educational spaces I had accessed, only that I had been permitted to participate in them for a while and that I had to find a way to understand the rules and abide by them in order to gain a faculty role somewhere. But I never felt smart enough, male enough, or rich enough to operate in the seamless, unconscious way that many of my peers seemed to. I was not alone in this feeling, and it was often clear that the presence of "difference" worked to legitimize the institutional belief that the institution itself was egalitarian, meritorious, and just.

I became a chief diversity officer, hired in inaugural roles several times, because I was interested in systems change, because I needed work in the academy after the bottom had fallen out of tenure-track jobs in my field after the 2008 recession, and because I was interested to see up close whether the inequities that seemed to surface year after year could be tinkered with, changed, or hot-wired to work in the service of racial equity or decolonization. It became quickly apparent that one could work *as* diversity or *on* diversity so long as it did not too dramatically unsettle the institutions' traditions and missions or seek to reassemble, crack open the systems that were the arteries of inequity, or dig around to find what needed to be abolished.

Despite the best efforts of highly competent people, diversity efforts, I have come to realize over a number of years, often function as a decorative "shield," as Brent K. Nakamura and Lauren B. Edelman describe it in their 2018 article "Diversity Structures as Symbolic Metrics in the Federal Courts." To understand diversity efforts as a tool that institutions wield to symbolize their antiracist commitment and to protect themselves against discrimination lawsuits is to grapple with how self-interested power maneuvers to use difference for its own benefit and how this has always been a defining feature of what we call *diversity work.*

Through my education at elite private institutions, I benefited from the college's and university's resources, faculty, and pedigree, but I incurred a significant amount of debt to obtain my degrees—so much so, that I allowed my debt to dictate the kinds of jobs I could and couldn't take. What I came to realize, through doing what is referred to often as "the work" for over a decade, is that while Sara Ahmed in *On Being Included: Racism and Diversity in Institutional Life* accurately captured the experience of diversity workers in higher education (this text became an intellectual life raft for me), the conceptual container that is diversity work is poorly understood. I began to see clearly that few people really understood what they meant when they talked about "diversity, equity, and inclusion" work, although lots of people had strong ideas about what they thought it should and shouldn't do. They either didn't understand what they were after or they believed that formulaic, mandatory workshops are what is needed to overcome racism and bias. The administrators I worked for and alongside often said that they didn't believe CDOs did anything effective at all; that I was there to manage the discontents of the non-white members of their institution; that my role would hinder free speech; that I would become the bias police. Few people I encountered had literally come to terms with DEI or what I term *diversity work* in the rest of this book.

Chief diversity officers or other administrators who work in the field are banging their heads against a brick wall for the many reasons that Ahmed describes in *On Belonging*: lack of resources, lack of authority, lack of support among them. But I also believe that "diversity" is an unproductive abstraction, a detour that permits powerful, heavily resourced institutions to ignore their role in the reparative actions necessary to move our society away from entrenched and relentlessly reproduced social and racial inequality. Although CDOs or diversity efforts are invited in, they are permitted to participate only under a framework of knowing difference, one that seeks to organize, define, place, and patrol the boundaries of efforts concerned with antiracism or anti-oppression. Diversity work that does not seek to reengineer systems by taking up the burdens of the past that formed their institutions or work to abolish exclusionary practices that privilege the wealthy, can never be the mechanism to bring about any amount of racial justice or social equity. I argue in this first part of the book that not only is diversity an unproductive concept for radical social transformation, but its conceptual genealogy reveals an epistemology of difference that has always been a tool to organize nondominant groups for the benefit of those in power. Diversity is not, I aim to explore, a reparative activity, though since the late 1970s it has become conflated and confused with historical responsibility-taking and the necessary undoing of persistent beliefs, attitudes, and values that sustain inequality.

I began to realize a few years in—particularly when I asked for data and files on tenure denials of BIPOC or first-generation faculty, hiring and promotion criteria or disciplinary records that included demographic information—that an inertia encumbered requests to peer into how the systems were working to prevent real discrimination or undo the conditions that facilitated discrimination. My asking for this kind of data was not to seek information on individuals in order to fire or discipline them, but rather to understand what kind of relationship the institution had with racialized people. More often than not, the relationship was either disciplinary, punitive, or apathetic: remedies if ever enacted, were always individually focused. There was rarely a mention of a problematic system or culture or set of practices. The remedy for or prevention of discrimination had little to do with what I was doing or had been charged to do. Some people were interested in talking about white privilege in the abstract, but not as much in investigating how the systems they relied on day after day were privileging whiteness, wealth, ability, or masculinity and how it might be possible to re-engineer or redesign how the institution, how higher education, functioned. With mounting evidence that, while I had been hired in these roles to inaugurate *something*, the presence of a CDO is, actually, what is most important to most institutions. The CDO's presence is a communications exercise, an attempt to signal to their campus, their alumni, and their prospective students that diversity matters in their mission. While this may come across as a cynical position, I assure my readers that this book arises from a spirit and a commitment to reparative action understood as an undoing, to interrogate why diversity work "isn't working," why its presence has facilitated an aggressive backlash, and how to maneuver in climates increasingly hostile to antiracist, decolonizing, or anti-oppressive efforts. The intent is to move higher educational institutions away from what Craig Wilder, author of *Ebony and Ivy,* describes as the third pillar in the processes of colonization and slavery, to a social force that may breach the wall of ongoing violence and inequities. In my work I began to want to unravel why DEI efforts seemed so "ineffective" and why they were being attacked from differing positions on the political spectrum. As someone who had spent a decade formally studying philosophy, I began to need to understand what "diversity," as a way of knowing and of being (epistemically and ontologically), meant. What was DEI anyway, and how had it come first to be assumed as a proxy for antiracist or anti-oppressive efforts and then rejected, by leftists, as a tool of neoliberal management? What was the source of its failures or breakdowns, and what could this tell me about its desired uses? In a 2007 article, *Diversity as a Dead End,* legal scholar Kenneth Nunn describes the US Supreme Court's cases on diversity as creating a condition by which practices and policies in higher education can evade the real power differentials and social inequities that affect Black, Latinx, and Indigenous people in the United States. He describes diversity as entering the practices of higher education with the 1978 US Supreme Court case *Regents of the University of California v. Bakke,* a case that I will spend some time examining in chapter 1, as the defining moment when race-conscious admission, created as a remedy for the exclusion of generations of Blacks from higher education, became subsumed as merely one among many aspects of difference that a college or university could consider in admissions. The moral argument, the need for remedy to undo the harm to generations of Black families whose social mobility had been limited due to racist discriminatory policies, was no longer a sufficiently compelling interest. Rather, in the present moment, affirmative action was an undue burden for the present. Diversity crept in as an AllLivesMatter predecessor, a way to dilute the historical imperative of racial inequality still present in segregated and raced opportunity. So when critiques like Pamela Newkirk's *Diversity Inc.* argue that diversity work "doesn't work," it is essential to understand what we thought it was supposed to do in the first place and whether it is the appropriate concept to abolish systemic racial and socioeconomic inequities. Pressure is on diversity work, rising from left and right political positions in the United States that, though dramatically different in their aims and reasons for critique, reveal that a frustration and discontent exists. Before continuing to unravel diversity, investigate its genealogical character and what this has to tell us about the ways of knowing and being it affords, let's examine more carefully what is meant when we say "diversity doesn't work" so as to help reveal what is lacking in our understanding of diversity and what diversity can hope to accomplish.

Diversity Doesn't Work?

Before delving into some of the key arguments in the critiques of diversity work, I would like to offer a provocation for consideration: Perhaps diversity is working exactly as it should? Perhaps it is doing what the epistemology of difference that undergirds it intends it to do? Critics of the inequities created by capitalism often point out that exploitation occurs not because capitalism isn't working well but because it's working exactly as it should. Maria Svart, the national director of the Democratic Socialists of America, wrote in a 2019 opinion piece in the *Guardian* that capitalism is not broken; instead, it is concentrating wealth gained through the exploitation of the many into the coffers of a miniscule portion of global society. Capitalism has never been interested in social equity or the eradication of poverty; exploitation is its progeny, and because of this, our current social inequalities are precisely what the system intends.

What I am attempting to provoke through this line of thinking is to ask my readers to take seriously the likelihood that diversity operates as a mechanism of power to organize the participation of difference and erase the need for remedy of historical violence that persists in the attitudes, values, policies, and behaviors of societies like the United States. Diversity provides a defining, organizing principle for how difference may participate in structures of power. Diversity, a value-laden concept for

the presence of difference, was not always invoked as a positive activity that would lead to more equitable conditions for
racially underrepresented people. Although diversity as a social idea was present in the United States and elsewhere prior
to the 1970s, it was not until challenges to affirmative action
placed diversity as a compelling interest in higher education
that it began to be employed, increasingly, as a way to dilute
the social reality of structural racism and inequality. Diversity
never sought to remedy persistent historical inequities; it was
a term to organize, identify, and control difference. Before
delving further into this idea, let us examine how diversity became detached from the reality of social inequity and consider how to begin the process of coming to terms, literally,
with diversity.

Legal scholar and president of Columbia University Lee
Bollinger, a fierce defender of and advocate for affirmative action, said in a 2018 interview with the university's student news-
paper, *The Spectator*: "In the current [debate], we can't talk about
past injustice; we can only talk about the educational benefits
of diversity [as if it is] some kind of abstraction that is not
rooted in an actual societal reality. I think that it was a real pity
to try to separate those two." The abstraction that Bollinger
laments has its origins in the legal challenges to affirmative action policy in higher education that began with the US Supreme
Court's decision in *Regents of the University of California v. Bakke*.
Justice Lewis F. Powell Jr, writing for the majority, stated that
it was inequitable to make innocent people bear the burdens
of the past. Essentially he put forward, as the decision's conceptual groundwork, that students in the present day should
not bear the burden of past harms and the present inequities
that these harms have yielded. In other words, our social reality should not bear the responsibility for past injustices. That
wealthy and white students continue to reap the benefits of

past privileges had no bearing on Powell's thinking. What the decision did was to push aside policies of "remedy" in favor of "diversity," which would come to be employed as a kind of conceptual cover for efforts to correct, through admissions practices, the chronic and systemic under-resourcing of K–12 education for Black, Latinx/Hispanic, Indigenous, and low-income white students that limited their access to institutions of higher learning. The move away from the need for remedy of systemic inequality fueled the use of diversity as a compelling interest; the presence of different identities on a college campus would become the rationale for alleviating chronic under-resourcing and discrimination. Detaching difference from social realities of structural racism became a way to expand the conversation around diversity to include ability, gender, sexual orientation, religion, and even geography. The social reality of racial inequities was removed from consideration, permitting higher education to engage not with remedy but with diversity: the organization and leveling of difference.

Preceding his arrival at Columbia, Bollinger had been president of the University of Michigan, where in 2003 he was the named defendant in two landmark affirmative action cases before the Supreme Court: *Grutter v. Bollinger* and *Gratz v. Bollinger*. The cases, brought by white students, claimed that the admissions policies disadvantaged their applications in favor of granting more weight to those of racially underrepresented students. Though the court in *Grutter* ruled that additional points could not be afforded to an applicant based on race, both cases upheld the 1978 *Bakke* decision that race could be a consideration in admissions practices so long as it could be shown that *diversity,* rather than *equity,* was a compelling educational interest of the university. However, in 2006 the state of Michigan voted by ballot initiative to ban affirmative action in university admissions.

Bollinger has continued to be an advocate for affirmative action policies, speaking and writing frequently on the ongoing challenges, most recently the 2014 case concerning Harvard University and Students for Fair Admissions, which claims that the university's admission practices discriminate against Asian and white students. In 2019 a federal appeals court ruled that Harvard's use of race in admissions decisions was consistent with Supreme Court precedent establishing the creation of a diverse student population as a compelling interest for education (Students for Fair Admissions 2019). What the most recent case against affirmative action failed to prove was the role of intentional discrimination against one identity among many diverse identities. The challenge to affirmative action that can prove intentional bias against Asian or white applicants, no matter if it is in favor of diversity, thus remains looming. What these cases reveal is that diversity as the conceptual foundation for remediation of the persistence of racial inequities in the form of de facto segregated and under-resourced K–12 schools and communities is not leading us toward increased access and participation in higher education for racial groups persistently underrepresented, nor is it leading higher education toward being a clarion call for remedying the social realities of racism. Diversity, as a remedy for racial exclusions and inequities, has led us further away from the need to seek social remedies for ongoing racial harm. As Bollinger points out, the abstraction of diversity has contributed to social detachment and collective amnesia from the continued need to redress a society still entangled in racist and discriminatory attitudes, values, and policy considerations. It has pulled away from the need to unplug the system blockages that facilitate discrimination, marginalization, and oppression. Within the systems of universities lie methods of exclusion and hierarchies that have become concealed as traditions or uncontestable, unmovable structures. The work of reparation, as distinct from that of diversity, is akin to an excavation, an undoing that pulls back the layers of sediment to show the operating system that has been running under the surface, one built on the bones of slaves and Indigenous people with enclosures to protect those who created the criteria of knowledge. Somehow many well-intentioned people have come to believe that the presence of diversity is sufficient to undo the perniciousness of oppressive and exclusionary operating systems.

In a 2019 *Chronicle of Higher Education* diversity report, Sarah Brown discussed the abysmal progress in racial diversity in the professoriate in spite of councils, task forces, and workshops on inclusive hiring. Even at Columbia University under Bollinger's leadership, the needle has moved only a few percentage points. In 2017 the National Center for Education Statistics reported that 76 percent of faculty in higher education were white in spite of efforts and investments in diversity on many college campuses. As a chief diversity officer, I frequently witnessed the persistent perception that hiring "more diverse" faculty (insert "Black" or "Latinx" usually) was an impossible task. "It's the pipeline," "it's the funding," "it's the competition with other institutions," "there is no open line in our department," "people aren't retiring" were among the reasons I heard most often. These oft-cited reasons led many administrators and department chairs to struggle and, if they were able to hire a single person of color, that individual became the only racially underrepresented person or entered a department hostile to difference. The percentage of full-time, tenure-track faculty in institutions of higher education remains overwhelmingly and persistently white, while the percentages of adjuncts from underrepresented racial groups continues to rise. According to the American Federation of Teachers (AFT) only 10.4 percent of all faculty positions are held by underrepresented

racial and ethnic groups, and of these, 7.6 percent are contingent positions (AFT 2010). If you are Black or Latinx person
seeking a faculty position, you are overwhelmingly likely to be
relegated to a contingent role. So while an institution may report that the presence of diverse faculty exists, that doesn't
mean that these individuals have permanent or tenured status,
or that they have the institutional power to make decisions concerning curriculum or pedagogy. Adjuncts are chronically un-
derpaid and excluded from institutional grants and external
fellowships requiring tenured status. Additionally, in my personal experience I witnessed the reluctance to disaggregate
international identities that are, while underrepresented in
the US professoriate, not members of groups historically excluded through law and policy such as African Americans
(Black), Latinx (Hispanic), and Native Americans. This reluctance to disaggregate is significant in that it reveals that institutional diversity hiring efforts can evade the need for historical remedy of the chronic exclusion of certain groups in favor
of the sprinkling of different identities and be lauded for it.
Diversity efforts, in these cases, are abstracted from the practice
of equity, which seeks to enact a remedy for historical and ongoing exclusions of particular groups from positions of power in
knowledge creation. Diversity benefits the self-interest of universities in serving as a self-congratulatory mechanism for the
appearance of difference while evading the prioritization of certain racial and ethnic identities, an effort that has increasingly
hamstrung universities through fear of liability. Diversity work
has, I believe, facilitated the drift away from practices needed for
redress of society's inequitable structures.

Diversity work, as evidenced in the following critiques of
diversity training and workshops in organizational spaces, is
proving insufficient for removing biased, racist, and other discriminatory practices. The ability to work with, study along-

side, and develop meaningful relationships with people different from oneself is a significant aspect of overcoming discriminatory practices and stereotypical beliefs. However, when abstracted from systems change that seeks to remedy inequities or abolish practices that uphold oppression, they become, regrettably, either forms of discipline and control or self-congratulatory feel-good activities. Diversity, as the legal challenges to affirmative action reveal, works along a logic of selection, ordering, and curation of higher education institutions to appear diverse, with images of different races, abilities, ethnicities, and genders populating their campuses. I want to emphasize that I am not opposed to this as a meaningful aspiration; our higher educational institutions should and must be filled with different kinds of people. But this kind of diversity is not to be confused with the practices of remedy and redress for generations of racial discrimination. Diversity works too often for the purposes of curating difference, making campuses (particularly the most elite ones) into carefully screened and scrutinized cabinets of diversity where Blackness, Latinidad, Indigeneity, and poverty become one among many forms of difference it seeks to include and, importantly, celebrate. The United States is not ready for a leveling of difference, a flattening of the need to build an actively anti-oppressive society where race is no longer a predictor of longevity, educational attainment, or incarceration. We are far from ready for an approach, as too many institutional leaders seem to reiterate, where all voices matter and everybody feels included. Diversity work formulated in this way diminishes the realities of power and inequality that persist in higher educational environments. All voices have never mattered, and the system is predicated on a hierarchical system of value where to say so lands disingenuously. Such statements assume that epistemic injustice, defined by Miranda Fricker in her 2007 work by the same name, as the devaluing of a knower on the basis of identity, does not exist. Diversity, equity, and inclusion work seeks to fill spaces with difference, to provide a seat at the proverbial table while doing little to rebuild a room that recalls the plantation. Reparative activity undoes the mechanisms that seek to curate difference. It is an activity of undoing, uncovering so that we may see clearly the substratum that we walk on, that we are educating through every single day. Though many strive for diversity to do the work of redressal, it does not and is not designed for this.

This is a perilous line to draw in climates where critical race theory, culturally responsive pedagogy, or even teaching children about slavery, Indigenous dispossession, and genocides and their afterlives is being banned in states like Texas and debated in many others. Where there are material consequences for public critiques of perceived white supremacist culture, such as when the president of Lyon College, likely intending to illuminate the realities of racial and class tensions that persist between colleges and their environs, resigned at the request of local officials. The resignation came after King told the *Chronicle of Higher Education* that the private Lyon College is a bubble "of inclusion and of diversity surrounded by a sea of angry, disenfranchised populations and a large white-supremacist population," according to an article published in 2021. This is just one example of how incendiary diversity work has become in certain areas of the United States, where the resistance to attend to the ongoing inequities that are facilitated by forces like racism and classism is digging in its heels and resenting any attempt to offer youth historical information that seeks to undo narratives that valorize symbols of oppression. Reparation as undoing has been, precisely for these reasons, excised from most diversity efforts. But what those of us committed to the possibility of higher education as a mechanism for social remedy must confront is the reality that perhaps our practices have facilitated in backing us into a corner; fear of lawsuits and liabilities has made us silent participants, complicit in the slip-slide backwards into diminishing access and opportunity for low-income students, who are disproportionately people of color. While we need diversity, it has not, nor will ever be, the mechanism that we need for creating a society that is actively antiracist, and anti-oppressive.

The theme of diversity work not working has been taken up by researchers in business and faculty in higher education as frustration with either the lack of systemic change or mandated disciplining practices grows. While many people on both sides of the political spectrum might agree that diversity work isn't working, what it *should* be working for and how is a vast and seemingly unbridgeable divide. The most frequently cited study, one that seems to undergird most current critiques of diversity work, is the 2016 report by Frank Dobbin and Alexandra Kalev published in the *Harvard Business Review*. Their report provoked a flurry of investigations and studies by firms such as Deloitte and corporations like Google to capture precisely what needs to be done to increase representation at the highest levels of industry. Pamela Newkirk provides a detailed and important investigation into the ways these industries (including higher education) have, in spite of spending millions, not made any substantial gains in diversifying their organizations. In fact, she observes that there has been a slide backwards since the 1980s. Most often cited as aspects of diversity work that are most likely to backfire or create a worse environment for racially underrepresented people are mandated activities—anti-bias workshops, hiring criteria, or diversity statements in courses or faculty files.

Dobbin and Kalev analyzed data from 829 firms over three decades and discovered that the diversity efforts of these organizations had remained relatively unchanged since the 1960s.

Where these programs existed, they found a *decrease* in the presence of women and people with underrepresented racial identities. Their report revealed that diversity training programs, particularly ones that instruct people to uncover their personal biases rather than focus on systemic interventions to bias and discrimination (such as the abolition of legacy admissions in higher education), were designed to police managers' intentions and that this "force-feeding" approach actually contributed to the erosion of diversity for the very groups whose representation it sought to increase. They concluded: "Decades of social science research point to a simple truth: You won't get managers on board by blaming and shaming them with rules and reeducation" (Dobbin and Kalev 2018). Neuroscience and behavioral sciences, they explain, show that shame is a powerful demotivator in changing human behavior. Even the attempts to use performance ratings and hiring tests designed to "level the playing field" were discovered to work in favor of cherry-picking results, leading to managers, who are frequently white, hiring people like them.

Amna Khalid and Jeffrey Aaron Snyder expressed similar discontent with and skepticism toward mandated training and diversity statements in their 2021 *Chronicle of Higher Education* article, "How to Fix Diversity and Equity." They describe the current state of diversity work in higher education as the application of metrics, rubrics, and requirements that create a state of affairs antithetical to transformative change; rather it is a stifling ideological etiquette with which academics can learn to game the system and check the box without meaningful reflection or change to their teaching, hiring, and research practices. Their critique focuses on their interpretation of such efforts as ideological indoctrination that stifles viewpoint diversity and is more concerned with public relations than equity. Like Dobbin and Kalev, they point out that one of the most critical and pressing needs is to change the ethno-racial composition of the professoriate to include faculty that have been historically and persistently underrepresented: Black, Latinx, and Indigenous faculty to be specific. In both cases the authors are quick to reiterate that they are not opposed to racial equity work or antiracism; what is problematic for them is the approaches that are taken within organizations.

In both higher education and the broad range of corporate organizations that Dobbin and Kalev studied, diversity work in the form of training, mandates, bias awareness, antiracism development has not resulted in any dramatic changes to representation or to discriminatory experiences. Diversity work, they argue, in its present form isn't shifting the demographics of power; in fact, it seems to be distancing people from the work of antiracism from disdain, shame, or anger and not doing much to change practices, procedures, or the systems that seem to, over and over, result in the same inequities.

Along with the critiques of diversity work are offered suggestions and ideas for what can work or what has been observed as working. Again, I want to track what we are seeking when we want diversity work to "work." A number of the critiques of diversity, from Dobbin and Kalev to Newkirk and Bollinger, identify representation as a critical area to move the needle. For diversity work to succeed, the numbers of BIPOC-identifying people holding professorships, Fortune 500 CEO positions, and manager-level positions need to reach thresholds that reflect national and local demographics. For instance, Latinx people make up approximately 18 percent of the total US population according to the 2020 census; to enact equity, a given organization should consist of a proportional representation of this community. This is often a guiding principle of diversity efforts. Inclusion then becomes the work of organizations to shift culture to ensure that the underrepresented sector feels and is included.

More often than not, in my experience, inclusion work operates at the level of offering workshops and affinity groups, not at the level of changing policy, practices, or structures that have upheld an oppressive environment. Most in the higher education space define effectiveness as more diverse representation on boards of trustees, college presidents and professors. Success in increasing numbers of racially underrepresented identities in these roles is often described as inclusion. Inclusion, as Verne Meyers has put it, is getting asked to dance, not just getting invited to the party. While this points in a good direction, the problem lies also with who gets to choose the music. Far too often in diversity work the focus is not on who and how the particular dance was selected in the first place or what kind of dance is included in the party. Suggestions for how to increase inclusion, get more diverse people into the dance, fall into several buckets that I will spend a bit of time summarizing before moving into a deeper discussion of coming to terms with diversity and how its conceptual framework is a precise navigational tool that, more often than not, leads us away from the past and conceals the operating systems of oppression.

Prestige Bias

Early on in my career I was an assistant dean for equity initiatives, working directly for the provost of a small liberal arts college. Part of my efforts were to support the provost in hiring plans to try to diversify the faculty, which at the time hovered around 90 percent white. The provost told me, after I suggested that we might think about recruitment from programs known to graduate high numbers of Black and Latinx PhDs, that the college wouldn't consider anyone who hadn't graduated from an Ivy League PhD program for faculty roles. She told me over tea in her office, leaning in as if to share a secret, that they just wouldn't be able to keep up with the research demands necessary for tenure. I pointed out that several senior faculty hadn't published anything in over a decade or more. One had published only a single article in his entire career. Well, yes, she said, but the institution has changed, it has become more prestigious, more rigorous in what is expected. I also pointed out that according to data tracked by the Survey of Earned Doctorates (SED), an annual census taken since 1957 of all individuals receiving a research credential from an accredited US institution, institutions producing the highest numbers of Black and Latinx PhDs were not Ivy League schools. If we were truly interested in hiring racially underrepresented faculty, I asked naively, why not recruit promising researchers from the institutions where they were graduating? The provost shook her head, echoing the president who had weighed in a few days before about new hiring plans; "excellence rises to the top," they said. This statement reveals the myth of meritocracy that dominates academic hierarchies; the vast majority of faculty at prestigious institutions have arrived there because they are the best and the brightest rather than because, more often than not, they come from privilege, economic and racial. Prestige, or pedigree, has been the litmus test for the brilliance or promise of a faculty member.

This conversation occurred over a decade ago, and still the institutions producing the highest numbers of racially underrepresented PhDs are not the Ivy Leagues; they are the large public state university systems. The SED reported that between 2013 and 2017 the top three institutions producing Black PhDs were Walden University (online), Howard University, and Jackson State University. For Latinx/Hispanic students, the top three PhD-producing institutions for the same period were

University of California, Berkeley, University of California, Los Angeles, and University of Texas, Austin. For Native American or Alaska Natives, the top three were Oklahoma State University, Stillwater, University of Arizona, and University of Oklahoma, Norman. No Ivy League institution appears among the top twenty for these three racial or ethnic categories. Cornell, Harvard, Yale, and Stanford appear, however, in the category "more than one race" collectively granting 253 PhDs in this demographic category. According to this provost's perspective (I encountered this belief frequently in my time as a CDO), we should be competing for these 253 because they must be the best of the best. One need only glance at the number of colleges and universities in the United States that would be competing to hire these 253 doctorates to realize that the efforts to recruit in this prestige-oriented way in order to diversify their ranks of professors is an activity destined for failure.

Meanwhile the approximately fifteen hundred Black PhD earners from the top three institutions mentioned are deemed, just on the basis of their degree-granting institution, as not possessing the correct "pedigree" for a tenure-track professorship at a small "prestigious" liberal arts institution, many likely ending up in contingent positions that do not pay a living wage or even offer health insurance. This way of thinking permits the lament of the "pipeline" to echo continually in the halls of institutions where their permanent faculty remain persistently white and from privileged backgrounds. As Khalid and Snyder suggest in their article on fixes to diversity, addressing the biases toward the degree-granting institutions as well as to where candidates have published might help shift the persistent underrepresentation of certain racial groups in the professoriate. Although shifting which institutions and journals are viewed as "acceptable" may support the cause of diversifying the professoriate, of collecting, accumulating, and organizing bodies of difference into its taxonomies, it does little or nothing to undo the epistemic exclusions and injustices that are the origin story for prestige bias. Such a "fix" will support the aims of diversification of identities, bodies, and cultures; it will not undo the ways of knowing that have built the belief systems of prestige and the enclosures that define hierarchies of value, increasingly invoking society's rejection. Such efforts may diversify the faculty ranks, but the undoing of prestige bias must operate at an epistemic level. How we determine what knowledge is worth studying, valuing, and reproducing and the methods of engagement have long determined the bodies and geographies that now dominate higher education.

Since its inception, higher education, understood as an institution that confers degrees in nonvocational subjects, has served as an important pillar in determining what is true, valid, and significant knowledge. Like museums these institutions have been the repository of what knowledge should be preserved by a society and reproduced through the education of new generations. Unlike museums, colleges and universities might also be thought of as locations where new contributions and breakthroughs in human understanding occur. Multiple volumes and journals have been dedicated to exploring the depth and complexity of higher education. Universities began in the United States and in Canada as an extension of European models, like Oxford University; they often served as institutions for training clergy and then as institutions where the sons of the wealthiest families were sent for education. Harvard University, the University of Pennsylvania, and William and Mary College are among the oldest institutions of higher education in the United States. While there is much to discuss about the origins of the physical institutions, which I will explore at length later in this book, their role in ascribing value to certain kinds of knowledge over others is pertinent to the discussion of addressing prestige bias as a way to make diversity efforts work.

Prestige bias must be understood as extending from a system of value that sought to determine the kinds of knowledge that were acceptable to the academy and the locations where that knowledge was held. Epistemic bias, or more accurately the epistemicide, of Indigenous and African lifeways has a direct relationship to the epistemology of difference, or the way that Westernized European perspectives came to develop the forms of canonical knowledge that we still consider to be the highest forms of knowledge production. Integral to the colonization procedures that were employed in the shaping of the United States and its institutions were efforts to eliminate forms of life and the ways of knowing held by nondominant groups. Integral to the processes of building higher education was the drawing of enclosures around whose knowledge, cultural productions, and ways of life were to be reproduced and whose were to be objects of collection, study, and lived annihilation. Prestige bias has an epistemic root that goes far deeper than simply changing the types of institutions deemed acceptable enough or rigorous enough for roles in the professoriate.

A recent study, *Socioeconomic Roots of Academic Faculty*, examined eight major disciplines of study and found that faculty are on average 25 percent more likely to have a parent with a PhD than the general population. Those getting PhDs, particularly from elite institutions, are much more likely to come from positions of socioeconomic privilege. Prestige, it turns out, is cultivated generationally, transferring the implicit and often opaque knowledge of how to gain advantage in academia through family ties.

An Option among Many

Many proposed solutions for more effective diversity work take up DEI as an accepted value, as something that, in order to make a difference, just needs different approaches, better funding, better preparation, more staff, or improved data-driven research. My inquiry seeks to challenge this premise by revealing that diversity work, as a conceptual container, will help organizations and societies do many things. It will help to absorb marginalized identities into the areas, positions, and fields that those in power decide they may participate in. It will increase different perspectives, identities, and abilities involved in decision-making. Many racially underrepresented people want and actively work to make this kind of inclusion happen. Black, Latinx/Hispanic, and Indigenous people have a broad range of perspectives about what inclusion should focus on and how it should be carried out. Racialized groups are often characterized as monolithic, but this tendency to essentialize any group must be avoided. Many people want to be included in the system as it presently exists but in an environment that is fair, unbiased, and supportive. I am not trying to say that race predetermines what position one will take on efforts to decolonize and commit to anticapitalism or antiracism. Seeking reparative activity, an engagement that undoes, is an option among many. What this book is interested in and committed to is an undoing that helps reveal that current systems of higher education seek to include historically marginalized identities in the practices of power that facilitate inequality, violence, and oppression. As the "diversity doesn't work" literature reveals, diversity work is occluding responsibility for unearthing the beasts (practices, policies, beliefs, and symbols) that feed off a festering and unhealed racism. Reparation is an activity concerned with undoing systems, practices, and beliefs that permit the reproduction of ways of knowing and existing that are descendants of the practices of settler colonialism and slavery. Reparative activity, unlike diversity, has the ability to undo present systems of power, not advance them. It should not be lost on readers of this book that Native Americans were "included" in education; they were included in order to violently subject them to the loss of their lifeways, to epistemicide, just as Blacks were included in higher education, relegated to certain kinds of institutions. Booker T. Washington and W. E. B. Du Bois debated whether Black Americans should study vocational or liberal arts in order to fully participate in society (Du Bois 1903). I do not believe we will gain greater equity or anti-oppressive and antiracist worlds by simply refining the tools of inclusion, making them subtler so that the absorption feels more comfortable and more acceptable. It should not, according to the ideologies that undergird this book, be considered a victory for commitments to decolonization, antiracism, or anti-oppression that BIPOC and LGBTQ people have the opportunity to lead the Central Intelligence Agency or serve as CEOs of arms manufacturing companies, sitting at the table providing diverse perspectives on how to help reproduce violence that disproportionately affects Black and Brown countries and communities. If those diverse bodies and perspectives lead to the ceasing of war in all its forms, then I will be more than happy to be called out as profoundly misguided. Identity matters less than a commitment to the activities of undoing, of revealing the matrices that entwine us to behaviors, beliefs, and imaginaries that fail over and over to stop the logics of violence and oppression. Too often, higher education engages in a model of diversity that avoids ideological commitments, believing that antiracism or anti-oppression can be achieved through a neutral position. Racism, as Ibram X. Kendi has shown in *Stamped from the Beginning*, develops from self-interest. Self-interest is highly ideological, and the ongoing production of racist systems will not be helped by the belief that this is not an ideological struggle for a more equitable and anti-oppressive world. So while I view diversity as a broken undertaking, my point is that diversity *is* working according to logics formed by the dominant epistemology, which maintains that the current concept is a sufficient container to operate within in order to achieve antiracism. So when it fails, as we have seen from some of the critiques, many believe that an improvement plan is the fix rather than coming to terms with diversity, as it is presently understood, as a set of activities and behaviors within a conceptual field that is insufficient for what many of us are trying to unravel. In order to get at this challenge of explaining more clearly *why* what is explained as "diversity work" has evolved into the set of practices, beliefs, and attitudes presently enacted in its name, tracing its genealogy may help us better understand why it has served as a force for detaching from social realities of inequitable and oppressive systems. It is possible to trace the way of knowing difference, what we now call "diversity" in countries shaped by colonialism, like the United States and Canada, to sets of beliefs, values, and attitudes that are largely the result of the dominant epistemology. Higher education serves as a socializing mechanism into varied forms of dominance, inculcating and rewarding particular forms of knowledge over others.

Object 2

Epistemic Dominance

Universities are hothouses of epistemic dominance, cultivating elaborate ceremonies to reproduce ways of knowing that breed competition, subjugation, evaluation, extinction, and extraction. While many scholars within academic fields are contesting forms of epistemic dominance, my interest here is in how universities continue to facilitate epistemic dominance, particularly in relation to attempts at diversity work. Epistemic dominance is defined as sets of knowledge that are identified and endorsed as superior to others (McDonnell 2014). They are ways of knowing that are the most rewarded and the most valuable to dominant groups. The very hierarchy of ways of knowing, such as deeming written works as more credible than oral works or intellectual production as superior to manual production, are examples of epistemic dominance. Among the traditions of higher education, prestige and power fall according to what position the institution occupies in this hierarchy. These hierarchies are direct descendants of the Divided Line that Plato outlines in *The Republic;* in the present day, they confer authority on particular forms of knowing and then classify, or place, other forms of knowledge in relation to this hierarchy. I will not spend a great deal of time discussing Plato's theory of knowledge here. Very simply put, the Divided Line offers a theory of knowledge that differentiates the visible world from the intelligible world, ascribing true knowledge as occurring through experiences of abstraction and intellect such as mathematics and philosophical theory. The visible world, that of perception, shadows, and experience, is not where we can experience truth and goodness. This division carried through to education, placing greater value on theoretical study—what we now call liberal arts—than on manual arts or labor. This valuing has long been connected to conceptions of who are the custodians of goodness and truth. This hierarchy of value is still visible today in social beliefs in the Western world about what kinds of education are the vehicles to power and authority. A vocational college producing carpenters and plumbers, according to this hierarchy, is not as powerful, well resourced, or prestigious in the way that elite private institutions such as Brown University or Princeton University are because of the types of knowledge reproduced within these educational spaces.

Another example can be found in the modes of existence and cosmologies of the Taino people, the first Indigenous groups encountered by Christopher Columbus in the Caribbean. These lifeways or epistemologies were, for Columbus and the stream of colonizers that followed, viewed as inferior to Christianity and European Renaissance thought. This epistemic collision led to the genocide and epistemicide that undergirded the development of colonial practices such as residential schools in which Indigenous children were taken to eliminate traditional ways of knowing as well as to enact genocide.* Epistemic dominance is a driver of social behaviors that result in the extinction of certain cultural groups, animals, and plants because the dominant form of knowledge does not perceive

---

*I understand epistemic collision as occurring when one or more theories of knowledge that are unintelligible to one another come into contact. This experience is best explained in the work of David Welchman Gegeo and Karen Ann Watson-Gegeo when dominant or colonizer groups encounter and attempt to organize or explain Indigenous groups and their needs. See Gegeo and Watson-Gegeo 2002.

them as holding truth, value, or intelligence. Many humans engage in brutal practices of killing animals, destroying forests, and polluting rivers because of a belief system that places the nonhuman far below or as lacking in intelligence that deserves rights.* The types of behaviors, values, and attitudes developed within locations of epistemic dominance have direct bearing on the way that difference is conceived, and the way that difference is conceived has shaped diversity work today. However, recent protests on campuses around climate change and antiracism can be framed as cracks within locations of epistemic dominance, attempts to undo dominant ways of knowing. They arise from modes of thinking and acting that, though now present and included within academic study, are not yet dominating the practices of institutions. What these protests mean for institutions and reparation will be taken up in part II of this book.

In higher education, no matter how much there seems to be spoken or performed commitment to principles such as equity, faculty and students are still instructed in how to compete, perform, brand themselves, write, speak, and engage in discourse that often "one-ups" or argues down another. Even faculty that teach in areas such as Africana studies or who are committed to working for equity in biology, for instance, struggle to find pedagogical and institutional forms to turn to that do not encourage or valorize individualized success, competition, or dominance. Their careers and academic survival are predicated on competition and dominance. I have rarely encountered institutions that center care, collectivity, decenter

---

* There is a growing legal movement that seeks to establish rights for nature (plants and animals). This movement builds from the subfield of animal ethics in philosophy. Importantly, Indigenous legal scholars such as Virginia Marshall criticize the concept of rights of nature as a non-Indigenous framework that is not guided by Indigenous ways of knowing and existing. See Marshall 2020.

the human, upend the notion of individual success, or undo accumulative behavior. How do we resist, refuse, and subvert dominance in how we know, create, and relate in universities? What does this have to do with diversity work? How do students, staff, administrators, and other university employees commit to this when power dynamics are so fixated on hierarchies and when the threat of losing one's job is a real material concern? Diversity—that which is distinct from the dominant group—arises as a method of the dominant epistemic regime as a result of the coloniality of power* and efforts to assimilate and accumulate difference. Diversity, equity, and inclusion efforts within universities have been shaped by their dependency on and relationship to the legacy of colonialism and slavery and the epistemic methods of domination that created them. Diversity does not know itself apart from its presence as a maneuver to organize difference in accordance with its hierarchies of value. Diversity, as we come to use the concept today, has evolved through an epistemology of difference that sought to categorize, organize, and dominate the non-white European human for use as material in financial gain— for capital. As Nick Mitchell points out (Mitchell 2018), interrogating diversity work can help illuminate how institutions use racial capital. To parse the distinctions between current diversity work and reparative or reconciliatory work, we need to understand diversity's entanglement with an epistemology of difference that was born from activities of profitmaking for a select

---

*The coloniality of power is a concept initially articulated by Aníbal Quijano to offer a way to define the colonial structure of power imposed through European conquest. The coloniality of power is defined by three central forms: systems of hierarchies, systems of knowledge, and cultural systems. Quijano and subsequently Catherine Walsh, Walter Mignolo, Sylvia Wynter, and Nelson Maldonado-Torres identify these forms as persisting today and focus on modes of delinking from coloniality. In part II, I take up delinking and Quijano's work. See Quijano 2000 for an introduction.

few. We cannot assume that DEI efforts will not work against or subvert reparative and reconciliatory aims, particularly given the absence of clarity about DEI's origins and its use as a mechanism for capital in the organization of nondominant epistemologies and ontologies. As Angela Davis said in a lecture at the University of Virginia in 2018, while diversity can do good work, in the absence of justice and structural transformation it "simply brings those who were previously excluded into a system as racist, as misogynist, as it was before." The work of reparation is an undoing of present systems that enact oppression and violence. These activities can shift how we perceive knowledge, existence, and the forms of life we take as truth. Diversity is not a proxy for reparative actions. Indeed, reparative activities seek to work against the absorption of difference into existing systems for what can be extracted from them in the pursuit of profit; reparative activity seeks to undo, separate from the forces that seek to accumulate.

Diversity work within universities is tethered to the birth of coloniality, the dark underbelly of modernity as Walter Mignolo aptly describes it, and its accumulation of Black and Indigenous bodies for capital by means of extraction, dispossession, and taxonimification. This epistemology of difference—the way that modernity formed thinking and relationships to what and who was encountered on the vast continent now described as the Americas, is detectable in how universities currently conceive of diversity work. Universities today still seek to include, count, interrogate, categorize, and accumulate BIPOC people, while attributing these epistemic behaviors to diversity efforts. The location of higher education is often a campus quite disassociated from the place it is, echoing the universalist perspectives of the Enlightenment. Institutional strategic indicators or fact sheets rarely lead with their demographics of white people. Instead, they highlight the amount of diversity that

has been accumulated: University X has a student population that is 62 percent white and a faculty population that is
78 percent white. Yet University X leads with its students of
color statistic of 38 percent. The story that institutions such
as these tell themselves, with the cheering diversity worker at
their side, is that they are doing a good job; they can call themselves a diverse institution, despite the "pipeline problems."
Meanwhile, down the street the local community college has
a student population that is 8 percent white, 58 percent Latinx,
and 28 percent Black. Why does this matter? Why do institutions report their accumulations of diverse racial identities?
They publish these statistics to ensure the appearance of inclusion, to show that their institution values and makes a little
bit of space for racially underrepresented students. In their conception, diversity work is an accumulative practice of drawing
in difference for use in their profitmaking mission. They do
this not necessarily only because it is just, but because it applies value to their institutions, one that they believe is favor-
able to the marketplace. These statistics represent the quantification of racial capital, how the presence of difference "adds
value" to their institution. It is rare to find an admissions staff
member who would be willing to characterize the work of creating a diverse class in such a way. University X, like other private
elite institutions that are gatekeepers of power and privilege,
do not redistribute wealth, foster open admissions, permit
collective self-governance, abolish trustee boards, or give land
back. They do not fire faculty who are known actors of racism
or sexism or fill their boards of trustees with the descendants
of the slaves they sold or the Indigenous people whose dispossessed land their institution sits on, or the indebted students who permit their institutions to continue to draw funding. They make gestures and statements, convene councils and
task forces, yet the structures remain fundamentally unchanged

because the logic,—the ways that higher education knows itself—has not changed. The unfortunate reality is that, as many of the critiques of diversity work reveal, shifting or transforming the environments of institutions to enact and embody the statements of commitments to antiracism or anti-oppressive environments happens far too infrequently. There are few material examples of dramatically transformed cities, institutions, or organizations that have amended, repaired, or redressed legacies of exclusion and violence. In the absence of such efforts to take reparative action, environments remain, for those now permitted to participate, monuments to the logics and practices of their exclusions.

Interrogating the roots and behaviors of diversity work is not to argue that the desire for justice or decolonization or equity in education should be discarded. Rather, what is needed, I believe, is a literal "coming to terms" with the words, their meanings, and what ways of knowing and acting must be discarded because they are leading us further into the solidification of how difference is used for ordering and dominating difference in the pursuit of power and profit. Why have so many institutions chosen to use these words instead of reparation or decolonization or culture? The words we use communicate more about our phenomenological experience, our belief in what existence is and who has rights to existence, than we often realize. Reparation or decolonization chafes against notions of diversity that are operationalized by higher education because, as Eve Tuck and K. Wayne Yang (2012) explain, such moves are incompatible with the logics of settler colonialism. Any attempt that seeks to alter the order of existence, of knowing, is incommensurable with a system that seeks to maintain order and control and that values domination. Diversity, as we will come to see, is a storehouse of colonial values, beliefs, and attitudes used to dominate and control difference unpacked and inserted into the context of the contemporary university. Unpacking this storehouse, or cabinet, reveals that DEI work is distinct from transformative or reparative-seeking activity. Unpacking this cabinet reveals that difference was created through positioning it as opposed to or in distinction to methods, structures, perspectives, and beliefs wrought from white, male, European experience in certain historical moments. This is not to say that all works developed from these identities, these perspectives, and these experiences should be discarded. Rather, there needs to be an undoing of their procedures of dominance, of the hierarchies of values that have contributed to so much oppression and destruction. The study of such texts, their disciplinary approaches, attends to how they have been instrumental in the production of racism and inequalities. There are examples of disciplines and academics struggling to attend and to undo the erasure of race and reveal the culpability of their disciplines in forming racism. The work of Dan-el Padilla Peralta in classics and the work of scholars such as Kim Hall (1996) are two such examples.* However, much work remains to be done in most disciplines to see how theories and practices have perpetuated ways of knowing that exerted extraction, collection, taxonomification, interrogation, and dispossession upon nondominant groups. Much work remains on how to unravel the way universities historically prioritize the works, practices, epistemologies, and imaginaries that center those cultures, people, and ideas that were placed at the top of hierarchies of value developed through colonization and slavery. If the ways we teach and learn how to know difference are ever to extricate themselves from legacies of racism, oppression, and

---

* See Hall 1995 and the Newberry Library's Race in Dialogue series.

other forms of violence, reparation is a necessary component of that work.

I recognize that this is sweeping rhetoric. But such moves are illustrative of men and whiteness, so why not here? Why not now? In the background of all this writing is the persistent voice that this is not rigorous, that I am illogical, that I can never offer something ironclad and do rhetorical gymnastics to please my prosecutors. These are the ways of knowing I have learned from the academy through my "difference." There isn't a correct beginning to an inquiry that tries to peek inside a cabinet or storehouse crammed with moments, artifacts, policies, behaviors, attitudes, and theories that form the substratum of how we currently understand diversity. To believe that such a process will be logical is not a concern that I undertake. My method here is akin to what happens when you open a closet and the residue—the detritus of generations—comes tumbling out, each indicating something of the collector's mindset. I pick up these artifacts with the hope that they might reveal the morphological character of diversity and why it is distinct from reparative moves. This is an effort to show that the needs for reparative moves are entangled with diversity practices. We begin now with an effort to consider the genealogy of diversity, to outline, by examining its transits (its morphological leavings), how it arrived within North American educational contexts through epistemic dominance as the concept that can deliver justice or goodness, as the mechanism that reconciles the engineered exclusions and suppressions. While there are many books on slavery and the university (see the anthology Harris et al. 2019), as well as on diversity, that explain and identify important historical events that resulted in policies and laws to desegregate, to integrate, and to distribute access to higher education, there are few efforts to unearth how diversity came to inhabit our social imagination as a value and a practice that we believed would help us achieve racial justice or equity. There are no inquiries that I am aware of that seek to track diversity as connected to an epistemology of difference born through epistemic dominance. Now, as many practitioners, theorists, and students try to make sense of how diversity became a neoliberal tool, one that is used to manage integration, quell discontent, organize the participation of difference, and accumulate BIPOC people, I argue that diversification, the concepts that fill this version of it (inclusion and equity) have always been an organizing method of coloniality intended to assist in upholding its dominance. It never was and will never be about power sharing or structural dismantling or embracing the provocations that arise from inviting those excluded to now participate. Rather, it is implemented as a safeguard against revealing the depth of the poor epistemic habits of the disciplines that prop up coloniality, their decadence, and self-interested posturing. Diversity, as presently used in North America to signify a set of values, a practice that signals equality, equity, and antiracism, absent of awareness of its colonial lineage, will always disappoint those of us interested in and committed to reparation and structural overhaul that encourages material transformation of social hierarchies and capital.

The intent of the next chapter is to locate diversity, its lineage, as birthed alongside the creation of universities with the processes of how those engaged in colonization developed, refined, and enacted an epistemology of difference. The manner of knowing difference, what came to be described as diversity, can be traced through its accretions, artifacts left behind that reveal the morphologies of what we now call diversity work. These morphologies are instructive in bringing clarity to how reparation stands in counterpoint to diversity work. Identifying the distinctions, the points of overlap and complementarity, between diversity work and reparation is an important step in an effort to elaborate on how higher education works on race and other forms of social inequality. Higher education engages a mode of diversity work that can often, I believe, work against reparative aims. Indeed, once diversity's lineage as a concept tethered to coloniality and slavery is confronted, it reveals that the reparative—acts of amending, atonement, and recompense—is always needed wherever diversity is invoked. The invocation of diversity work signals that the realm of the reparative is not far behind. Diversity efforts signal a problem to be managed, a body to accumulate; they are fundamentally present-focused, ignoring the past and the future. Diversity efforts perform for where we are now and work to cloak or conceal the methods of coloniality or neoliberalism in new clothing. Reparation describes the future as contingent on what we do now through revealing the suppressions of the past. We are so accustomed to the incantations of diversity in higher education contexts that we no longer understand what we mean when we invoke it. If reconciliation and justice for past injustice is an aim of diversity (which perhaps it is really not) and after many decades of efforts, higher education still holds deep inequities, exclusions, and violence, it is important to understand why and whether reparation, if realized in all its form, activates these aims? It asks us to consider whether vice presidents of reparation, reconciliation, and decolonization are both possible and a more accurate title of the work that many expect to undertake within CDO roles. Finding diversity work's origins is a step toward drawing distinctions, coming to terms with its fundamentally colonial character and methods, a lineage not well suited for reconciling, amending, and atonement for injustices that persist in present forms.

The creation of curiosity cabinets, a practice that emerged as a method of recording and providing organization for Europe's process of conquest and colonial expansion, provides insight into epistemic habits that sought distinctiveness, difference, oddities, or the exotic as objects for possession, classification, extraction, and interrogation. I argue that the practice of curiosity cabinets reveals modes of thinking and behaving that shaped how universities came to relate to and define difference. Seventeenth-century European curiosity cabinets laid an important foundation for the development of higher education (Roberston 2006). They exhibit the organizing logics and modalities of coloniality and provide the lineage of present-day diversity work. The next chapter traces the morphology of coloniality's epistemology of difference by examining several artifacts from its North American context. It will show that this notion of diversity—difference—is central to how universities organize themselves and that diversity is epistemically linked to accumulation, ownership, possession, and the patrol of difference. Reparation is when coloniality of power acknowledges the harms that have been committed for its power and enacts responsibility-taking actions to relieve burdens for those historically harmed. Diversity efforts, regrettably, often work to solidify the coloniality of power. But this, I argue, has always been bound up with diversity. I will excavate several objects to reveal diversity's boundedness to coloniality and to argue that the service of justice in higher education must contend with the challenges and limitations that exist within diversity and diversity work as a concept that came into existence as a means to control, discipline, accumulate, steal, and erase non-European people and cultures.

From Wunderkammern to the Majors

The Discipling of Difference

As someone who has been in a higher education institution for more than half of my life as either student, professor, or administrator, I have always felt in-between, interstitial within disciplinary work. At times, the rigidity of disciplines and their taxonomic form make the university resemble an eccentric collector's cabinet of human thought-experiments over centuries. I have often, as a hired diversity worker, attempted to understand how difference is organized, interrogated, questioned, and included by universities through distinct disciplines that use organizing principles to generate hierarchies of value. I have spent a significant percentage of my professional time convincing leadership or faculty of several things that, while a CDO is often hired to do such work, they are rarely positioned in such a way so as to be able to have power to enact them. Some of these things included integrating texts or theories or approaches to learning from the global South or anywhere outside Europe, that are authored by Black, Indigenous, or Queer people; offering learning opportunities to help the academic community understand the difference between tokenized insertions into curriculum and developing a critical race perspective of their class, discipline, or department; convincing people that the examination and discussion of institutional history matters to present policies about inclusion; and, finally, proving that an understanding of higher education as a settler colonial construct matters if they are to, as so many nonperformatives around race in higher education do, articulate a concern for enacting justice.

According to Edouard Glissant in *Poetics of Relation*, this drive to organize, categorize, and squeeze life into tiny examination boxes for display is an attempt to enact dominion over the opacity of the world (Glissant 1997). This desire for disciplining or bringing the unfamiliar, the opaque, under control is not, for Glissant, the work of relation; it is the work of dominance—an effort to subsume difference into discernible and controlled categories, so as to present it as subsumable under a universal organizing principle passed off as truth. The Taino people whom Christopher Columbus encountered were not perceived by him or other Europeans as human in the same way that he was. One of Columbus's first comments recorded in his journals was that the Taino would be good servants, due to what he perceived as their gentle and childlike nature. They are permitted existence only in terms of how they serve the empire; they are undeserving, due to their difference, of the right to opacity, the right to exist, to change, to be as they are without control. They exist for how they are useful to power. Glissant explains that empire is the absolute manifestation of totality (Glissant 1997, 28). Columbus attempted to bring back evidence of what he had encountered. It is recorded that his death ships tried bringing several Tainos, parrots, and gold back to Spain. It is recorded that the Tainos died during the voyage and that the parrots escaped.

The more we can see, from multiple vantage points, in the first encounters between Europeans and Indigenous people of the Western Hemisphere, the more we can comprehend the significance of epistemic encounters. The more we can comprehend that the ways of knowing that settlers such as Columbus brought with them, the clearer it becomes, for me, how diversity arose from the violent disciplining of difference that had likely been learned from the Inquisition and the expulsion of the Moorish and Jewish people from Spain. It is important to note this here because I ask my readers to operate from a place where standpoint is a reality for how we develop our ways of knowing: our beliefs, values, attitudes, and approach to existence. It matters that individuals like Columbus and the other conquistadores were emerging from a moment when difference was viewed as a threat to empire, and bringing it under control, through violence or fascination or exclusion, was core to who they understood themselves to be. I believe that this manner of knowing is perpetuated through generations that have been socialized in colonial geographies into what Walter Mignolo and others describe as the coloniality of power.

An example of how coloniality approached difference and developed knowledge, was through the invention of the curiosity cabinet, or *Wunderkammer*. *Wunderkammern*, also known as cabinets of curiosities, were originally rooms that displayed collections of various objects, plants, and animals. The process of collecting and categorizing objects, plants, animals, and humans encountered during the travels of wealthy white European men, conquerors, or missionaries came to underlie the modes of knowledge production that shaped the museum and the modern university. Bruce Robertson writes, "the practice of collection, organization and taxonomifying of the unfamiliar, expressed and shaped an epistemology of difference, one that underlies the modern university" (Robertson 2006, 43). He argues that not only is the curiosity cabinet the ancestor of these institutions, but importantly the *Wunderkammern* shaped how many of the disciplines that constitute the modern university came to conceptualize and relate to difference; particularly differences that were encountered through conquest, colonization, and slavery. In this chapter I will examine how the practice of creating curiosity cabinets, which provide an epistemic foundation for universities today, have also shaped contemporary diversity work. Our current use and understanding of diversity in higher education and other contexts are a direct descendant of the collectors who sought to exert domination through taxonomic and organizational hierarchies that signaled wealth and power. The logics of diversity work are intertwined with the disciplining of difference first introduced in the curiosity cabinets of the ruling classes of Europe that developed power from the activities of conquest and colonization.

In the late 1700s, the Spanish monarchy commissioned the Portuguese naturalist Antonio Parra to create a *Natural History of Cuba*. Such collections and drawings of the flora, fauna, and curiosities of a country or exotic region were common during the seventeenth and eighteenth centuries, but Parra's was one of the earliest commissions of illustrations from the American continent. Until this point, voyagers had returned with artifacts and specimens for cataloging in curiosity cabinets. Contained among pages illustrating the flora and fauna of Cuba in this book was an image of a single human being.

All that is known of this man, Domingo Fernandez, is what Antonio Parra recorded underneath the last three plates of his *Descripción de historia natural de Cuba* (1787) in which Fernandez is the only human subject. An excerpt from Parra's description reads: "Domingo Fernandez, Negro of the Congo nation; 32 years old (who worked as a coach driver or coachman) Spherical sarcocele hernia (testicular elephantiasis) in its circumference of one and a half varas and six inches; and from top to bottom three quarters and five inches: its weight of four and two pounds" (author's translation from the Spanish).

Parra's images of Fernandez were among the earliest renderings that the Spanish in Europe saw of a Black person from the colonization of the Caribbean and the "new worlds." I do not know for sure, but they may have been among the first images of an "actual" living Black person of the colonized territory. There is no mention of whether he is enslaved or free, but at the time in Cuba had a sizable free Black community. His image was the accepted type of representation of a Black person of the time: as collected property. The method of his categorization—as an object of curiosity among plants and animals to be studied, gazed upon, and cataloged—was a widely accepted epistemology by the 1700s. The dominant regime of slave portraiture at the time rarely depicted black people in positions of authority, as possessing a cultural identity, social world, family members, or as intellectual as white people. These observations took the form of curiosity cabinets, emblem books, and travel notebooks filled with images of specimens from the "new world."* They served as aesthetic instruments through which the European elite were "educated" on what inhabited their colonial possessions. Such objects created, in Jacques Rancièrean terms, a regime of perception that framed Black and Indigenous people as specimens, logged and identified, in the curiosity cabinets of the seventeenth, eighteenth, and nineteenth centuries alongside flora and fauna. In *Aisthesis: Scenes from the Aesthetic Regime of Art,* Rancière defines the regime of perception as the "sensible fabric" of experience within which the work of art or culture may be interpreted. He defines this sensible fabric as exhibition spaces, modes of production and consumption as well as thought patterns, values, and emotions that circumscribe visions of the social world.

Present universities resemble such practices. Collecting and studying specimens, the separation of the human and nonhuman, the organization of production and consumption

---

*For an in-depth study of portraiture and the Caribbean at this time, see the digital humanities project *Digital Aponte* (https://aponte.hosting.nyu.edu/; Govantes 1937; Palmié 2002; Pavez Ojeda 2012.

of knowledge are present preoccupations of the academy. Universities need "difference"; they have always needed it in order to have specimens, to practice their discipling. Parra's manuscript, where I was able to see the portrait of Domingo Fernandez is kept in the Princeton Library Collections. To read it or touch it, you need a special ID card, state your research purposes, sit in a special room where you cannot leave with it or have food or water. Access to the manuscript, a possession of the university, is highly controlled. Your use of it is disciplined; access to it is possible only by passing through Princeton's castle-like campus and the fortress that is the library; through a series of gatekeeping practices to the knowledge artifact. There are a number of requirements that have to be fulfilled in order to be allowed into the archives. These methods of possession and archiving are signals of what it means to be educated.

The Princeton archives are an amazing place, full of documents, objects, and artifacts that provide essential material for intellectual creation, social memory, and a record of human existence. However, they are also a testament to how universities claim ownership, use, and control the residue of human experience. Such practices conceal the procedures and belief systems that led to accumulating objects and artifacts in this way, and through these spaces. Though rarely identified as such, many objects are spoils of theft, items acquired through a long chain of exploitation, war, and oppression. They are a record of how universities with such collections are repositories for the reproduction of epistemic exclusions and serve as gatekeepers for how history is engaged and accessed. Within these archives one can find, such as in the Parra manuscript, a genealogical record of the accumulation of difference for study and how universities have participated in their control. A recent example of contestation of who owns or has rights to archival material acquired through exploitation and/or theft was brought into public discourse in 2019 and explored in a series of articles in *Hyperallergic*. In 2019 Tamara Lanier, a descendant of enslaved people, sued Harvard University for wrongful possession and expropriation of two images of her ancestors, Renty and Delia, stored at Harvard University's Peabody Museum of Archaeology and Ethnology (Di Liscia 2021). This is only one of many contests around possession that people and countries have made against university archives and museum collections.

The daguerreotypes, used in Louis Agassiz's 1850 study that sought to prove the theory of polygenism, or the belief that Black people did not have the same genetic roots as whites, have been licensed for use from Harvard for book covers, conferences, and documentaries. The images of Renty and Delia are among the earliest photographs of enslaved people. Lanier's lawsuit claims that as a descendant of Renty, she has the right to damages for Harvard's "wrongful seizure, possession, and expropriation" of the images (Whalen 2019). The lawsuit calls upon the university to condemn Agassiz's racist work and turn the photographs over to Lanier. The case is complicated for many reasons and, at the time of writing this book, remains unresolved. In early 2021 the case against Harvard was dismissed by Massachusetts Superior Court citing legal precedents that had established that photographs are the legal property of the photographer. Lanier has submitted an appeal, the opening arguments were heard on November 1, 2021. The legal and archival structures through which she must prove her link to the images was engineered to sever links and occlude connection for enslaved families. The lawsuit reveals a significant area for reparative work within universities, particularly those whose collections are the descendants of the curiosity cabinets that were created as a result of encounters with a continent that had been unknown to Europeans. While Lanier must "prove" her lineage to Renty and Delia, what must Harvard do to take responsibility for housing, sustaining and elevating Agassiz or for possessing and using these images? Harvard's use of the images for financial gain, however negligible the amount of money earned, exemplifies the nature of the relationship to difference embedded within universities. Renty and Delia, photographed without their consent for study and taxonification, are testaments to an epistemology of difference that is intertwined through higher education in North America; that difference—diversity—is valuable to universities for study, for accumulation, and for capital. Without the presence of difference, here in the form of Renty and Delia the university, its theories, its work, and its value, could scarcely be comprehended; the practice of organizing, categorizing, gatekeeping, and disciplining difference is integral to the phenomenon that we call the "academy." What universities owe and what responsibility they should assume, beyond returning spoils of theft to family, communities, cultures, and countries, is an open question. The "use" of Renty and Delia insists on a set of values that sees the image as property whose use is determined by the criteria set forth by the discipline or the university. How we undo and reinvent the conditions for encountering images or artifacts that are compelled through violence, theft, and domination is, I argue, a reparative move—a move that assumes responsibility for and commits to repair of the epistemology that has facilitated procedures of continued exploitation. The epistemology that defines difference is bound to dominance and accumulation. Diversity work is a kind of effort within this circumscription; it is a boundary whose methods make it nearly impossible to transgress.

In Saidiya Hartman's *Wayward Lives, Beautiful Experiments: Intimate Stories of Social Upheaval,* she makes a choice to conceal a particular photograph as a palimpsest behind her words. She obscures the photograph, covering it with her words so we cannot fully see the little girl. Hartman writes, "was it possible to annotate the image? To make my words into a shield that might protect her, a barricade to deflect the gaze and cloak what had been exposed?" (Hartman 2019, 26). To confront the banality of the violence and terror captured in the obscured image, through the protective barrier offered by Hartman's words is a reparative act that moves at the level of our epistemology. To view it over and over, make it transparent again and again, many of us are taught is truth-seeking. But Hartman's maneuver encourages us to ask whether granting opacity is a method of liberation from oppression. To resist the need to see its violence reproduced again and again. The child in the photograph, the circumstances of her life, the abuse endured, cannot be changed by tracking down her descendants and providing financial recompense. But it can be changed by refusing to continue participating in the ways of knowing that permitted such violence in the first place. If we can open ourselves to the possibility of amending, what is owed to this horror in the present and to how to choose not to reproduce the subjugation, we might find a path toward modes of relating that are freed from disciplining, capturing, and subjugating difference. To relive it, to see the image clearly, to place it in a museum with no barricade of words to deflect the gaze, reproduces the harm committed in another form.

Hartman's method of working with the image provides me with an example of how to know reparatively—how to acknowledge the importance of bringing historical harms forward without using the same ways of knowing that created the horror. It instructs, for me, how to make small interventions that undo

academic methods that many have taken as sacrosanct. Hartman has recast how we might relate to past harm to make a
future liberated from its procedures and practices of terror.
She writes about this and other images not as objects for taxonomification and accumulation but rather as human experiences whose terror and subjugation should not be perpetuated
through the same methods of capture that contributed to these
conditions to begin with. Hartman works with the photograph
differently than Harvard does with the images of Delia and
Renty; Harvard seems to think that more visibility, more reproduction will do the work of undoing racism, extending capture
in a sense. While Hartman used an episteme of evasion and dis-
guise, a manner of fugitivity that permits us to imagine what is
there, to know of it without continuing the spectacle of violence, she does not assume or engage with the photograph as
property, making no claim to ownership. Even after Agassiz's racist theories were exposed, the photographs were still treated as
property for use in whatever manner the owner believed suitable. Lanier's lawsuit asked, arguably, for precisely what Hartman does with the photograph of the little girl; to provide protection, self-determination for how it is used. Lanier, much like
Hartman, seeks to "possess" these images so as to guard them
from further exploitation and theft of their existence. The
splashing of Renty and Delia across book covers, websites, and
conference programs makes no amends in the present for such
atrocities. The way in which the university permitted the image
to be used was intended to signify that they embraced diversity,
that they could "stomach" the ugly past. But this misses the
ways of knowing, the methods of capture, to which diversity is
tethered.

Increasingly institutions, particularly those with archeo-
logical and anthropological collections, are facing pressure to
be held accountable for the theft and hoarding of artifacts and

remains that belong to tribal nations, the descendants of enslaved people, and other cultures around the world whose knowledge or sacred objects have been taken and held in universities as items in their collections for study. This pressure is coming not only from students who are learning about repatriation/rematriation efforts by Indigenous groups but also from faculty in these fields who have been awakened to the harmful methodologies of their disciplines, such as anthropology, to objectify and exploit non-European cultures. These collections, some of which hold the human remains of Indigenous people, are reflections of the curiosity cabinet logics that undergird diversity as an organizing concept for universities. The lifeblood of universities has long depended upon the study of the other, the collection and examination of that which was defined as less than human because of its distinctiveness from the dominant regime of whiteness, Europeanness, and textuality. Archives and their ancestor, the curiosity cabinet, matter for an inquiry concerned with exposing how diversity work is bound to the very colonial behaviors that necessitate remedy. When a university, like Harvard University, possesses an archive that holds the remains of Indigenous people or images such as those of Renty and Delia, their holding and capture not only enables the accumulation of power; it also tells us something of how higher education thinks and behaves in relation to oppressed communities. The power is bound up in its understanding of itself as having the right to determine how difference is allowed or not allowed to exist. The university exerts an ontological dominance through how diversity is wielded. It often feels that universities function like small kingdoms, heavenly ones, populated with many terrible and glorious small gods. It captures the theodicy of the West, the belief that all that is done is divinely given and inherently good as decreed by God. Universities, like churches, believe themselves to be an essential civilizing and disciplining social force, though this position, particularly in the United States, is increasingly being challenged. A number of mission statements of colleges and universities outline their purpose as being to develop citizens or global leaders who will spread their knowledge across the world. It is an essentially inward-looking position, one that maintains that all that emanates from its campuses is goodness, civility, and light to spread across the world, any difference that enters it being sufficiently assimilated and imprinted with the ways of knowing and behavior that are quintessentially "educated." But many of the challenges to higher education today arise from this positioning: from the claim to moral superiority while exerting, with the assistance of government, profound exclusionary forces that draw in difference according to particular criteria.

Universities, particularly the most elite, which hoard resources, often act to sanction values of existence; a person or culture exists so long as the university can dictate the methods of its participation and definition. How often do staff and faculty of institutions tell students, particularly those who come from low-income or first-generation families, that they come to university to better themselves, to advance their station in life. As the case of Renty and Delia reveals, universities have the power to gain possessions, which may or may not translate into material wealth, from harmful acts. The university determines the mode of their continued existence. If we consider how diversity relates to this, to the criterion of existence, difference can exist only according to how power defines it and seeks to patrol its existence.

Patrol / The Ordering of Difference

He reaches up, stretching to place something into a cabinet. He appears to me to be a child. A white woman, studying science at a college in 1895, leans intently over a microscope, her hair piled fashionably high, her ruffled dress immaculate. We are supposed to read the image as an example of overcoming gender expectations and stereotypes. But it is, to me and others, a relic of the function of anti-Blackness in higher education, its roots and processes. The college posted the photograph on Instagram to celebrate its long tradition of women in science. The Black person in the background is, though named by the archivist, unlabeled in the Instagram post, his presence unremarked. He is unseen, yet again. I imagine that his presence as an essential participant in her education was unseen as well. The tools necessary for study, food, and cleanliness appear as if by magic, the stuff of princesses in fairy tales who are served not by people but by small mice or birds, a trope that helped cultivate generations who believed that domestic work was done by enchanted animals, not enslaved humans. Willy is necessary for her study; he continues, through the unseeing of him in the photograph, to exist as an instrument for the white woman's achievement.

I asked why the picture was used without any acknowledgment of the Black person's presence. He had, it turns out, simply not been noticed by the unit responsible for publicity at the college. The college responded that there is a mention of someone named "Willy" in the caption of the photograph; he is also mentioned in a letter that describes him using a derogatory term for a Black person. He is never described as a child. All that exists in several archival documents are descriptions of his diminutive size. He might indeed have been a child, but he might not. The absence of further detail tells us that it wasn't considered important to include his last name or information about what he did for the college. The rest of the description of "Willy" that was shared with me is one sentence in a letter from an early graduate of the college that describes him falling asleep often, snoring outside the classroom door, and as someone who from their perspective loved the college so much he believed that its dignity depended on him. This sentiment reflects, to me, a way of knowing similar to that expressed in plantation history or justifications for the continuance of slavery: that the Black workers enjoyed the backbreaking labor required of them. The belief that laborers should be grateful and honored for working in such esteemed environments persists in the academy today. During the COVID pandemic the service workers of college campuses suddenly became "essential." What informs such logics of unseeing and the hypervisibility of Blackness and poverty, and where are they still rooted in the academy? What do the archives of any institution of higher education reveal about the practice of diversity, its evolution, and its persistence? Why does it matter to tell Willy's story, to value his contribution to the institution's history? Why is his image not shown as one of the earliest forms of "diversity" at this institution? How should this image of Willy be captioned, and what should it communicate or remind the present institution of? These questions are answered by looking at the persistence of classism, the hierarchies of value, still largely unremarked and peripheral. Most students take for granted that someone cleans their dormitories, cooks meals for them, tends the gardens, and patrols the perimeter. The most elite of these institutions train the ruling class to reproduce the behaviors of classism that in North America are in lockstep with racism.

The archives unearthed another image of Willy, where now his face is visible as he stands outside a room in which white students are studying. He is foregrounded in the photograph, gazing directly at the camera. I'm still not sure whether he is a child or a young teenager. I'm fixated on this and want to understand why this matters so much to me. The label describes the photograph as a study hall with Willy, the doorman, standing outside.

These images provide an example of how elite private universities have placed difference—what is now referred to as "diversity"—outside the life of study yet as essential to its function. "Difference" in Willy's case is his Blackness, class, and male identity present in a women's college. What such images illustrate, when held up against many institutions' reckoning with their participation in slavery, is higher education's continued practice of circumscribing the way Black, Latinx, Indigenous, and poor white people participate in higher education and its unabated need for low-wage labor. I work, in this section, with the concept of "patrol" defined as a mode of behavior detectable in universities of ordering difference, racial difference in particular, in an effort to maintain control of its participation. A *Chronicle of Higher Education* report by Sarah Brown provides yet another piece of evidence that racial diversity efforts to shift representation in higher education continue to fall short. The report documents that although student demographics have continued to shift, the racial representation at the highest-level positions in academe remains persistently white. According to the report, Black and Latinx staff often constitute the majority of the lowest-paying positions on campuses. The whiteness of the highest-level positions also communicates the lack of internal development, education, and resources allocated to the people laboring in the lowest-level positions. For example, when shifting class times was proposed at an institution I worked at as a way to allow facilities, operations, and dining staff to take advantage of the college benefit to earn a degree, it was instantly shot down as an impossibility. When administration was asked how these staff were supposed to take advantage of their benefit to earn a degree, the question was met with shrugs or indifference.

The low-wage labor of people, most of whom, though not all, are Black or Latinx, is necessary for universities to function, and their modes of participation are heavily patrolled. Meaning, higher education operates through sets of values and behaviors that position difference where it is needed, its participation is patrolled through categories, disciplines, and institutional policies. This is the hallmark of what often passes as inclusion. Inclusion work is often only a thinly veiled reinvention, a reinscription, of patrolling, classifying the criteria of participation of so much that is not male, white, Northern, written, able bodied, or wealthy. Willy's presence is instructive in how racialized and low-income people have been permitted to participate in the structures of education. The structure of higher education dictates the modes, pathways, and permissions of inclusion. Threaded through the history of elite universities is the dependence on the labor, existence, and control of Black, Latinx, and Indigenous people. This is what is meant by "racial capital": that institutions of higher education rely upon Black people for social and economic value. They have arrived at this through the colonial logics of difference (Robinson 2019).

At the college where Willy worked and grew into adulthood, the role of doorman—the individuals responsible for monitoring people's comings and goings—remains Black, Latinx, or low-income. The patrol outside classrooms and dormitories, the keeping track of visitors' comings and goings, and the maintenance of buildings are largely conducted by a workforce that is composed of low-income people, a disproportionate number of whom are Black or Latinx. Though titles are altered and staff unionize to create improved working conditions, the modes of relation remain relatively unchanged. The static nature of racialized roles within higher education is one signal of how universities persist in patrolling difference or serve as a sorting mechanism for where and how difference belongs. What has participation in such an epistemic structure, one in which difference is both placed outside and allowed in according to specific criteria, yielded to us over time? Willy is not included as part of the institution's history, as heralding its early work at "diversity" because his difference cannot easily be reconciled to the narrative the institution has told about itself. Those who cared for the buildings, cleaned, secured and fetched are rendered invisible, insignificant in contrast to the sweeping balustrades emblazoned with the names of wealthy donors, or trustees, or dead white men. This continued participation is unintelligible to the epistemology that dominates institutions, expressed by the common question, "well, what can we do about it?" and "why does it matter?" There has always been "diversity" at work within institutions. Why Willy's diversity didn't "work" for the institution, as representative of the institution, communicates to us today, patrol as a behavior of what we understand as diversity. The institution needed Willy, though that need was unacknowledged, probably viewed at the time as unimportant or interchangeable for another body in a way that the students, despite their transience, were never described. His presence may present as a problem to be solved, repaired, or met with an indifference attributable to a historical moment that is over. What redress can be given, and why should we bother to interrogate it? What does his life matter to how the institution knows itself? These are questions that I will seek to interrogate more deeply and answer. To acknowledge that Willy and the people who labored within and for an institution mattered for its survival and development is an act of reparation, an act that undoes hierarchies of value embedded in higher education and exposes that difference is seen as diversity insofar as it assigns benefit or capital to the location.

Diversity frequently functions as a method of patrolling the participation of difference in education. Willy's presence reminds that higher education is dependent on hierarchies of labor as well as class and race distinctions and that inclusion is linked to identifying what is outside, what must be invited in because it is different or kept out through the construction of elaborate gatekeeping procedures.

Increasingly, thanks to the work of scholars such as Craig Wilder, Leslie Harris, and Alfred Brophy, to name only a few in the growing field of slavery and university studies, we have evidence that early colleges and universities were full of "diversity" but, importantly, that they were *not* full of antiracists nor full of reparative spirit and action except, arguably, in the locations where abolition was discussed and idealized though not necessarily enacted. There are far too many examples of self-proclaimed abolitionists in the academy who also argued for the subhuman status and perpetrated theories of biological inferiority of the Black person. Agassiz, like other abolitionists of his time, wanted to eliminate slavery because, he believed, it put whites into too close contact with Blacks; there were few social mechanisms for keeping the races separate, he believed, under a slave economy.* This is, for me, an early example of the dangers

---

* See Irmscher 2013 for an in-depth overview of Agassiz's work on racial taxonomy and his personal views on race.

of conflating diversity with antiracist and reparations work; diversity can and has been a method for identifying, ordering, and creating hierarchies for difference. Methods of organizing Black and Indigenous people into appropriately defined enclosures were needed at the turn of the century in particular to ensure subjugation and separation. Diversity, as an epistemology of difference connected to ordering so as to monitor and control the participation of difference, has a conceptual link to this history. Early institutions of higher education provide a stark example of how diversity, understood through its rootedness in coloniality's epistemology of difference, can work as a mode for facilitating racist or segregationist relations. This effort to reveal the epistemic underpinnings of diversity aims to reveal its significant limitations for undoing the ways of thinking and existing that have contributed to racist and oppressive social structures. It is critically important, as affirmative action and DEI-related work are increasingly under threat and derided, that those of us committed to antiracism, the abolition of the prison industrial complex, or decolonization are clear about what diversity works for and what it does not.

Early universities in North America, thanks to the research of many historians who have been developing the field of slavery and university studies, were full of Black people, many enslaved, some freed, who toiled to build and keep the institutions we value today running. They were also full of the extractions, human and sacred, of Indigenous communities.* But they were

---

* One case that I struggled with the ethics of "reexamining" in this book, is the story of a Yahi man who, after years of massacres against his people, was "discovered" nearly starving to death outside Sacramento. Anthropologist Alfred Kroeber took him to live at the University of California's anthropology museum in San Francisco where "Ishi" (which means *man* in Yahi) worked and lived as Kroeber's research subject and live display for museum visitors. When Ishi died of tuberculosis, Kroeber cut out his brain for study and sent it to the Smithsonian Institution. In 1999, after much advocacy by Native groups in California, Ishi's

also filled with ideas that worked to actively uphold a social imaginary that wealthy white men and, much later, wealthy white women, were the tiny gods of culture—the intellectuals, producers, discerners, and owners—and that they were destined by birth and by God to have dominion over all things, to be the creators of the enclosures, the sentinels of the gates of truth, and were, like all gods, able to have ownership everywhere and of all things. Universities were elaborate cabinets filled with ideas where having an enslaved person serve you while you studied Enlightenment thinkers writing about equality, freedom, and the natural rights of man was perfectly congruent; all things existed in their proper place.

In *Darkwater*, W. E. B. Du Bois writes: "But what on earth is whiteness that one should so desire it? Then always, somehow, some way, silently but clearly, I am given to understand that whiteness is the ownership of the earth forever and ever, Amen" (Du Bois 1999, 18). Institutions of higher education such as Harvard University, Yale University, and even St. Stephens College (now Bard College) were beginning to enroll students who were Black, from Puerto Rico, or Indigenous as early as the mid-1800s (Wilder 2014). These enrollments have recently become part of the narrative of difference at many institutions. They are often cited in institutional histories as accomplishments even if the enrollment was limited to one person who was Black or Indigenous. Little can often be found about that person's experience within institutional narratives. The "inclusions" of such students are used as an

remains were laid to rest on the land of the remaining descendants of the Yahi. In January 2021, Kroeber's name was removed from a building on Berkeley's campus (Day 2016/2018). I cite this case here to remind readers that the logics of universities in settler colonial societies cannot be remedied only through the renaming or removal of names from buildings but must operate at the epistemic level, the level of knowledge that believed such practices were just and in the service of goodness and truth.

effort not to reveal the abysmal persistence of whiteness, the rigor with which admissions departments monitored and patrolled the enrollment of non-white groups; rather they are used to celebrate that the institution was attempting to enact diversity and inclusion even in the nineteenth century. While these are signs we can take as miniscule positive acts to permit access to higher education for more than the children of the white ruling classes, they cannot serve as evidence of institutions radically committed to a moral imperative of educational access to all regardless of race, religion, ability, class, or gender. The agonizingly small numbers of racialized and religiously othered people admitted into the most elite institutions in North American education before the Higher Education Act of 1965 makes me uninterested in celebrating such revelations. We are proud of how many students we decide to exclude rather than proud of the availability of the education we are attempting to provide to many. Again, the positive positioning of the few racialized students who did participate, who were permitted to enter, leaves out the other racialized people, like Willy, who were there—who were part of the institution but not permitted access to learning.

The person who came upon the photograph of Willy, who made the decision to use it to celebrate the college's long legacy of women scientists without seeing the need to attribute presence or existence to the other person in the photograph, is not a "bad" person. Willy was unimaginable as a person with a contributing role to play in early women in science. So what is it to learn from Willy? Does the omission reveal something to us about the shifts that diversity makes as a mechanism for value and prestige? Imagining that the study of science by a white woman in 1865 was made possible because of the labor of Willy raises a cognitive dissonance in the presently held imaginary of diversity in higher education. That Willy and so many other people who labored, enslaved and free, within and for universities are not readily included under the term *diversity* reveals that diversity has a genealogy of shifting value—one bound up in social artifacts such as political documents, monuments, and pieces of legislation—that requires careful tracing. What is *diversity* presently to higher education? The next chapter traces the absence and appearance of the term *diversity* in higher education in an effort to expose its intertwining with an epistemology of difference with racial capital and the discipling logics of colonialism. It will work to illuminate the tensions between diversity work and reparative moves in an effort to lay the groundwork for institutional transformation that operates at ontological and epistemological levels.

Willy reveals something of the paradox in which higher education is bound up. *Not* seeing Willy is anti-Black, yet elevating his role for the benefit of institutional optics is also potentially exploitive. His imaginative resuscitation—the critical fabulation of his life within the archives of the institution—and the revelation that such laboring made possible the advancement of white women (in this case) is a reparative move. But for what cause? If the cause is to acknowledge the essential labor of marginalized and racialized bodies to the functioning of the institution and to share decision-making, provide adequate real raises, promotions, and access to knowledge production, then perhaps it is a just cause. But this would mean a fundamental reconstitution of power within the university. So who does such amending and repair? What role do university diversity approaches have to play in a country where reparation is still, often, unimaginable? Diversity work, in its present form, straddles this tenuous line. Is diversity work intended to "correct" the person who failed to see Willy through implicit bias training or to take down the image? Or is it to do both? Is it to commission a study named after Willy, as the

Lemon Project at the College of William and Mary, as an attempt to amend institutional history, provide correction and amending of the institution's understanding of itself? It is to name Willy? Or is it to reframe the narrative? To say, "Willy labors in the background, enabling an unnamed white woman to pursue science." Willy's life is included and excluded in the institutional conception of diversity because his existence contains value for the institution insofar as it can participate in the politics of racial capital. His inclusion and exclusion depend upon the social moment. At this moment, society is witnessing a range of institutions saying BlackLivesMatter but failing to interrogate how this serves to uphold their financial stability rather than interrogating how their structure upholds an exploitative system descended from those first moments of dictating the participation of difference. Higher education is not immune from using racial capital as an empty gesture to assuage the burden of history in the United States; yet it continually fails to connect statements to material redress of the enduring racial inequities embedded within its daily functions.

Accumulation / Difference That Makes
No Difference

Diversity, according to Nick Mitchell, "is about difference but also about its overcoming—the promise that difference, properly conditioned, either will make no difference or, better yet, will transform difference into an asset primed for accumulation" (Mitchell 2018, 68). Mitchell's definition is an astute critique of the limitations of present-day diversity work in higher education. Diversity work seeks to systematize difference so as to control and manipulate it for easier absorption as a resource. It is an exercise distinct from reparative action because the focus is on its additive benefit rather than on what undoes and pulls away; it is focused on conditioning difference for use in a social world in which it fuels or bolsters existing institutions. Diversity, in this sense, begins from the premise that difference is, as W. E. B. Du Bois reminds us throughout *The Souls of Black Folks*, perceived as a problem to be studied, collected, and organized—an opacity to be penetrated for manipulation and use. A key function of universities has been to accumulate difference in an effort to assimilate it into the dominant social imaginary. The accumulation of difference by higher education has, historically, not been for difference to change or unsettle, but rather for its study, monetization, and attempted assimilation in an effort to ensure that it remains a form of capital necessary to the institution's survival. This is evidenced by a long history of protest and struggle, such as the circumstances that led to the creation of Black studies and ethnic studies programs.

These protests were an intervention in the way groups previously excluded from higher education shifted the production and focus of knowledge. When such protests erupt, they are viewed as unrest, as a public relations task for the diversity worker to manage. When difference seeks to make a difference, it is often met with control tactics rather than epistemic and ontological shifts in the institution. Control tactics are often foisted on the hired diversity worker as a mechanism of patrol.

The persistence of the control of difference in higher education emerges as a logic critical to its function. From its earliest instantiations, higher education participated in the behaviors of collecting and organizing differences into taxonomies. The practice of colonizing cultures to collect nature, other human beings, and animals as objects of study is a central episteme that persists in higher education today. The ways that universities use diversity tells us something important about the ways of knowing it produces.* The ways that institutions accumulate differences holds intentions around its use. A close examination of how higher education has used diversity illuminates why diversity work has struggled to fundamentally transform it into the antiracist or decolonized places so many desire.

The growing field of the study of slavery and universities has revealed that the history of higher education in the United States and other colonial countries is the history of how, as Craig Wilder describes, the labor and bodies of unfree black people paid for the institutions we hold as bastions of progress and enlightenment today. It is also the history of land

---

*I employ the term *use* in the spirit of Sara Ahmed's work on the uses of use. In *What's the Use?* she traces the term back to nineteenth-century values that ascribed value to how things, people, animals, and plants were used: usefulness was a shaping force, one that directed purposes of life and identity. She seeks to queer use, to show how marginalized identities enter institutions and frequently use them for something other than the institutions' original intent.

grabs, expulsion of indigenous people, and accumulation of their lives as objects of study. Carefully documented, particularly in the anthology *Slavery and the University,* this research provides evidence that what we now call "diversity"—that is, bodies and cultures of difference—has always been present in higher education. Diversity, in the form of the accumulation of non-white bodies for sale, for study, for labor, is bound up in the ontology of universities. None of this is to claim that higher education is irrelevant or that higher education is solely responsible for a racial imaginary that contributes to the daily subjugation of and violence against non-white people. Rather, I seek to unravel a persistent self-perception that universities are bastions of meritocracy and egalitarianism and that they are exempt from the perniciousness of structural racism and inequality. How is this history located in the manner in which the university teaches, knows, values, and operates? What responsibility does higher education to redress its role in contributing to the cultivation of a social imaginary that perpetuates racial and social inequality? Difference makes a difference but, even in some of the founding documents that formed the Constitution can be found expressions of diversity in the United States, evidence of it as a concept in the service of what we now call "colorblindness" or an impulse to have race or class hold no difference, can be found.

Colorblindness / Federalist Paper No. 6

Diversity was not always the positive social value that it is now. Its root etymology is a fourteenth-century century French word: *Diversete,* meaning difference or divergence but also oddness, perversion, or wickedness (Mitchell 2018). Importantly, Diversity did not become a social virtue in the United States until the 1790s, when evidence of the concept's growing importance can be discerned in Federalist Paper no. 60. Alexander Hamilton wrote:

> The dissimilarity in the ingredients which will compose the national government, and still more in the manner in which they will be brought into action in its various branches, must form a powerful obstacle to a concert of views in any partial scheme of elections. There is sufficient diversity in the state of property, in the genius, manners, and habits of the people of the different parts of the Union, to occasion a material diversity of disposition in their representatives towards the different ranks and conditions in society. And though an intimate intercourse under the same government will promote a gradual assimilation in some of these respects, yet there are causes, as well physical as moral, which may, in a greater or less degree, permanently nourish different propensities and inclinations in this respect.

This form of diversity was not intended to serve for the protection, integration, or equality of people of different ethnic, racial, or gender identities, though some commentators extrapolate this intent. Diversity was not a celebration of racial, gender, or economic difference. The concept of diversity that Hamilton outlines here seeks to ensure that representative government is not dominated by a singular viewpoint. This diversity is described as dispositional, as one that though expected to assimilate under a single system of government, will serve to permit a range of desires and perspectives. His view is that a range of dispositions and beliefs are a positive balancing effect for representational democracy. This conception of diversity is not so different from the present struggle to ensure that diversity is inclusive of everyone and all viewpoints, while attempting to prioritize those works, groups, cultures and viewpoints that have been systematically prevented from participation. Diversity, in this sense, has deep roots in American tradition, but it is quite distinct from what it began to replace in the late 1970s: affirmative action. Diversity suddenly, through the rulings of the US Supreme Court on affirmative action cases, became conceptually linked with the work of enacting equitable remedy for discrimination. Yet diversity was never a suitable proxy.

Diversity, from this small snippet of history, becomes a social virtue working in the interest of representative democracy. What becomes sticky for the United States is how this concept was developed through a society that actively facilitated racial subjugation and unequal rights. The idea of diversity did not extend to racial equality at the time of the Federalist Papers; rather it was fostered as a phenomenon relegated to those who were white and male, the wealthiest of whom were educated within the newly developing universities of North America. Diversity, as distinct from legal and political efforts to abolish slavery, was alive and well within early higher education in the form of debate: a favorite topic was often slavery and the question of its morality and abolition (Brophy 2016). The notion that diversity could be a method of achieving racial equity and justice would have been inconceivable in the 1800s.

Alfred Brophy has traced debates at a number of early universities, such as Washington College in 1850, in an effort to show that the morality and its constitutionality of slavery were regular topics of discussion (Brophy 2016). While these debates gave rise to a diversity of viewpoints, they were, for the most part, intellectual exercises with little bearing on the lived conditions of enslaved Black people at the time. Overwhelmingly, students at a range of institutions, Washington and Lee being one example Brophy discusses in his work, would debate slavery, acknowledge its immorality yet vote, at the end of debates, against abolition. This practice, while showing that slavery was a regular topic of university debate, also reveals something of the ontology of universities in the face of serious social injustice. It shows that the exercise of different perspectives is ascribed greater value than working to change the material conditions of human suffering. This exposes something of the colonial mindset being reproduced: that education was most valuable in how it created space to study, think, and speak about difference not to enact social transformation on the structures that facilitated inequity. Diversity, in this sense as a virtue of higher educational institutions, has always placed viewpoints and the free exercise of rhetorical maneuvers above the urgency to remedy lived conditions of inequality. The problem raised by efforts to shift the machine of higher education to be a location for enacting racial equity or decolonization is that diversity is a maneuver that reasserts the value of viewpoint above structural change. When diversity came to replace affirmative action in how education sought to remedy generations of material exclusions and systemic under-resourcing, its conceptual foundation worked to edge back in, through rhetorical maneuvers of groups with epistemic authority in higher education, this value hierarchy; to elevate viewpoint difference above material remedy of racial inequality.

The recent concerted effort by political conservatives and many liberals to actively block diversity efforts to enact systemic changes in higher education in the service of equity has been successful. Free speech and academic freedom are wielded as institutional virtues free from considerations of how epistemic power and injustice are employed within our institutional structures through these logics. The inherent foundational problems with academic freedom—who it protects in the academy and how academic freedom continues to be stratified according to race, gender, and income—is subsumed under an immutable virtue. The discussion of academic freedom is often approached in the absence of its connection to historical harm. How the lack of conditions to express oneself freely due to fear of violent reprisal or loss of employment has shaped our collective understanding of free speech. To engage in the debate as if those historical conditions have no bearing on free speech belies the present reality that still exists for many racialized people in the form of power imbalances that are raced and classed. Academic freedom does not extend to the most vulnerable within institutions; it does not extend to adjuncts, to at-will administrators, to groups of people within universities who are the most vulnerable to repercussions for complaints of discrimination. Diversity work has been increasingly demonized as a threat to free speech and academic freedom by a range of organizations and faculty groups, particularly when it veers away from propping up viewpoint diversity and attempts to change systems and challenge traditionally held concepts such as merit and fairness.

According to the American Project on the Future of Conservatism, "in no American institution is the literal battle over what should define conservatives and progressives being fought more publicly than on our college campuses." This is not only true outside the classroom, but inside the classroom, through bipartisan movements like "Heterodox Academy" and others, scholars, students, and donors who are pushing for greater "viewpoint diversity" in the teaching of the social sciences and return of the university to its original identity as a place open to civil debate over great ideas. All with an end to preparing citizens who can deliberate with others over the future of their city, state, and nation.

The project of viewpoint diversity maintains that the university has an original "sacred" identity to return to—that at some point in the past epistemic justice existed and that the only difference that needs safeguarding by higher education is the capacity to debate with others and hear their perspectives. It is clear to me, through attending to the use of diversity in Hamilton's Federalist Paper, that diversity has a long conceptual history and interest not in achieving racial equity but rather in ensuring that a range of differing viewpoints exist. In a sense the argument for diversity to ensure viewpoint difference is not new nor misleading; what is misleading is to believe that diversity is the concept that will lead us toward repairing systems still engineering racial injustice.

Within these present debates I have heard very few references to the power imbalances that still exist in the expression of viewpoints between those identities that have power in the academy and those who do not. Tenured faculty, in the face of social media campaigns that attempt to force change for racist and sexist practices, believe they hold less power than a group of precarious graduate students. Tenured faculty and trustees worry about cancel culture, about how to safeguard free and unfettered inquiry from the ideological "mobs" of antiracist students while enjoying comfortable paychecks, health care to offset their stress, and easy access to media and political representatives through well connected boards of trustees. Rarely in the discussion is it taken seriously that the entire edifice of higher education, particularly elite private universities, is the story of the wealthiest, the most educated, reproducing themselves, claiming epistemic authority with little acknowledgement of the long tradition of epistemic injustice (what Kristie Dotson [2011] describes as testimonial quieting),* or the epistemic challenge that is already present when a Black or Latinx CDO seeks to identify bias within the institution.

Diversity holds an epistemic failure—an inability to realize that one's perspective is deeply shaped by history, race, and culture; to escape this requires a transformation that operates at the epistemic and personal level,† which I discuss in part II as epistemic reparation. Since the inception of the United States, the engineering of race inequality has occurred through our social epistemology: how we are socialized to believe and value. In the United States the persistence of a deep epistemology which maintains that if we could only learn to talk more openly about our differences, enable universities to be the places where truth seeking and diverse viewpoints are celebrated, where everyone sits around a table respectfully listening to one another, our society would find deeper solutions to the grave social inequities and injustices that we see all around us. This is the epistemic root of a colonial mindset that places the responsibility on the individual to work harder

---

* Dotson builds on Gayatri Spivek's concept of epistemic violence to offer testimonial quieting. In her paper "Tracking Epistemic Violence, Tracking Practices of Silence," Dotson defines testimonial quieting as "when people are dismissed as knowers, capable of giving testimony worthy of consideration." She connects this to an epistemic framework that hinges on racial identity to confirm or deny if a person is a valid producer of truth.

† See the work of L. A. Paul on transformative experience.

to shift their thinking rather than restructuring a social system to root out the mechanisms by which people are held in poverty, in detention, in debt, unhoused, and starving. Taking responsibility through rebuilding social systems as a way to unsettle the injustices of the past is the urgent work of the present.

Partition / Grievances Not of Their Making

In 1978 Allan Bakke, a young white man, sued the University of California Davis Medical School for reverse discrimination. He claimed that he met the school's admission criteria and was denied admission, twice, because of his race. At the time, the university reserved 16 percent of the seats in its incoming class for minority applicants under its affirmative action program. The US Supreme Court ultimately ruled that the university could not apply racial quotas in the service of affirmative action, but that diversity, or the presence of difference, was a compelling educational interest. The *Bakke* decision marks a line in the transition of race equity policy in the United States; it marks the birth of the diversity defense that would come to be used by higher education in its efforts to increase the participation of Black, Latinx, and Native Americans in historically white institutions. It also marks the birth of white-identifying people claiming discrimination in the face of actions that seek to affirm the nation's history of discrimination against Black, Latinx, and Indigenous people. This claim that diversity and anti-racist efforts signal or enact discrimination against white people, in spite of evidence that shows whites still outpace Blacks in earnings, health outcomes and social mobility, is, according to the research of social psychologists such as Cheryl Kaiser, on the rise in the United States. Before tracing the rise of the diversity defense after the *Bakke* decision, let us turn to the words of Justice Lewis Powell Jr. in the opinion.

Justice Powell wrote, "There is a measure of inequity in forcing innocent persons in [*Bakke's*] position to bear the burdens of redressing grievances not of their making" (*Regents of the University of California v. Bakke*). This statement reveals an epistemic failure, one that has permeated a persistent social imaginary around redress, reparation, or equity-based policies in the United State. *Bakke* pushed early desegregation and diversity efforts away from a direct consideration of how hundreds of years of oppression and disenfranchisement of Black and Indigenous people could be ameliorated or redressed in the present through the redistribution of resources, increased access to education, and the restructuring of system and policies that disproportionately work in favor of those who have wealth, power, or prestige. Powell maintained that rights and redress should not be applied to the experience of individuals in the present, no matter how much the structure of education had been engineered to advantage wealthy white males. It reveals that the failure of the Fourteenth Amendment to mention Black and Indigenous identity in particular allows the Equal Protection Clause to serve, in the case of Allan Bakke, the interests of colorblindness, perpetuating the belief that individuals in the present moment are direct beneficiaries of a prolonged system of conferring privileges to white people. Powell's statement reveals an epistemic structure that fails to acknowledge structural racism, a system upheld through participation in a complex network of the varied ways that wealth, educational access, health care, and the justice system have advantaged white identity.

This is not intended to be a legal analysis of the Powell decision nor of affirmative action policies. Numerous sources deconstruct that decision as well as the numerous subsequent challenges to affirmative action. This is a brief attempt to show that Powell's opinion reveals yet another type of content for the diversity cabinet or container—contents which reveal that diversity untethered from history and a belief that the present bears a relationship and responsibility to it, can be easily used to continue its long tradition of being filled by colorblindness. Diversity, untethered from what responsibility to truth telling and history means remains a mechanism that works to diminish efforts that operate at the level of structures and redistribution. I am also interested in exploring the *Bakke* decision as revelatory of a social belief; that present social experience can be and is disconnected from the harms (or privileges) of the past. Powell's decision, as well as the Affirmative Action decisions that came after it, such as *Fischer v. University of Texas* and the recent *FAIR v. Harvard University*, are examples not only of how the United States has struggled to form policies that account for the system of privilege and exclusions on the basis of race and income. The collective social value of redress, furthermore, is revealed in this decision, as one fundamentally in opposition to the bootstrap individualism that characterized US culture.

Redress, after the *Bakke* decision, became pulled apart from diversity and placed outside of it as something burdensome to its present work. However, reparative modes are not necessarily compatible with diversity as a conceptual category, as a procedure of undoing; in some ways, they actively work against the diversity defense. Powell treats historical harm not as a responsibility but rather as a burden that ought not to be shifted to individuals in the present, essentially short-circuiting the potential for ending continued harm in the future. What we ought to do now, because of the past, conditions the future. This is a mode of being that the majority in the *Bakke* decision does not encourage or seek to cultivate as a social responsibility.

Diversity, as Powell outlines, works to buffer those in the present who benefit from the harms from assuming responsibility for systems that enable them to avoid criminalization, acquire wealth and property, or live in areas free from the worst forms of environmental pollution. The notion of the present individual as free from any form of responsibility for past harm, from the idea that present existence is conditioned on past events, is poured into the diversity concept. The decision helps frame the belief that one can participate in a society, benefit from its systems of distributing resources based on predetermined characteristics, without any responsibility for the atrocities of the past.

The imperative to attend to the presence and existence of the afterlife of slavery and colonization is effectively erased by invoking diversity, the presence of difference, as the balm for historical crimes. It is then used by institutions as a convenient concept to help rationalize the dominant political and social needs of the moment, whether those needs include the invocation of BlackLivesMatter or the inclusion of trans people; it is fluid not because the historical harm is fluid, but because the concept can be used as a way to continue to hold power to dictate the means of participation and distribution. It is telling that antiracist work meets with the greatest resistance when it calls for power sharing, monetary recompense, or any form of perceived privileging of those historically marginalized. In 2016, President Barack Obama issued a statement on the Supreme Court's decision in *Fischer v. University of Texas*: "First, in the affirmative action case, I'm pleased that the Supreme Court upheld the basic notion that diversity is an important value in our society, and that this country should provide a high-quality education to all our young people, regardless of their background. We are not a country that guarantees equal outcomes, but we do strive to provide an equal shot to everybody. And that's what was upheld today."

Obama's brief statement, from the first Black president in the history of the United States, makes no mention of race in the concept of diversity and characterizes affirmative action as a forward-looking policy. He frames it as a mechanism that ensures all people, regardless of their background, can access higher education. He disconnects, in this rhetorical move, the exercise of diversity from the consideration of a person's background. Their difference, put another way, should make no difference—except that it does, deeply and persistently, in communities all across the United States and the globe where the practices of systematizing disenfranchisement, under resourcing, and criminalization begin from birth. The exercise of diversity here is encouraged as something that takes no account of history or of how the location of its persistence is essential to its redress. Let's imagine for a moment that President Obama had instead said, "First, in the affirmative action case, I'm pleased that the Supreme Court upheld the basic notion that *redress of persistent racial inequities* is an important value in our society, and that this country should instruct in the collective responsibility for the burden of backgrounds still ensnared by systems that are the legacy of racial privilege and violence. We are not a country that guarantees equal outcomes, but we do strive to create conditions that work, over generations, toward the equality we dream of achieving. And that's what was upheld today."

Fisher v. University of Texas is one recent example of the persistence of the diversity defense as well as the perception, as shown in research conducted by social psychologist Cheryl Kaiser, held by some white people that they are increasingly devalued under efforts connected to remedying racial discrimination and violence. The shift from affirmative action—an effort to remedy past discrimination in higher education against Black, Latinx/Hispanic, Indigenous, and female students—to diversity is an example of the pull away from nurturing a collective social value for a society still burdened by past injustices through systemic racism. The diversity rationale for admissions aligns with the belief that higher education should focus on meritocracy, regardless of race, in admissions, without recognition that meritocracy is an illusion built from a system that confers privilege through inherited wealth, preferred admissions, well-resourced schools, and adequate health care largely, though not exclusively, through race. Yale law professor Daniel Markovitz explores the myth of meritocracy as a sham in his 2019 book, *The Meritocracy Trap: How America's Foundational Myth Feeds Inequality, Dismantles the Middle Class and Devours the Elites,* a myth that undercuts the reality of inherited wealth and privileges, working to obscure the harsh realities of generational and systemic racism and classism.

The *Fisher* case provided yet another example of how diversity is put forward as a greater compelling educational interest than responsibility taking for decades of engineered exclusions and how beliefs about merit, that one's present is somehow void of historical privilege or disadvantage, is core to the social imaginary of the United States. In 2008 Abigail Fisher and Rachel Multer Michalewicz, both white women, applied for admission at the University of Texas at Austin and were denied. They subsequently brought a lawsuit against the university, claiming they had been discriminated against on the basis of their race and in violation of the Equal Protection Clause of the Fourteenth Amendment, as they believed their high school performance, test scores, and extracurriculars made them deserving of admission. The lawsuit was eventually heard by the US Supreme Court, with the justices deciding that the University of Texas at Austin's use of race in admissions satisfied the use of diversity as a compelling educational interest established from the precedents of the decisions in prior challenges to affirmative action in *Bakke*, *Gratz*, and *Grutter*, the latter two affirmative action cases brought against the University of Michigan. In all cases racial preference in admission to remedy or rectify past exclusions were rendered in violation of the equal protection clause and the use of diversity, weighing factors of difference in their contribution to the educational mission, were upheld.

In the years since these landmark affirmative action cases, nine states, including Michigan and California, have enacted bans on race-based affirmative action practices in higher education. In October 2020 California voters considered Proposition 16, which would strike down the twenty-four-year ban on race and gender considerations in university admissions. The proposition was voted down in spite of evidence that revealed statistically significant drops in the enrollment of Black and Latinx students in the University of California system. Edsource, a California educational research and analysis organization, found that in 1997, just before the ban would have affected enrollment, Black students comprised 8 percent of students at California State University and have fallen to 4 percent, while their high school graduation rate has increased. Many states that enacted a ban put into place new methods to uphold diversity such as percent plans and socioeconomically based admissions strategies. Concurrent with the diversity defense has been the growth in diversity, equity, and inclusion–related positions in higher education, offered in place of policies that systematically ensure equitable and socially just access to higher education.

The socially held value that those in the present should not be burdened with grievances that they did not create persists and has, arguably, become even more intractable in the face of a rising tide of emboldened white supremacy in North America. Currently efforts to increase equity, to acknowledge the persistence of a history that weaves a persistent system of racial and class-based violence are a tinderbox on which white supremacists seek to stoke a rising campaign of hate. The grievances of the past are the material called upon to ignite the present, and attempts to rectify inequality that hesitate to unapologetically take responsibility for the past must be considered in the ongoing work of oppression.

The Morrill Acts

The "Land-Grab University"

The Morrill Land-Grant Acts were federal statutes enacted in 1862 and 1890 to facilitate the development of college and universities in the United States using territory that had been taken from Indigenous tribes, mostly through acts of violent seizure. The acts were conceived as a stride forward for equity in higher education, and even today they are often described as monumental achievements in the creation of public higher education in the United States. They helped establish the large public universities that we describe as "land-grant universities" and many of the historically Black colleges and universities (HBCUs). Their passage, which allowed for a massive theft of land from Native Americans, created the institutions that enabled generations of low-income, working-class, and Black people to attain higher education, fundamentally changing the trajectory of social mobility in the United States. However, just as colonialism is the "dark underbelly of modernity," the creation of these institutions has a violent and unreconciled history.

To fully communicate the violence and devastation that the Morrill Land-Grant Acts exerted on Native Americans deserves a book-length examination. The paradox of the land-grant universities contributing to the development of many HBCUs, as well as setting the track for separate but equal institutions, reveals that within the founding of universities is the partitioning of Blackness and the erasure of Indigeneity from higher education. The separation of Indigeneity and Blackness is a repeated

mechanism of empire. The founding of these institutions relied on an epistemology of human value based on race. Even
in contemporary diversity work in the United States, reparations to Indigenous groups or even enrollment of Native students remain persistently marginal in comparison with efforts
to enroll Black students in historically white institutions. These
processes of using Black and Indigenous people as forms of
capital to facilitate the growth of universities reveals the processes universities have relied on to patrol the participation of
difference in higher educational institutions.

The digital journalism project Land-Grab Universities (land-
grabu.org) provides a comprehensive view of how many of the
nation's most prestigious universities owe their existence to the
violent seizure of territory from Native American people and
calculates, to the dollar, what tribes are owed for the loss of territory through the Morrill Acts. During the period from the
passage of the first Morrill Act in 1862 to passage of the second in 1890, 10.7 million acres of land owned by 245 tribal nations were stolen from Indigenous people and divided into
roughly 80,000 parcels for redistribution. Even in the present-
day, as the United States Congress holds hearings on reparations for slavery, attention to the losses inflicted on Native
Americans remains negligible.

The Morrill Act of 1890 barred allocating funds to states
that made distinctions of race in admissions to colleges and
universities. But it offered a caveat: if a state sought to bar admission based on race, at least one land-grant college for African
Americans had to be established. This led to the creation of 19
public colleges for Black students. This Act provided the foundation for the development of many of the public HBCUs,
which would provide a footing for a Black middle class. The
creation of the land-grant colleges, which enabled greater
numbers of working-class white people and Black people to

access higher education, was widely seen as a victory for early diversity efforts in higher education. Also worthy of attention is how the creation of these institutions was the direct result of subjugation and violence toward Native Americans as well as how their creation provided a powerful foundation for separate but equal education. Including Blacks in higher education through procedures of patrol and enclosure provided a rationale for segregated institutions. These founding institutions furthered a rationale that divided education, mainly vocational and agricultural at the time, along principles of class and racial hierarchies. The elite private institutions, founded on the same practices of dispossession and enslavement, were reserved mainly for the white and male wealthy with a few scholarships available for low-income white people and the occasional person of color. As early as 1900, universities in the so-called Ivy League enrolled Black American students and students from China and parts of Latin America. The founding of separate institutional systems of higher education for whites and Blacks also contributed to a collective imaginary which maintained that prosperity was the result of access to education; the systems, however, were engineered to facilitate discrimination and unequal resourcing based on racial identity.

The passage of the second Morrill Act diversified the range of people who could access higher education in the United States. The creation of the land-grant universities and HBCUs created a system that opened the door for Black and low-income people to access a critical mechanism of social mobility. It must also be understood, however, as an example of epistemologies that attempt to erase the Native American from the landscape of higher education, the violence of the dispossession that led to the founding of these institutions is only recently receiving attention from the universities themselves and Tribal Colleges. The first Morrill Act arose on the heels of the emancipation struggles in the United States, as the republic sought to prove to Europe that its ideals of freedom and prosperity were available to all. It sought to appear as if the stain of slavery was, under the ideals of a fresh Civil War, being redressed through the creation of systems, though separate, that provided access to skills and training needed for self-sufficiency. As a new society seeking to prove its egalitarian and democratic character, success had to be framed not as race privilege but as an effort at self-making.

The myth of grit and hard work as necessarily leading to wealth is woven into the social imaginary of the United States. That hard work equals financial gains persists in spite of grow-ing degrees of wealth inequality in the United States. This prosperity myth serves to support a racist imaginary because it works well to justify the poverty and challenges to maintaining wealth among Black, Latino, and Indigenous people. In 2019, prior to the COVID-19 pandemic, white Americans held seven times the wealth of Black Americans. The median family net worth for white people is $171,000, compared with $17,600 for Black people (Lee 2019). The median family wealth for Latino/Hispanic and Asian American families is only slightly higher than that of Black people. In a social environment in which gen-erations have been socialized to believe that hard work results in financial success, the bitter pill of structural racism that arises through practices such as redlining, evictions, and debt is internalized and narrated, for many, as an individual failure. The prosperity myth serves diversity through social imagi-naries such as bootstrap narratives and the exceptional per-son of color. In the case of the Morrill Acts, establishing a sep-arate higher education system for Black people in the form of HBCUs served to reinforce the white imaginary that because education was available, prosperity could be engaged as at-tainable, no matter your race. This ideology still haunts our society today, though such mythologies are being torn down all around us, their hollow promise to people of color increasingly revealed. The modes of "opportunity" granted to people of color who remain persistently precarious in terms of wealth acquisition are engineered to uphold the prosperity myth, blaming the individual for lack of success while rewarding those who have the benefit of race and intergenerational wealth privileges.

Higher education debt plays a significant role in this mythology. Institutions actively work to accumulate Black and Brown bodies through diversity-recruiting practices that provide access to education but at the cost of crushing lifetime debt. These institutions capitalize, in various ways, on their acceptance into the institution. Free education, without indebtedness, when argued for as a reparative move that would significantly contribute to social equity and providing a somewhat equal footing after graduation, is often dismissed as financially impossible on a widespread basis. A number of Ivy League and elite liberal arts colleges, such as Bowdoin College and Amherst College, offer reduced fees for students whose families are below a certain income threshold. These graduates, though many incur debt for their graduate-level studies, show the significance of an undergraduate education free of debt, evidenced in a higher degree of social mobility. The work of economist Raj Chetty has relentlessly illustrated that attaining higher education matters to intergenerational social mobility. However, it also matters which schools one attends and how much debt is incurred for the people in the low- and middle-income quartiles. (Chetty 2017) Mere access to higher education is, as Chetty's work has shown, insufficient to support the myth of prosperity. It matters where one goes to school, as it always has, and the creation of institutions to help working-class people enter into lesser resourced institutions, begins with the Morrill Acts. Important to this discussion is why, in spite of efforts to diversify the most elite institutions, the children at the top 1 percent of income distribution are still 77 percent more likely to attend Ivy League and Ivy-plus institutions (Chetty 2017). This fact challenges the notion that the most elite institutions are "diverse" or intend to serve causes of justice or affirmative action. From the earliest moments, higher education has committed itself to the creation of a segregated system in which the most elite institutions control the levers of power to determine when and how those not from the most elite classes may participate. Diversity serves as a justificatory mechanism for resource hoarding, exclusion, and theft—a means of cloaking how higher education (particularly private elite education) has been used to reinforce class station, ensure the reproduction of intergenerational wealth, and serve as an amnesia mechanism to forget the responsibility that institutions hold for injustices such as land theft.

Bound up in diversity work is the work of forgetting. It is the work of celebrating the identity diversity of the present individual, which holds little interest in how Indigenous people are persistently erased in the United States' collective imaginary. Survival is predicated on whom the ruling classes decide lives and dies. Diversity as a concept that works to patrol and manage difference enters when emphasis on the use of bodies of culture needs concealing. This is a primary strategy underlying settler colonialism, of which the Morrill Acts provide a critical example. Land-grant universities and HCBUs were necessary to protect elite institutions from the masses and to create a mechanism to ensure that human capital could be transformed into the kind of resource that industry needed. These institutions used the egalitarian language of "access to education for all" to conceal the extraction of the land from Native communities and the chronic underfunding that would arise from establishing a segregated higher education system.

Afterthoughts

Diversity, as a concept laden with the promise of a social good is best understood through how it shows up in social artifacts, how it has been used and is used. Concepts like happiness are given shape through how a culture uses them over time. This manner of knowing is inherited and often replicated without critical analysis of whether it aligns with a group's or society's moral aspirations. The moments and artifacts that I have enlisted in exploring how diversity manifests and is applied are an effort to reveal that diversity work is not only an insufficient engine for the abolition of racism or decolonization in higher education; diversity may, in fact, be contributing to greater divisiveness toward racial equity efforts as well as weakening initiatives to balance unequal systems. Diversity, as a practice of assimilation, must always be understood in air quotes because when we say *diversity,* not everyone holds similar values or beliefs about what it is and what it is supposed to do for society. Diversity holds great interest in ordering, controlling, and accumulating representation; it is less interested, I argue, in the procedures and processes that perpetuate inequality. In the absence of practices, habits, and values, a collection of different kinds of people grappling with diversity can yield hostility or, it can through attentiveness to processes lead to transformative experiences. The morphology of diversity into a social good that will remedy racial and other forms of inequality is, from my own perspective and experience, a misguided notion. Diversity, as a social practice in institutions such as higher education, has its conceptual roots, as I have sought to show, in an epistemology of difference that developed from the self-interested needs of colonists to generate ways of controlling, defining, and accumulating bodies and cultures that were distinct from those of white Europeans. Within its genealogy, it holds an ontology of control of difference.

It is and will remain an insufficient and misapprehended concept for efforts to advance taking responsibility or to recompense, amend or make restitution for higher education's collusion with facilitating a hierarchy of human value originally predicated on maleness, whiteness, and wealth and now based on maintaining the interests of the ruling class. Diversity work, in spite of all the good, dedicated, earnest, and intelligent people putting their energy into it, is fundamentally the wrong concept if we are seeking to unsettle systems that have facilitated racism and classism. Reparative activity, its epistemological and ontological character, is where those interested in contributing to efforts to abolish carceral systems, to create antiracist policies or to end economic injustice should turn our energy and attention. Reparation is, I believe, a complex way of knowing that may enable us to create educational institutions that rather than reproducing colonial ways of knowing that have enabled a mass exploitation of humans and animals, facilitate transformative futures conditioned by present responsibility for past harm. But first, reparation as an activity of undoing must be examined.

PART II

The Constellation of Reparation

A supernova is the final luminous stage in the death of a star. It occurs during the last evolutionary moment as the star collapses, undoes itself, its brilliance shooting innumerable points of light into darkness. What is unleashed is pure matter dispersed as material for new forms. In dialogue with Saidiya Hartman in their 2003 essay "The Position of the Unthought," Frank Wilderson III explains that when reparations are distributed to redress a past historical injustice unlinked from how anti-Blackness continually operates, its varied behaviors of subjugation unaddressed, they lose their potential for revolutionary transformation. Reparations fail to provide material necessary for the creation of new forms, which they have the potential to unleash. Reparations, in the case of slavery, are often raised as recompense for past harm; but they do not always connect to ways of knowing and existing, the way in which institutions *relate* to, think about, Blackness or the Other. Increasingly, as evidenced in the policy platform outlined by the Movement for Black Lives on their website, reparative actions across policing, housing, health care, prisons, and education are proposed as steps to end the ongoing violence exerted on Black people. If reparations are, as David Ragland (2019) says, a peace treaty, then there is a growing awareness that this peace treaty must be material. As Wilderson's 2013 short film *Reparations . . . Now* posits, the experience of racist harm is found in racism's constant presence, the way it constantly stalks those who are seen as Black in this society, the way perception is backgrounded by thoughts about what Blackness is and is not. In the film he describes (replaying the loop in different ways) being asked whether he is out on parole while reading the paper and drinking a low-fat decaf latte on a Sunday morning. He reveals, through this work, the impossibility of recovering or repairing the multitude of incessant and perpetual harms of slavery and its afterlife, for there is a specter that lingers in perception, action, and knowledge. In other words, reparation is also an activity of undoing, unsettling, and unraveling how we understand, through truth telling, how our systems and structures perpetuate ways of knowing and being bequeathed to us from slavery and settler colonialism. When unleashed, reparation is an unraveling force that works to unsettle habitual and comfortable modes of perceiving existence. This part of its character often conceals, paradoxically, how repair is connected not simply to fixing but also to undoing, ripping, and tearing in order to make ready for the new.

Conversations about reparations, particularly in higher education, fall short of the kind of unleashing that Wilderson describes. Far too often even uttering the word elicits ridicule or disbelief that the inequalities of our present life have any connection or responsibility for past harm. Comments in online chats about reparations, even from earnest progressives, can be summed up as both a skepticism that responsibility-taking moves for the past can ever affect anything in the present and a resentment that people in the present should benefit from material recompense for the suffering of their ancestors. Our epistemology in settler colonial states facilitates forgetting and innocence for the generational benefits of wealth and educational privilege that have been conferred along color lines. These examples are found all around us. Even as we watch the United States erupt in protests against a persistent structure of state violence against Black people, reparations remain side-stepped as a possible option, uninterrogated for what their conceptual richness might provide in the struggle to move into a less violent, racist, and oppressive society. This is connected to the epistemic, to what happens when a concept not readily available within a society brings us to a boundary in our social imagination. New concepts or ideas can present a horizon that we have difficulty perceiving how to get to or knowing what might be found beyond as it presses against the limits of an imagination that is socially conditioned and produced. An example of this can be identified in current efforts to abolish the prison industrial complex (known as PIC abolition) in the United States. When presented with the idea that a society could exist without police or prisons, it is challenging to imagine how society might grapple with harm. Mariame Kaba, a lead activist and theorist in PIC abolition work, often tells people that abolition work does not provide a preconceived picture or framework for what comes next (Kaba et al. 2021). Rather, what is created comes from the collective work of undoing the manner in which we relate to one another through harm in communities. What we need to ask is why reparations are met with marginalization and most importantly, why it is so challenging for many to imagine that reparations might be a liberative rather than limiting force? Or, put another way, why are reparations *not* a set of activities in settler colonial societies like the United States? Is it that the concept of reparation is simply insufficient to offer social and political mechanisms to account for persistent structural racism; or is that reparations cut against ways we are socialized to learn, exist, and imagine? I want to explore the following questions in this part of the book: What are some ways that reparations as a multifaceted phenomenon have been understood and employed within higher education in particular?

What happens when the onto-epistemic (ways of knowing and being) dimension of reparations is engaged? What implications do reparations engaged as an onto-epistemic phenomena hold for the work of antiracism, decolonization, or antioppressive efforts in higher education? What happens when reparative thinking and acting, rather than diversity, are engaged in the educational environment?

I will explore reparative activities as life-affirming choices, as active commitments made to facilitate undoing as a method for creating new modes of existence detached from the violent unrelenting generational chain of white supremacy and capitalism. When the full promise of the reparative dimensions of existence and knowing is engaged, the character of reparations as a source of life-affirming energy is revealed; undoing can offer space for new life to emerge. When a statue is knocked from its plinth and tossed in the river, a space is revealed to imagine otherwise. The work it took to remove the statue from its plinth opens potential; it ruptures the accustomed gaze and provides a gap through which to imagine what could be. But, as philosopher of education Maxine Greene warns, imagining otherwise is not necessarily a virtuous endeavor. In the gaps can rush all manner of oppressive or liberative imaginings.

Reparative activities are provocations to transform, to perceive the ruptures that harmful histories have caused to human behavior in the present. What is imagined is the risky work of uncertainty; it is the epistemic shift from classifications to something else, something unwieldy, unsettling—some life-generating energy. To imagine and realize what might exist in its place exercises the muscles we need in order to shift behaviors, attitudes, policies, and systems. It allows us to develop new onto-epistemic resources to describe what we need, what has been missing, and what we might build or grow in the rubble left from monuments to terror and violence.

To place the statue of Jen Reid, a BlackLivesMatter activist, in the space where a statue of slave trader Edward Colston once stood in Bristol provides imaginative material for a society to begin the structural work of creating many worlds that no longer honor domination and oppression based on race and gender. This offer of a new epistemic resource, a new statue for imagining, is necessary yet it is not sufficient for altering the material conditions of Black, Indigenous, and gender-oppressed people; it is one star in the activities of a reparative constellation. Policies, law, and systems overhaul are needed in addition to massive shifts in our epistemic structures: we need to change not only *what* we know, but *how* we know. Universities have a central role to play in shifting the way that settler colonial societies construct, reconstitute, and imagine knowledge. Why they do not take up such a role? Collective social and cultural understanding of reparation and its broader constellation of reparative activities is an educational concern that can be traced to education understood as the social and political institution that deeply shapes credibility, truth, and values.

Reparations efforts, in higher education and in politics, often focus primarily on economic recompense and redistribution as a way to redress harm. Less often emphasized, though increasingly witnessed, is the role of the aesthetic, specifically the symbolic, in reparative activities. The removal of monuments and portraiture as well as the renaming of buildings honoring people who upheld slavery or were involved in violence against Indigenous people has increased in the United States, Canada, South Africa, and the United Kingdom, revealing the significance of the symbolic in the work of redress and reconciliation. In 2005 the United Nations identified cultural restitution as one of several ways to enact remedy in cases of war, building from efforts begun after World War II with the 1954 Hague

Convention on the Protection of Cultural Property in the Event of Armed Conflict.

One recent high-profile example of the ways symbolic interventions have been part of efforts to rupture, through truth telling, dominant images of power was the 2015 Rhodes Must Fall protest movement. Students at the University of Cape Town campaigned to remove a statue of Cecil Rhodes, claiming that the statue's presence was a daily reminder that the university honored those who had helped engineer apartheid and institutional racism and that the impact of this history on the present university had not been reckoned with. The monumentalizing of Cecil Rhodes, an undisputed racist, communicated that the ways of knowing embedded within the university that are the descendants of apartheid have yet to be undone. Rhodes, the founder of Rhodesia, publicly expounded on the virtues of settler colonialism and the superiority of what he described as the white race (Rotberg and Shore 1988). Rhodes Must Fall ignited similar protests against monuments on university campuses in the United States, the United Kingdom, and Canada. The removal of monuments or altering of signage to more accurately reflect the harm that occurred is identified by the United Nations as one way to satisfy reparations defined as compensation given for abuse or injury.

Reparative activities are cultural, aesthetic, and symbolic actions revealing that domination, oppression, and violence are inflicted through a range of modalities and therefore must be redressed through a multifaceted approach, which scholars such as W. E. B Du Bois knew and spent much of his life's work articulating. Oppression occurs through language, cultural devaluing, or erasure as well as through violence exerted on bodies. Monuments and symbols are reminders that harm can be inflicted through the creation of social myths, ways of socializing people over many generations, into ways of erasing and reconfiguring narratives to evade responsibility and account-ability to truth. The placing of a monument or symbol was used by dominant groups to claim or uphold power; it is one way that the Empire reminds its victims of their place and how power works to shape the historical narrative. Sociologist James Loewen described this in the context of US history in a 2015 *Washington Post* article: "the Confederates won with the pen (and the noose) what they could not win on the battlefield: the cause of white supremacy and the dominant understanding of what the war was all about. We are still digging ourselves out from under the misinformation they spread, which has manifested in our public monuments and our history books". The removal of a monument affirms that violence and white supremacy will no longer be valorized or be allowed to shroud themselves in thin narratives of remembrance for war, for sacrifice without responsibility. A core concern driving this inquiry is to understand how so many people have *not* been able to perceive what monuments to Robert E. Lee, Christopher Columbus, or Cecil Rhodes represented or why, despite the persistent testimony of Black and Indigenous people, that these monuments were daily testimonies to terrorism. It is not simply that people don't know or understand what happened historically; it is that this fails to matter to their present experience and that imaginative options beyond what they experience as "normal" are lacking. This is why the onto-epistemic character of reparation needs examination; we need to understand why, as societies shaped by settler colonialism, we have not found sufficient ways to enact recompense and amends for its harm. Furthermore, why our structures of existence provide knowledge frameworks that support and reward the evasion of social responsibility for past harm is a persistent question. Our ways of knowing all too readily facilitate modes of existence that have little relationship to how our present privileges are connected to a long chain of exploitation. If we understand higher education to be a primary mechanism for the reproduction of social imaginaries that shape our sense of truth and provide meaning to our existences, then it is necessarily a site for critically examining how we might begin to develop ways of knowing that no longer reproduce settler dreams of accumulation, extraction, subjugation of life, and patrol of difference.

Societies whose cultures are interwoven with legacies of racist violence have experienced a new wave of reckoning that demands accountability for how institutions and ways of knowing within them continually facilitate the production of racism and oppression. In other words, if we attend to reparation as a concept that is a constellation of ways of knowing and existing that unravel, undo, and unsettle, then perhaps we may begin to see that its activities hold potential for transformative relations to emerge. Accountability is a different turn in social movements; it requires an epistemic shift for groups that have been habituated to a one-sided freedom, a freedom that conducts itself as if there were no impact, no responsibility. If the truth is obscured about how past harm persists in the construction of knowledge today, then we cannot see where and why that harm is still inflicted, nor can we create the means of transformation. Without developing critical perspectives on how we may stop the various present manifestations of the logics of slavery and settlerism, I fear that we will continue to operate within cycles of domination that evade responsibility-taking and change. Our diversity efforts, as I outlined in part I, are not necessarily attempts at rupture and responsibility-taking. They are often efforts due to the morphology of diversity to provide management and comfort to those who continue to benefit from systems that facilitate inequality and to assimilate previously excluded people and cultures into these systems as yet another iteration in how difference is used according to its value. Time spent building elaborate, costly apparatus in the form of bias awareness workshops to buffer the pain and guilt of those who control resources and own the means of production is a distraction from efforts to unsettle structures, to undo them so as to put something else in their place.

Reparative knowing and action assist in understanding the root cause of the violence that we witness around us every single day. It can awaken us from this hallucinatory dreamworld in which we wander, believing that we have little agency, that the system around us that is killing so many of us and our planetary home, is the way it is, not the experience of the after-shocks, the undulating transformation of the ways of existence learned through slavery and settler colonialism. The confrontation of truth is painful in societies that have benefited from slavery and Indigenous dispossession and genocide, because it shakes the order of our world. It is not seeing the truth for the first time that shakes the order; it is when it becomes irrevocably clear that responsibility requires giving up ways of living and knowing that have conferred comfort or privileges. Truth, for many in the United States in particular right now, reveals that its social fabric is built upon a grand lie, but it is not the realization of the lie that matters so much as the actions to take responsibility, to enact accountability for it. This presents a challenge to the deepest parts of how we exist and know, our onto-epistemology, and provokes us to face the fact that social institutions, like higher education, have socialized participation in a system that has permitted— in fact rewarded people—the evasion of responsibility for ongoing suffering. Higher education has been a key social organism for the perfection of this onto-epistemology through its place as a social reproductive mechanism, a mechanism that has facilitated socialization into the grand lie of white supremacy that frames daily existence and knowledge. But to be clear, attentiveness to the white person is a waste of time. Responsibility-taking for the way systems confer social privileges disproportionately on white people and undoing them is, from this perspective, where energy should be directed. I cannot change the degree to which a white person stands in a classroom and enacts racism; only they can. I can, however, work to undo systems, such as exclusionary college admissions practices, that privilege the engineered confluence of whiteness and wealth. Reparative work, unlike diversity work, is a weapon that unsettles the structures of knowing and existing that have operated without account for its impact.

We often hear the refrain "let the past be past." But the past can never be past, just as our DNA weaves into our very bodies the experiences, illnesses, and strengths of our ancestors. The past is, as is our genetic material, always present in our attitudes, behaviors, values, and actions. Telling the truth about how our society was constructed—the origin stories—opens us to perceive the social forms that are its legacy. Repair, which reparative activities can enable, allows us to participate in the possibilities of renewal, re-creation, and hope that existence can be more than this violent hallucinatory dream. Without this, I worry that quests for liberation from racist modes of knowing and existence will fail.

Attempts at redress for slavery and Indigenous dispossession in the United States and other countries have occurred in fits and starts—always with contestation, always through the labor of those victimized by the system—and redress rarely ever permeates the collective imaginary, our onto-epistemic structures. Yet slowly we are seeing signs and signals of reparative activity. Policies such as affirmative action are increasingly forgotten or so challenged as to become ineffective as systemic efforts to redress generations of systemic exclusion from higher education and employment based on race. In its early years, affirmative action policies enabled real material shifts for Blacks, Latinx/Hispanics, and Indigenous people who were deliberately excluded from higher education. Yet it still brings some of the greatest benefits to white women. The Americans with Disabilities Act, enacted in 1990, is now a policy and practice that we rarely question yet still struggle to integrate into our daily decision-making because, for many, it does not yet shift how they think and know. Disabilities are often an afterthought, an add-on, an accommodation to the existing structure rather than a way to fundamentally redesign how time and space are ordered. The institutions of higher education, as locations where people are socialized into values about knowledge, are potential sites for undoing or unsettling epistemes that facilitate oppression and inequality.

Reparative movements are, I believe, arising all around us. Universities will decide to meaningfully participate through identifying responsibility-taking maneuvers or will be subject to significant challenges from their students and their employees. Higher education should see this as a critical activity to embrace meaningfully, even if unleashing reparative activity leads to fundamental changes in its identity, function, and power.

The varied dimensions of reparation can assist humans in the creation of new systems for life to flourish within, built from healing and atonement. It is my hope that this inquiry may illuminate the varied kinds of activities that higher education can commit to in efforts to abolish systems of social exploitation and violence. The epistemic dimension of reparative activity—a way of knowing that undoes long-held modes of relating to difference, opens empathy and accountability to the past, connecting its legacy in the present—is a most urgently needed capacity to develop. Whether higher education can participate as a transformative mechanism, a reparative force, lies first with its own truth telling and accountability to the ripple effects of the harms it has participated in, perpetrated, and continues to perpetrate. This is not intended to encourage exercises in apology or control. Taking responsibility for how actions result in harmful policies must be material, thoughtful, and collective. The controlling behaviors associated with diversity cut against efforts to unsettle and undo. There are no predetermined sets of criteria to follow. Though statements of apology and verbal acknowledgments of harms are important, they are insufficient. Material commitment and the changes such commitments require is what works to shift structures of knowing and existing. The social imaginary that we inhabit, our values, behaviors, beliefs, and attitudes, have been crafted and reinforced over generations to reproduce an existence that relates to all life, particularly Black life, as capital to be extracted from, dominated, subjugated, and used in service of the self-interested power of a few.

Reparation is, as evidenced in responses to Ta-Nehisi Coates's essay "The Case for Reparations" (2014), a concept that elicits strong reactions in multiple political directions. Critics like Kevin Williamson who wrote a response to Coates in the *National Review* titled "The Case against Reparations," engage with the economic dimension of reparative activities and the impact of wealth redistribution as a form of "moral primitivism," which Williamson identifies as divisive, imperfect, and impossible to administer equitably. Critics like Williamson overlook the epistemic framework that surrounds the way wealth and race are considered. Policies that worked to disenfranchise Blacks and create a foundation of distrust of the financial system in Black communities are driven by a way of knowing that views Black identity as a location for theft whether through subprime mortgages or interest-based debt for college. The concern should lie less with the mechanisms of who gets financial recompense and how it is possible that whole communities, as Raj Chetty's research on social mobility by geographic region in the United States reveals, have remained impoverished along color lines? What epistemic frameworks govern the use of Blackness for theft, for control, or for consumption? Critics like Williamson overlook how Black communities in the United States built wealth, acquired land, and built institutions, and that every time it happened outside the control of those in power, it was destroyed and people were slaughtered, as in the case of the Tulsa Massacre, or defunded as in the case of HBCUs or the ongoing dispossession through finance capital of land owned by Black farmers.* The focus of such critics targets the social challenges of unequal wealth distribution that is historically conditioned rather than the epistemic frameworks that undergird beliefs about why race and money are continually, perpetually in the United States, a tension, linked in their maneuvers of oppression.

Critics also cite reparations as financial recompense as a practice that is "un-American," because Americans just have to work harder for financial gains, make sure to get the right financial planner, or learn to better manage money. Rather than focusing on why the economic system needs poverty—needs oppression—for wealth to happen, the focus is on the moral failings of low-income people, who in the United States are disproportionately Black, Latinx, or Indigenous. These mythologies are deeply embedded in our bodies, our daily lives, and our educational systems. As the year 2020 unfolded, the world witnessed the destabilization of forms of existence that had once been taken for granted. Going to school, to an office or a workplace, socializing with friends and strangers in crowded

---

* See Newkirk 2019. The article outlines the procedures of finance capital, most recently the retirement fund held by almost all higher education workers (TIAA) to dispossess Black farmers in the southern United States.

spaces were suddenly, overnight, transformed. The COVID-19 pandemic unsettled our order; it left ways of life undone; it opened possibilities of reparative knowing because it intervened in accepted modes of existence, asking us to see otherwise.

In this part of the book I explore some of the ways reparation is already understood and practiced, investigate its historical evolution in relation to white supremacy and higher education, discuss the social imaginary as explained by Lorraine Code and Cornelius Castoriadis, examine why understanding reparation as a socio-imaginative activity is important to higher education, and explore what happens when we think about reparation as a form of energy, a human activity that provides a life force necessary for epistemic, aesthetic, and ontological transformation of human existence. I work with reparation as an energy concept in the sense that its force and promise for responsibility-taking, accountability, and restoring society into balanced relationships with one another and with the planet—one that has been lacking since colonialism and industrialization—lies in understanding it not only as an object or an end, but as an activity or process of collective human effort, a form that arises from collective commitment, from principles of care and love rather than of patrol, accumulation, and theft. I will explore reparation as a force of undoing that makes way for new forms of existence to arise. I offer higher education as an apparatus for energy conversion, shifting how and where human activity focuses collective efforts of undoing.

Reparation, I aim to illuminate, functions onto-epistemically; it is not, as it is often understood, an end or an object, such as money, to be doled out. Reparative existence is the practice of directing energy toward what needs undoing for "right" relations to emerge. By right relations I mean the obligation to enact responsibility-taking for what arises in relationship with other humans, with animals and with the planet. Glenn Coulthard in

Red Skins, White Masks (2014) describes the ethical orientation to land and to others as grounded normativity. Land is not a commodity or a discrete thing to be used but rather a relationship of obligation to humans and other-than-humans. In the case of reparative epistemology, it is a process of undoing ways of knowing and existing that have not seen the responsibility required to land or nonhuman others, whose modes of knowing continue to facilitate violence and exploitation in the name of freedom. Ownership of everything and domination to serve the dividends of a few have guided existence and beliefs around the progress of success for generations.

Imagining into the spaces revealed by undoing, unsettlement, and engaging rigorously with what remains is urgently needed. I realize, as I write this, how dramatic it sounds. How we amend, undo knowing and existence through reimagining the structures and procedures that ensnare even the most committed of us, allows us to participate in the reproduction of racist and settler colonial attitudes, beliefs, and practices, is an activity laden with choice; it is an activity of identifying what to say *yes* to and what to leave behind. The reparative, I will try to describe, is an onto-epistemic activity that can help move people into behaviors and attitudes of undoing and un-settlement needed for rebuilding, re-engineering the structures of the present. The law of the conservation of energy says that energy cannot be created or destroyed, it can only be changed from one form to another. Extending this analogy, in this part I will work to explain reparative activity as a force of conversion that generates energy necessary to change one form of society into another.

As I experience this historical moment of a global pandemic providing, for many people, a crack into yet another face of climate change and increased mobilization for racial justice, people are calling to build the apparatus needed for transformative activity. How humans, particularly those who are the beneficiaries of the oppressive violence of coloniality, figure out how to stop doing requires undoing, unsettling, and cleaning up before we enact remedies. Within universities, particularly those shaped by long legacies of white supremacist ruling-class interests, the heat and work of reparative activity is already underway, undoing and unsettling. Whether it can lead to a transformative undoing or be managed out through the epistemology of difference that favors patrol and classification, remains to be seen.

Attempted Remedies

Exploring the conceptual constellation of reparation requires inquiry into origins, into how its existence as an act—as a concept or social practice—arose and is presently used. Reparation, atonement, or the seeking of amends is an ancient concept, appearing in various manifestations from the Bible to the Qur'an. Along with the concept of sin or the infliction of harm came actions to enact remedies. The creation of white supremacy, of capitalism founded on the creation of race and its associated behaviors of dominance, extraction, oppression, and erasure through slavery and settler colonialism, gave rise to a distinct form of reparations: one that transited geographies through patterns of exacting horrors upon difference by means of control, tortures of classifications so horrific that their consequences are still echoing within our social structures. The term "white supremacy" is often uttered these days, as if its invocation will serve as an undoing, an accusation leveled at people born into white skin, as if their patrol will undo the strictures binding hundreds of years of habituation. Perception and acknowledgment matter, but in the absence of collectively working to undo them, these structures of oppression will continue.

Over the last decade, whiteness studies have sought to examine how whiteness is a problem not simply of white bodies but also of ways of knowing and acting that confer privileges through practices of subjugation. Rather than citing current scholars of whiteness,* I will turn to one of the earliest voices to explain the working of whiteness, its identity tightly bound to practices of extraction and enclosures, and its effect on culture, our collective imagination, and frameworks of existence.

W. E. B. Du Bois, writing in 1919, captured whiteness succinctly. In *Darkwater: Voices from within the Veil* he writes:

> I do not laugh. I am quite straight-faced as I ask soberly:
> "But what on earth is whiteness that one should so desire it?" Then always, somehow, some way, silently but clearly, I am given to understand that whiteness is the ownership of the earth forever and ever, Amen!
>
> . . .
>
> After the more comic manifestations and the chilling of generous enthusiasm come subtler, darker deeds. Everything considered, the title to the universe claimed by White Folk is faulty. It ought, at least, to look plausible. How easy, then, by emphasis and omission to make children believe that every great soul the world ever saw was a white man's soul; that every great thought the world ever knew was a white man's thought; that every great deed the world ever did was a white man's deed; that every great dream the world ever sang was a white man's dream. In fine, that if from the world were dropped everything that could not fairly be attributed to White Folk, the world would, if anything, be even greater, truer, better than now. And if all this be a lie, is it not a lie in a great cause? (Du Bois 1999, 33)

I quote Du Bois at length here to emphasize that reparative activity is connected to undoing imaginaries of racial dominance and logics of ownership. Education—elite higher education in particular—has been an unapologetic celebration of the superiority of Europe, of a form of capitalism predicated

---

* See Alcoff 2020 for a philosophical grounding in whiteness.

on violence, although there have been strides over many generations to make the curriculum more "multicultural," more "ethnic," or to decenter it from the global North, the epistemic framework of classification, ordering, and patrolling where and how difference still operates. Through emphasis and omission, higher education has consistently viewed bodies of culture, as Resmaa Menakem (2017) describes them, as peripheral, significant only as the object of study, neither the creator of knowledge nor an equal participant. There is an appropriate manner and place where difference is permitted to appear. While institutions have sought to diversify their curricula, by adding texts from underrepresented identities and geographies, reparative moves and approaches have been minimally part of these efforts.

Du Bois identifies whiteness as a relatively new construction by the West. He describes it as ownership over everything, a presumption that whiteness has birthed the world and thus owns it. Efforts to uphold whiteness, its bundle of behaviors, values, and attitudes, are done through collective energy, which perpetuates a lie within a great cause. The great cause, as Du Bois identifies it later in the essay, is connected to European culture and its need to create a perception of race in order to justify the use of humans for the benefit of masters—for the acquisition of wealth. It is the creation of a hierarchy of life that is a lie, that places Black and Indigenous human life in particular at the bottom of this hierarchy. This hierarchy of existence, ordered according to difference as explored in the first part of this book, served the wealth and power acquisition of Europeans in their quest to own the lands now described as the Americas. Higher education is entangled in the perfection of this hierarchy of life. This entanglement has implications for the role of universities in reparative activity because, in spite of many earnest efforts, universities in the United States in

particular remain largely engines of social inequality structured on the basis of race and income (see Chetty et al. 2017).
The turn toward diversity as a remedy has not brought us
much closer to eradicating structural and interpersonal value
hierarchies that facilitate oppression in our societies. It has
been increasingly criticized as taking us further away from
transformative change. Reparations are not new; there are
many books on the topic, and global efforts at reparation have
been underway for decades.* This book is not intended as an
exhaustive overview of the history or evolution of reparations
work. Rather, it seeks to expand how reparative activity is understood epistemically and to examine the role of universities
as sites where its unsettling character may be learned and cultivated. But first it is important to highlight a few key moments in
the history of reparations work.

Reparations as a Peace Treaty

In 2019, David Ragland, the director of the Campaign for
Truth and Reparations, wrote a series of essays in *YES* magazine, in which he compellingly outlined how the work of Nelson
Maldonado-Torres assists us in understanding how reparations
are an active set of procedures intended to halt the relentless
violence exerted on Black and Indigenous people. Ragland explores reparations as a peace treaty, working with the United
Nations' Basic Principles and Guidelines on the Right to a Remedy and Reparation for Victims of Gross Violations of International Human Rights Law and Serious Violations of International
Humanitarian Law, adopted in 2005 by General Assembly Resolution 60/147. The UN principles and guidelines state that

---

* In 2020 William Darity and A. Kristen Mullen published one of the most
comprehensive reviews of economic reparations for Black Americans to date. See
also the Reparations Syllabus project: https://reparations.lib.umn.edu/sections/,
as well as the work of Mireille Fanon-Mendes with the United Nations.

reparations are connected to achieving peace and resolution of harm for groups victimized by war, slavery, and colonization. Reparations, as Maldonado Torres illuminates in his *Ten Theses on Coloniality and Decoloniality* (2016), are inextricably connected to the procedures needed to end the perpetuation of colonial violence. Higher education, with few exceptions, has yet to examine itself as a social mechanism that has been an organ of war, epistemic and ontological, against BIPOC people and cultures. This is evidenced through attempts at remedy such as affirmative action, the Civil Rights Acts, and the ongoing struggle to establish pathways of access through scholarships, specialized advising, and recruitment. The presence of affirmative action reveals that the morphology of higher education has developed a need for restitution; it requires, given the prolonged infliction of exclusion and marginalization, a mechanism that provides a means of correction for the exertion of harm. Another way to think about this is that higher education exists in relation to/because of exclusions; it is, fairly consistently since the late nineteenth century in the United States, for which various modes of redress have been prescribed. It is one reason that, I believe, reparations for colonization and slavery in particular have yet to be truly enacted in higher education; the harm is still wrapped up in the need for exclusion and patrol behaviors. Undoing these persistent logics is wrapped up in a bundle of behaviors and beliefs about knowledge that are difficult to unravel because the oppressions are varied; they have changed their forms but not their intentions and are ongoing.

The restitution given to Japanese-identifying/-identified Americans interned at camps during World War II was connected to a particular point in time, with a start, a finish, and a list of people who had lost property and been subjected to internment. The ongoing war against Black and Indigenous people is less easy to identify as a single moment or singular event. Japanese Americans who received restitution or experienced internment camps and racial discrimination feel, still, that the restitution was insufficient and that the anti-Asian hatred experienced in the United States has a long history that has gone unaddressed. Reparations in settler colonial societies such as the United States and Canada must be cultivated as part of the social imaginary, with aesthetic, political, and moral value. Affirmative action, though widely employed, met and continues to meet many contestations: though offered as a remedy for the violence exerted by higher education through persistent exclusion (it should not be understood solely as a remedy offered for dispossession or profit from owning slaves), it still fails to enter the collective social consciousness as a core belief, value, and disposition.

The UN Basic Principles and Guidelines describe five types of reparations: restitution, compensation, rehabilitation, satisfaction, and guarantees of nonrepetition.

1. Restitution: measures which serve to "restore the victim to the original situation before the gross violations occurred." This can include: restoration of liberty, enjoyment of human rights, identity, family life and citizenship, return of one's place of residence, restoration of employment, and return of property.
2. Damages Compensation: the provision of compensation "for any economically accessible damage, as appropriate and proportional to the gravity of the violation and the circumstances of each case." Such damage includes: physical or mental harm, lost opportunities, material damages and loss of earnings, moral damage, and the cost of legal, medical, psychological, and social services.
3. Rehabilitation: medical, psychological, social services, and legal assistance

4. Satisfaction: various measures that include the cessa-
   tion of human rights violations and abuses, truth-
   seeking, searches for the disappeared, recovery and
   reburial of remains, judicial and administrative sanc-
   tions, public apologies, commemoration, and
   memorialization.

5. Guarantees of nonrepetition: reforms ensuring the
   prevention of future abuses, including civilian control of
   the military and security forces, strengthening an indepen-
   dent judiciary, protection of civil service and human rights
   workers, the overall promotion of human rights standards,
   and the establishment of mechanisms to prevent and
   monitor social conflict and conflict resolution.

The outline of reparation offered and the various means that
must be engaged in order to facilitate support, healing, and
compensation for communities affected by systemic violence
and violation of human rights is multilayered. The United
Nations, as well as many scholars, notably Charles Ogletree Jr.
and Mireille Fanon, has engaged in a substantive review of
why reparation extends beyond financial compensation. At
the core of the five types of reparations is the notion that the
process necessary to move beyond abuse and injury must include more than money; it must be material but also symbolic,
imaginative, spiritual, and psychological. This is why describing
reparations as a peace treaty offers a means to grapple with its
character; reparative knowing and action must be able to perceive where the violence and injury persist in order to undo and
unsettle them. To establish peace necessitates an undoing, an
unraveling of where and how oppression persists. Understanding reparations in this way reveals it as a complex set of values,
beliefs, and practices that a society recognizes as an essential
part of healthy and just governments and institutions.

How education, the institutions of schooling, can become locations where reparation, as a collective value—its practices and its need to enact modes of undoing present practices imbued with past injuries and violence—is what drives this inquiry. Reparation, as outlined by the United Nations' resolution, requires an attentiveness to its epistemic framework, one, like all our forms of knowing and conceptions of truth, into which our communities are socialized. Higher education, I believe, has a role in how we are socialized to learn reparative activity.

Reparation and the Social Imaginary

Across the street from where I sit and write, a United States flag flaps in the wind. There are many flags on the street where I live. What we collectively see, or are taught to see, when we see the flag has a dominant narrative. The flag symbolizes freedom, liberty, and justice. This is the flag of the dominant social imaginary of the United States. When nondominant or marginal voices articulate an opposing position or question the dominant narrative as untrue or founded upon a false premise and not applicable to everyone living under the flag, many respond with disbelief, anger, and accusations. When Colin Kaepernick kneeled during the national anthem, many understood his position as disrespect for what the flag stands for, not as a protest that the flag as a symbol of freedom, liberty, and justice does not apply to Black lives in the United States. It does not apply to Native American lives in the United States, or Puerto Rican lives, or the lives of Alaska Natives and Pacific Islanders. There are colonies of suppression and injustice scattered, like the fifty stars, all across the United States. Kaepernick's gesture revealed also that the dominant way of knowing and behaving in relation to the flag seeks to avoid responsibility for the lived injustices and hypocrisies that are carried out every day. But as a Puerto Rican, I have always known that the US Constitution does not necessarily follow the flag.

Truth telling about harms and injustice inflicted within locations that believe themselves to be bastions of human rights and liberty causes ruptures within the social imaginary. It presses against the dominant way of understanding social orders. It unsettles and provokes inquiry into how such harm could have occurred or, importantly in the case of universities, have been suppressed and ignored. If universities are, as so many of them state, beacons of truth and justice in society, then truth-telling activities about institutional, disciplinary, and social histories along with the material changes necessary to provide recompense must be integral to their missions. Universities are potential locations where reparative activity may occur so as to unleash life activity necessary for social transformation.

A number of institutions of higher education, including Georgetown University, Princeton Theological Seminary, and Cornell University, have begun to engage in acts of recompense through the establishment of commissions, dispersal of funds, and issuance of apologies for slavery.* While Georgetown has offered a financial settlement and preferred admission to descendants of the 272 enslaved people that the Jesuits sold in order to provide a financial future for the university, few universities have offered recompense in any form to First Nations communities that were dispossessed for their institutions to exist and whose communities' history, sacred artifacts, and

---

* Cornell University, one the largest beneficiaries of the land dispossession of Indigenous people that occurred under the Morrill Acts, initiated a project in 2020 through the leadership of the university's American Indian and Indigenous Studies program to reckon with this history. See Cornell University, American Indian and Indigenous Studies Program, Indigenous Dispossession Project, https://blogs .cornell.edu/cornelluniversityindigenousdispossession/indigenous-dispossession/.

very bodies have been extracted as objects of study. Apologies and recompense administered in the absence of shifts in the social imaginary, understood as the dominant values, beliefs, attitudes, and behaviors in a given society, run the risk of circumnavigating systemic change because the ways of knowing and being within universities remain unaltered. People may listen to a truth-telling about harms exerted from racism, such as the 1921 Tulsa Race Massacre, or support administering funds to communities still entrenched in poverty from persistent Jim Crow practices yet still be unable to perceive or alter behaviors and policies that uphold anti-Blackness and Indigenous erasure. How higher education continues practices of dispossession must be interrogated and undone as part of efforts to enact remedies for historical acts of injustice.

The Land-Grab Universities project reveals how land taken through the Morrill Acts sustains endowment growth and profit making for universities such as Cornell. Indigenous dispossession is not the taking of property in a singular moment but rather the ongoing assertion of settler domination. Higher education institutions are frequently guilty of performances of racial justice without the necessary onto-epistemic and material shifts needed to co-create antiracist institutions. Reparations, practiced apart from shifts in our social imaginary, as in a discrete allocation of funds adjudicated by those already in control of the resources, will not end racism and the system it perpetuates. The subjugation and injustices exerted on Black and Indigenous people will continue if we are unable to make epistemic and ontological shifts that undo structures of white supremacy and domination. The toppling of monuments and financial redress for slavery are essential aspects of the struggle to abolish racism and settler colonialist legacies. However, how we know reparation, how we learn it as an emergent and generative activity, as a way of knowing and being that seeks to undo systems of self-interest that have perpetuated racial inequality, is an opportunity as yet not fully realized in higher education.

Present reparations efforts in universities have yet to locate the residues that linger, coating modes of existence that were birthed through and flourished after the supernova of slavery and settler colonialism. The onto-epistemic dimensions of universities—that is, the forms of life that emerged from their persistent engagement with values, beliefs, attitudes, and behaviors that facilitated slavery and settler colonialism as true and real modes of existence—must be examined if we are to understand where these modes of existence remain. Reparation in universities, practiced as a verb rather than a noun, has dramatically different implications for revealing the onto-epistemic persistence of slavery and settler colonialism. The former unleashes reparation as an activity, as a way of thinking, acting, and being that holds the potential to unsettle everything that it encounters.

As a noun, reparation may act as a singular discrete thing, an inert object whose influence on the present has little ontological significance; it was not—it is not—still. In the history of reparations, particularly in relation to education, its invocation and use have often fallen along decisions to administer reparation as an object, as a thing that was not and is not still, rather than as an action, a state of being that works to unravel dominant modes of power and control. This way of understanding reparation facilitates power; it upholds a hierarchical strategy and requires little change to the present behaviors of higher education. It is a way of using reparation as a management tool, an attempt to distract from real structural recompense such as power-sharing in governance, the elimination of exclusionary admissions practices if private institutions accept public dollars, or the turning over of the funds garnered from decades of siphoning money from stolen land. Discussing the recent case of Georgetown University enacting reparations will help better ground this distinction between reparations as object and as an epistemic and ontological activity of undoing.

In 1838 Jesuit priests who owned Georgetown University sold 272 enslaved people in order to keep the institution alive. I use the term "alive" to assert that, at that time, the existence of an institution mattered more than the life conditions of Black humans. This hierarchy of value finds its present-day successor in how frequently and easily institutions privilege their financial stability over providing a living wage and health benefits for adjunct faculty. While not at all the same, there is a throughline in how institutions exert oppression and hierarchies of human value in relation to their "survival." The lives of the 272 people mattered far less than the survival of the institution. Recently Georgetown, like many other institutions since 2002, has sought to identify modes of redress and restitution (Harris, Campbell, and Brophy 2019). The Jesuits kept detailed records, so the names and locations of the people who were sold were uncovered in the institutional archives. The decision to administer restitution by distributing money to the descendants of people sold by the institution and putting in place an admissions policy that gives preference to descendants, provides a window into what I am describing as the onto-epistemic life of universities contending with their entanglement in legacies of slavery and settler colonialism. What it reveals, without knowledge of the discussions that must have occurred between the president, the trustees, and Georgetown's senior administration, is that the university could not think beyond the same transactional logics that defined the Jesuits' 1832 decision. Though the outcome was dramatically different, it was decided that money would be given to the descendants; ultimately it was a transaction, as in a checkout line where at the end, one is handed a receipt for atonement. To my knowledge, descendants, while invited into open forums and town halls, were not ultimately part of the decision-making process of what manner of reparation to administer. If power is located in social behaviors, values, and attitudes, then locating oppression in the processes of institutions, in how the people within it behave in accordance with tradition or expectations or requirements is connected to identifying how, in a decision-making process such as restitution, the marginalized are included or excluded. William Darity and Kristen Mullens, authors of *From Here to Equality* and experts on reparations, criticized Georgetown's approach: "One of the problems with the Jesuit program is the Jesuits focusing on 'our enslaved people', so there is still this mindset that 'we owned these people and we own the solution as well'" (Merelli 2021). The processes related to the creation of the reparations fund, a $100 million trust held by JPMorgan Chase, have been criticized by descendants as opaque. The process and criteria by which the funds will be used and administered has been made by a small number of descendants with significant involvement by the Jesuits (Merelli 2021). While there exist few examples of how to go about reparations for slavery, self-determination—ownership of the processes for remedying harm and a redistribution of power—is critical if social transformation rather than a perpetuation of transactional morality is desired.

The behaviors of inclusion and exclusion by universities often communicate far more than the statements that professional communications teams spend days and weeks crafting. If power cannot relinquish itself in order to offer a participatory process in which the harmed can set the criteria for their amends, then power continues to exert itself as it always has: setting the criteria of existence for the other in whatever way it best serves to uphold the institution's self-interest. In the case of many universities, the self-interest is to preserve the institution and its financial viability, particularly as it relates to its existence as an asset, an attribute of economic and social capital.

Reparative activity works to change the processes through which we have been taught to participate as well as to offer financial recompense to communities that have been subjected to discriminatory policies and practices over many generations. It is not only to remember the acts, the harm, the "willful amnesia," as W. E. B. Du Bois describes it, but also to perceive the modes of knowing that hold us still and repeat the same procedures that permitted the exertion of harm. If those harmed are not included in the decision-making about the modes of alleviating the harm, then we must question whether the outcome can ever lead to societies that cease to reproduce oppression.

Financial recompense enacted by higher education institutions, particularly those that hold billions of dollars in endowments, does little to unsettle the institution beyond putting a dent in finances or giving over spaces in an incoming class. An example of how the onto-epistemic structure of universities could be shifted through reparative action would be to direct energy toward redistributing decision-making, or land, or assets to dispossessed First Nations communities, or to give over a percentage of the assets belonging to the university to descendants of those sold for the institution to survive; or to construct the board of trustees with descendants and First Nations people; or to stop placing the survival of the institution above adjuncts who barely earn a living wage. Any of these are examples of how, through unleashing attentiveness to undoing as a mechanism toward amends, universities have come to exert power, as ownership, as dominance, to how universities only know themselves through such logics, begins processes that may create new apparatuses through which transformation may flow. Diversity officers, though rooted in historical events that seem to logically dovetail with reparative effort such as affirmative action in the United States, are frequently tasked not to unsettle institutions or expose how the afterlife of slavery and settler colonialism still appears in what is taught, but rather to manage the difference that enters. Reparation pushes against the gap between present knowledge habits and how to undo, in an effort to take responsibility, those very ways of knowing that facilitate reproducing systems of oppression. If, as a country, we are ever to heal from the violence of racism—and I use *heal* as fundamentally related to abolition—where and how do we break the chains of racism and domination that cause the behaviors of patrol, accumulation, and domination? Is the sphere of education that site?

Higher education has been shaped through an epistemology of difference that has facilitated turning racialized people and nonhuman life into capital for accumulation and extraction. Diversity work that remains unconscious of its own identity becomes a reinforcing mechanism rather than a means of antiracist or abolitionist effort. In other words, diversity work that is unconscious of how an institution of higher education works to preserve its wealth and power will, despite the best intentions of the individual hired to do such work, become a tool for patrol, accumulation, and continued extraction. Those committed to redress, repair, or amending—to the reparative as a verb in higher education—must be attentive to how disinclined most institutions are to fundamentally share or redistribute power, to enact systemic changes. Diversity workers, as this part aims to explore, can, more often than not, become used to managing challenges to power through inclusion as an assimilative endeavor rather than facilitating and creating space for the undoing that reparative activity reveals. This is often why institutions that have attempted recompense may prefer the form of reparation that Frank Wilderson III cautions against. It is safer for the survival of the institution to pay a settlement to descendants of people sold to bankroll its survival than to apply reparations as a political weapon in the present, one that has the potential to reveal that higher education still relies upon the accumulation of racialized people while it remains complicit in their indebtedness and has created a precarious workforce of undercompensated, overworked adjuncts who are disproportionately people of color. Reparative moves are fundamentally connected to redistributing property and power. Whether universities can commit to this work beyond taking down monuments and creating new signage remains an open question.

Where do slavery and settler colonialism lurk in our universities today? Where do the ripples from these seismic events extend to? As I walk the halls of some of these institutions, the specter of their existence are all around. The epistemic frameworks that have produced and reproduced hierarchies of human value are the weather, as Christina Sharpe describes it in *In the Wake: On Blackness and Being*, of so many higher education institutions. As a diversity worker, I feel haunted by what so many of these institutions have been complicit with, what they perpetuate still in evolved forms. I often meditate on what universities need to remember to facilitate reparative knowledge and action within their institution and in society. I seek to commit daily to teaching, thinking, and feeling reparatively, to daily work to undo practices, behaviors, and attitudes that participate in oppression. Evelyn Brooks Higginbotham writes, "The new field of slavery and universities thus calls for greater analysis of the ripple effect of ideas and information taught in American colleges, universities and seminaries" (Harris, Campbell, Brophy 2019, 338). Indeed, the truth-telling activities about the history of slavery and settler colonialism arising in numerous universities reveal that the need to contend with the identification and dismantling of its legacy in the form of present practices is necessarily connected. Reparation for past participation and facilitation of racist ideas and practices must also work to locate how the truth of the past persists in the present functioning of colleges and universities. While many in higher education are increasingly engaging in revealing the historical underpinnings of racism and settler colonialism in the academy, the ripple effects on present ideas, behaviors, values, attitudes, and practices, or what I term the social imaginary, needs more analysis, particularly as it relates to current diversity, equity, and inclusion efforts.

Writing on reparations is not new, nor is it my intention to offer a comprehensive overview of the range of reparations that have been administered historically, nor to delve too deeply into the technicalities of how reparations, particularly in the form of economic redress, have been and can be distributed. My interest in this project and in this chapter is to offer insight into why reparation, both its administrative life and its conceptual formulation, should be considered an essential focus of higher education today. It is to argue for education to take up the challenge of finding ways to educate in reparative knowing and being as well as to identify actionable ways that institutions of higher education may integrate reparative activities into their systems. If so many people in this country have been so miseducated that they have difficulty connecting the legacy of slavery and settler colonialism to the violence and inequality experienced by Black and Indigenous people today, then we must ask ourselves if education has morally and epistemically failed. The gap between those who support a range of forms that reparations may take is vast, and it is racialized. How do we bridge this gap if we are not committing to the creation of new social imaginaries or revealing that so much of what we know must be unlearned? The history of the events that have precipitated a need for the redress of harm are best articulated in the recent books *Slavery and the University, Ebony and Ivy,* and *Stamped from the Beginning,* among many others. While this next part of the book will not spend a great deal of time outlining the historical events and myriad terrors that higher education facilitated against Black and Indigenous people, it will provide an overview of the history of the reparations struggle in the United States and its relationship to reparative efforts in universities.

Outlines of Epistemic Reparation

As a philosopher who studies education and has worked as a diversity administrator, I rely on my education to help provide frameworks to explain what it is that I am experiencing. As I approached trying to articulate what I encountered in the use of diversity within higher education, I thought a great deal about the expediency of using terms such as *ontological* and *epistemic*, particularly in an inquiry critical of the persistent logics of settler colonialism and the European legacy of excluding other epistemologies. Philosophy is an essential tool, yet it is a field that I have migrated away from because of its persistent marginalization of women and women of color in particular. Yet philosophy is one of my first loves and a helpful tool for describing and articulating aspects of experience.

Epistemology is the study of knowledge: how we come to understand what we believe we know and what constitutes true belief. Epistemology has a long history in Western philosophy, but many cultures have their own epistemologies: a manner of meta-comprehension of the knowledge they hold and the ability to identify what constitutes truth. The range of differences in epistemic structures (how we know that our beliefs are true and valid sources of knowledge) was integral to the subjugation of the civilizations encountered by the settler colonialists. Antiracist and decolonizing work, particularly when it speaks to those identities that hold power, has to be able to explain and illuminate that oppression occurs at the level of how we justify what we know and believe to be truth—in other words, how we know what we know. The climate within which we live, how we exist on a daily basis, shapes what we call knowledge. It is important to explore the onto-epistemic dimension of reparation because it assists us in understanding it as energy, as a life activity that opens a conceptual apparatus through which we may collectively create new forms of existence and knowing. Reparation is not only an object or an end; it is a way of knowing, a constellation of activities, that opens a modality of being. I write from the standpoint that being and knowing are entangled; I know what I know because of where I am and where I find myself. What I know is also because of a long chain of cultural productions created by other people who were in specific places where events shaped their beliefs, attitudes, values, and behaviors. I understand this as the social imaginary described by Cornelius Castoriadis (1998) and Lorraine Code (2011).

Knowing does not come ex-nihilo, disembodied and de-historicized. Humans enter a world thick with beliefs, values, attitudes, and behaviors. Depending on how one's identity tracks along a given social imaginary, individuals are socialized and subjected to deeply historicized perceptions and beliefs that can cause oppression of others. In the present social imaginary of the United States, persistent anti-Blackness and Indigenous erasure are signals of a dominant social imaginary that works to use and control how difference participates in the present social hierarchies, particularly in the form of access to and control of land and labor. Yet how even the most well-intentioned diversity workers delink or undo the ways of knowing and treating difference—a way of knowing that results in behaviors of patrol, accumulation, and extraction—necessitates a form of reparative activity that operates at the epistemic level. Delinking or decolonizing from the colonial matrix of power is an activity that necessitates a significant disruption in a social imaginary.

Delinking and the Affective Borderlands of Epistemic Reparation

In *Borderlands / La Frontera: The New Mestiza*, Gloria Anzaldúa offers insight into the radical epistemic shift necessary to delink from the tyranny of coloniality. The borderlands, the place where one finds oneself in the search for an unshrouded self free from oppression, is at first a terrifying and unrecognizable place. We are afraid to go home, and we are afraid to go on. A state of immobilization arises within us. "Petrified, she can't respond, her face caught between 'los intersticios', the spaces between the different worlds she inhabits" (Anzaldúa 1987, 20). Decolonial knowledge, which I understand here as epistemic delinking, arises in and works within and upon our bodies. It holds an affective dimension. Anzaldúa's canonical work captures this affective dimension of delinking, one that is felt in the body as anxiety, shame, confusion, and antagonism toward once seemingly friendly or innocuous institutions, people, beliefs, values, and attitudes. Delinking, as it operates on epistemic, social, and political levels, engages an embodied subject, one that feels acutely the ways the body, the self, endures decolonial movements. Delinking engages whole communities, which come to perceive structures and systems they have once valued as the very entities that have suppressed, oppressed, and extinguished histories, cultures, and people and that they sometimes have ignorantly participated in and perpetuated. There comes a moment, for some, where it becomes clear that the systems they live within are the result of maladjusted beliefs, beliefs that have inflicted or permitted oppression, and they need to leave them, depart, as Anzaldúa does, into new unknown territories. Her work provides insight into the significance of considering the affective, felt, dimension from engaging with activities that attempt to undo or delink from accepted or dominant modes of knowing and existing.

The psychological toll of colonization and decolonization was central to Frantz Fanon's work and laid the foundation for the philosophical consideration of the embodied impact of political processes. While Fanon's affective theory regarding colonialism undergirds this project, I will not undertake an analysis of his theory here. One way, among many, the psychological toll of colonialism and its legacies is manifested is in the form of antagonism, shame, and anger toward universities as epistemic communities that have reproduced beliefs and values about, for instance, Black and Indigenous people, as can be observed through student and faculty protest movements such as #ConcernedStudent1950 in the United States and #FeesMustFall in South Africa.

Epistemic delinking, how we may begin to decolonize beliefs and attitudes, was first given clear philosophical articulation with the work of Anibal Quijano. He introduced the idea of coloniality, the oppressive violent creation of modernity, as a means of articulating how, after the historical moment of colonialism had ended, its character and procedures endured through the colonial matrix of power (Mignolo 2011). In *Colonialidad y Modernidad-Racionalidad* published in 1989 soon after Anzaldúa's *Borderlands*, he articulates how coloniality works to suppress Indigenous knowledge, to colonize it, as a means of suppression and control. Quijano opened a pathway to grapple with the task and possibility of decolonizing knowledge, to contending with universities as a social imaginary of modernity and thus a social mechanism for reproducing the logics associated with coloniality, such as white supremacy, human civilization as beginning in Europe, knowledge as abstracted from place, time, or identity, and land as capital or property. The affective dimensions of these delinking activities, the possibility of the resurgence of suppressed epistemologies, is made visible through the work of Anzaldúa, who moves insurgently against accepted academic modes of doing "theory" to exercise the kind of radical epistemic shift that the program of delinking asks. She abandons the need for English, replacing it with Spanish-Spanglish-Nahuatl, uses personal narrative, activates Mayan and Aztec myths as contemporary modes of truth-making, and places the body as a source of knowledge. Her work pushes against the formal, and it is within this consideration of the rupture, the undoing of form, that reparative activity is best detected. Her work fractures dominant epistemic modes and through those fractures, releases an energy of undoing, unraveling flows into academic discourse. Importantly and unlike Quijano, she offers a vision of the role of aesthetic/aisthesis, a play with forms, in enduring the interticios of the ontological onslaught, the Fanonian struggle, that delinking elicits.

Epistemic reparation is a movement of embodied wakefulness, an affective engagement, that may arise from delinking and responsibility-taking moves. Its need arises in the borderlands, in the interstitial moments of fear, anxiety, anger, and shame a person or community may feel as they pull away, become responsible for harmful beliefs and oppressive habits they have carried. As Frank Wilderson III directs, reparative activity must be understood not as a fixed condition, an endpoint, but as a weapon used to upend continuously the institutions and behaviors that perpetuate its need (Hartman and Wilderson 2003). It must be understood in its ongoing character, for the wake, the afterlife of enslavement and colonization, is ever present and flows through all social structures. An effort to illuminate reparative activity requires an attentiveness to its affective dimension, to the powerful range of feelings and emotions that undoing evokes. Wilderson aptly describes reparative activity as a weapon; it releases powerful sentiments. This affective dimension of the reparative, and the centrality of feelings of shame, doubt, and hesitation when realizing symbols, beliefs, or values that have facilitated oppression, was first articulated by psychoanalyst Melanie Klein in 1934 and taken up by Eve Kosovsky Sedgwick in her work on paranoid and reparative reading (Sedgwick and Frank 2003). Both Klein and Sedgwick identify the role of guilt and shame in reparative activities, describing it as a powerful force in what hinders and drives the work of liberation or responsibility-taking moves. It implies continuous, vigilant, and restless movement, knowledge that risks becoming stuck or immobile, as Anzaldúa warns. It warns that making amends is an iterative endeavor, better characterized as undoing, to capture its infinite procedure. Engaging in epistemic reparation is a process of developing through wandering into lesser-known corners and resurging suffocated histories, social imaginaries necessary to widen epistemic communities and to abolish logics, beliefs, and values that are the source of ongoing oppression and destruction. But the process, the release into undoing, is fraught with many human emotions: security, predictability, ritual, tradition, and routine are all parts of human existence that societies rely on to make sense of the ineffability of existence. Oppression—engineered deeply into the structures of knowing and existence of cultures such as the United States—is a frightening procedure at first to undo; it is hard to decipher where it leads. I have often felt that the conceptual structure of diversity work is content to shove people into small boxes and make them ashamed if they attempt to flee or escape. Through this, in the procedures of my own epistemic reparation, my own undoing, I have looked to the examples of fugitives and maroons to remember that the movement into the unknown, the activities to undo the frameworks that have been forced, is where liberation is detectable; what comes remains to be created, but the movement out of the boxes, the enframing of engineered modes of existing and knowing, is the first undoing.

Epistemic reparation is not a project of impossible return but rather one that seeks to undo and amend belief systems that have attempted to distort, erase, deny, and disfigure the history, knowledge contributions, and epistemic existence of colonized and enslaved communities and illuminate its connection to the affective dimension of the delinking and decolonization processes. When we situate this process of delinking within the setting of the university, when the learner—a student for instance—begins to experience epistemic fractures or shifts, an antagonism, an anger, and a shame can arise toward the institution. So the university, in such a case, becomes, potentially both a facilitator of *desprenderse* and also responsible for its perpetuation of coloniality of power: of values, beliefs, and practices such as extraction, erasure, and racial injustice. Understanding epistemic responsibility can further support the outline of epistemic reparation and its significance in higher education that I am offering here.

Responsibility and the Social Imaginary

The decolonial and the process of decolonization is, as Walter Mignolo (2018) and many others state, an option. It is not an option desired by everyone and not necessarily desired by all identities that have been the object of oppression. The desire to delink from the colonial matrix is a first act, one might say, in a series of acts that a knower or community might take in assuming responsibility for the perpetuation of and participation in harmful or maladjusted beliefs. The affective dimension of delinking opens space to feel the impacts of maladjusted beliefs, or beliefs that have caused social harm in some way and to desire another way, even if that way is unknown or uncharted. My own effort as described throughout this book, to delink and engage processes of undoing not only what I knew of diversity but what I believed could be valid forms of social justice work and philosophical research was deeply unsettling It was a choice to not ignore the glimmer, the pull, that appeared, but to follow it and see where it led me despite heading into the unknown, off familiar and accepted professional and analytical paths. It was, and is, an errant movement that once understood, became a responsibility to not participate in the continued perpetuation of doing philosophy as abstracted from experience and ignorant of diverse epistemic manifestation of what we describe in the Westernized university as "philosophy." How we take responsibility for our beliefs, for the ways we develop and reproduce knowledge, particularly beliefs that exert oppression, is bound up with epistemic reparation and with the work of higher education.

Lorraine Code first articulated epistemic responsibility in 1987 as a contribution or intervention into what she describes as the Eurocentric epistemological practice of investigating beliefs in abstraction from a particular epistemic community (Code 1987). Although she is not an epistemologist, we can see the resonance with Quijano and other decolonial theorists concerned with how to delink from Eurocentric knowledge systems. Epistemology, as a philosophical subfield, was traditionally focused on the individual knower, what the individual could possibly know to be justified or true (such as the cup is on the table or the car is moving fast), and paid little attention to the role of socialization into a particular epistemic community. Code significantly deepens the concept of epistemic responsibility in her 2007 book, *Ecological Thinking*, in which, according to Catherine Maloney, she undertakes a significant shift in epistemic responsibility to include greater consideration of power imbalances in given epistemic communities and their connection to social imaginaries. Epistemic responsibility, understood within the ecological model happens within a network of interactions, limited by the meaning-making that may arise from the relational frameworks of a given community (Maloney 2016). Epistemic responsibility, in its simplest form, is defined as the responsibility we have regarding the beliefs that we hold. Every society or community holds beliefs and attitudes that may be understood as instituted social imaginaries. Code, working from Cornelius Castoriadis's theory of a social instituting imaginary explains it as, "the normative social meanings, customs, expectations, assumptions, values, prohibitions, and permissions-the habitus and ethos-into which human beings are nurtured from childhood and which they internalize, affirm, challenge, or contest as they make sense of their place, options, responsibilities within a world, both social and physical whose 'nature' and meaning are also instituted within these imaginary significations" (Code 2006, 30).

The way in which a society lives, sees, makes, and expresses its existence is interwoven to generate a nonstatic imaginary through which individuals exist. Within this weaving, the intersections of individual decision-making or responsibility for the beliefs that are perpetuated or enacted may be found. The facets or fragments expressive of a social imaginary are experienced in a variety of ways, one of which is through physical institutions like higher education, museums, or through their symbolic products such as monuments, art, and the architectures that shape daily modern existence in the United States. Let us consider, for a moment, that colleges and universities are a kind of epistemic community that embodies aspects of the instituted social imaginary, expressing it through monuments, architecture, or even curriculum design. Given Castoriadis's and Code's definition of the social imaginary, universities and colleges—schooling—become a central organ for the confrontation, socialization, and perpetuation or destruction of meanings, customs, expectations, assumptions, values, prohibitions, and permissions of their society. And "their" society, as Code and others point out, is most often the dominant group. This is where Code's consideration of power and privilege enters her articulation of epistemic responsibility and becomes key to remembering that instituted social imaginaries are not experienced the same way by all members nor can they be ethically or politically neutral. If we are part of a social environment and participate in social institutions like schools, the beliefs that we come to hold are not developed ex nihilo; they are developed through socialization processes that occur not only through family and subcultures but through the "fellow-feeling," as John Dewey described it, cultivated through common institutions such as the public school. Responsible knowing, or what Code describes as knowing well, is possible because of and limited by our epistemic community. So our ability to take responsibility for harmful or maladjusted beliefs is connected to what epistemic resources are available to us in our given communities. "Good" or responsible knowing, for Code and other social epistemologists, is interdependent knowing; it is knowing that may ethically and politically account for the impact of attitudes, values, permissions, or the social imaginary. Put another way, responsible knowing assumes accountability for the impact of the social imaginary. Reparative knowing connects here in that it works at the level of undoing and amending to create new directions.

In *Ecological Thinking,* understanding is no longer individual or autonomous but happens within an "ecosystem of meaning making" (Maloney 2016, 2). But knowers do not necessarily have equal access to epistemic resources to understand well or take responsibility for their beliefs and this ability, in an ecosystems approach, shifts with "the innumerable relations, events, circumstances, and histories that make the knower and the known what they are, at that time" (Code 1991, 269). The normative social meanings of a given community may permit the oppression or epistemic subjugation of another group based on an identity category. This knower is bound to and by the limits of her community's imaginary (Maloney 2016), and the sociopolitical implications of this. As the knower navigates her epistemic community, her ability to take responsibility for beliefs that may be harmful, oppressive, or maladjusted is bound up in the events, circumstances, and histories that are available to her as epistemic resources to, as Code describes, empathically imagine, or feel the impact of what she knows of the "other." For instance, if a knower is bound by a community that believes there is no legitimate form of economic life possible beyond capitalism, then the knower is limited by this instituted social imaginary. However, the knower may encounter subjugated or conflicting conceptions to the dominant social imaginary; they may encounter the harm that capitalism has wrought on the planet or see the working conditions of fast fashion in countries far away from the United States and feel a desire to delink from the instituted social imaginary that capitalism is the only possible reality. At this moment, they may become an advocate for socialism or communism or anarchism or seek to stop participating in or undo lifestyle behaviors that they perceive as contributing to the harmful effects of capitalism. This wandering away, driven by an attempt to understand the impacts of capitalism and embrace or develop alternative instituting social imaginaries, or the perception that the experience of social imaginaries while liberative for some is oppressive for others, is where I begin to connect epistemic reparation to Code's theory. Connecting to Code's theory is to support my readers in locating epistemic reparation as a form of socially constructed undoing that arises from responsibility-taking moves.

In a given community, Code acknowledges in her 2015 article, "Care, Concern, and Advocacy," conflicting conceptions of epistemic responsibility and agency exist. She explains these as socially entrenched and related to power imbalances, imbalances well articulated through Miranda Fricker's notion of hermeneutical injustice and Kristie Dotson's epistemic oppression. So an individual knower may attempt to advocate for a particular belief, such as that most North American universities are settler colonial institutions and must be decolonized in order to actualize justice, healing, or liberation and be viewed as untrustworthy because they are advocating strongly for something for which people have limited social imagination. Code writes that advocacy practices work to illuminate truths that glimmer beneath the collectively assumed status quo (2006, 176). Important to the work of advocacy is that the advocate must endure risk in destabilizing the instituted social imaginary making, as Edouard Glissant would tell us, tremors the means of creating, developing the epistemic shifts necessary to open the way for reparative knowing to flow. The institutional workers who embrace reparative activity become, I believe, a source of energy for destabilizing the instituted social imaginary.

If we apply Code's concept of epistemic responsibility to colleges and universities to formal schooling systems, we can locate any number of attitudes and beliefs (which in turn create and perpetuate systems of knowing) that have a collective impact. Taking responsibility for beliefs is the step (if we are attempting to create a thinking model) that begins the undoing quality of epistemic reparation. Again, this project is particularly interested in how we engage in undoing and amending (in the sense of reconstituting) those epistemic beliefs and attitudes that reproduce oppressive ideas, values, and beliefs that emanate from the residue of coloniality. While epistemic reparation may surely have a role to play in reconstituting knowledge related to other knowledge systems (I sincerely hope so), I am decidedly interested in illuminating its potential for transitioning the ways of knowing instituted through the legacies of settler colonialism and coloniality toward anti-oppression and antiracism; toward societies that are characterized by peace, healing, liberation, or what some describe as justice. We can often observe these oppressive epistemic habits at play in higher education, where socialization into a hierarchy of value is central.

When I was a newly hired diversity worker at a small liberal arts institution, a well-respected academic center convened a talk on labor unions and the contemporary US workforce. The lead faculty member and director of the center invited well-known academics in labor studies, an activist, and a renowned performance artist. The service workers on the campus, including food service, cleaning, and construction-related jobs, were unionized and very active. The faculty member did not invite the head of the labor union on campus to participate nor extend an invitation to the event. During the event Q and A, the head of the labor union on campus, a carpenter, asked the panel why he wasn't invited to participate. The professor who convened the panel responded, in front of the fairly large audience, that the event was dedicated to the study of labor unions, not the practice of them. The professor made a common epistemic distinction between the role of higher education as one where topics are studied, not practiced. Practice and experience are valued less than theory; this is a widely held and practiced value hierarchy in liberal arts higher education. The faculty member believed that valid testimony regarding knowledge about labor is made through those with professional credentials, not through the lived daily experience of running a union. The responsibility he failed to take up is the perpetuation of knowledge exclusions, which frequently devalue the testimony of lived experience as an essential part of the production of knowledge. This is a maladjusted epistemic habit because, frequently, as I explored in the first part of this book, the relationship the academy has had to difference has been characterized by behaviors of control, subjugation, and removal of self-determination.

The epistemic habit of knowledge hierarchies that this vignette illustrates has material outcomes that are most readily witnessed by ideas, policies, or decisions that are made for groups under analysis rather than with or alongside those who are impacted. This is fundamentally, I believe, a different orientation to knowledge creation, to how we know about phenomena and engage with difference. A hierarchy that values credentials, ones accessed through layers of applications, gates, and various systems of sorting and privileging, frequently rewards the most powerful, leaving those, such as refugees, at the mercy of the scholar who studies them, defines them, and patrols their participation while denying that any responsibility should be taken because it is "just theory."

If, as a result of the question the union leader posed, the faculty member were to see the question as an option, an opening, or a crack to investigate further, he might begin to undo an epistemic habit that facilitates oppression. But in that moment, in that Anzaldúan *intersticio*, what makes that person keep going, keep unraveling into the discomfort of the unknown horizon? If Code's work on epistemic responsibility can be applied, particularly as she articulates in her work *Ecological Responsibility*, one can understand that the professor has been socialized, is reproducing a hierarchy of value within the social imaginary, to believe that valid testimony arises from those with a similar pathway of approaching the task of knowledge construction and that his values, beliefs, and attitudes are after taking responsibility for the exclusion they produce, in need of reparative activity. Yet, how the individual or the institution takes up such affective responsibility needs further clarification.

Amend/Reconstitute/Undo

In her 2012 book, *On Being Included,* Sara Ahmed accurately depicts the philosophical and practical pitfalls of employing repair in diversity work. To repair, she warns, is to potentially engage the impulse toward making racism, inequality, and injustice more comfortable and more bearable to the white majority in higher education (Ahmed 2012). To "repair" implies that something can be fixed so that it will no longer be problematic, shameful, or hinder performance. Repair can be used as a patch, as a means of claiming something has been "taken care of" and can no longer cause difficulty or harm. Ahmed warns, correctly, that the institution can utilize repair in order to inoculate itself against the work of reparation, of detecting and dismantling structures that conceal the persistence of past injustice—that the problem has been fixed so that it is no longer a problem. The history of slavery and colonialism in the United States cannot ever be repaired in this sense. We cannot fix the millions of past lives tortured, tormented, lynched, raped, and degraded. Thinking that we can exerts another degree of harm. We cannot believe we can offer a clean "fix" to the conditions of our society that have arisen because of this history. Mass incarceration, racialized income inequality, racism, and sexism are creolized versions of slavery and colonization that, as Sarah Nuttell describes comprehensively and poetically in *Entanglement: Literary and Cultural Reflections on Postapartheid,* societies like South Africa, the United States, and Canada (to name a few) are entangled. Where in an entanglement does one begin to repair? To attempt to "repair" in this sense the present prison system, for example, has a logic akin to attempting to fix the system of chattel slavery; it cannot be made better. Rather, the unraveling, undoing of the wreckage to make way for the new is what I am after in offering an expansive, thick concept of reparation. Abolition is closely akin, a distant goal of undoing; even the demolition of a house leaves traces, wreckage, material that may be of use or beauty in its reconstituted state. Reparative epistemology leads us toward such new modes of being that are, as my reader is likely thinking, seemingly impossible. The reparative action, in an epistemological sense, aims at the possibilities of thinking/feeling/imagining the undoing needed to amend, to alter modes of knowing that believe past injustices are not still playing in our present systems—that cannot see a way toward new futures such as abolition.

The outward expression of the students in two protest movements of 2015, #FeesMustFall and #ConcernedStudent1950, gesture of a kind of reparative activity, an undoing that does not seek to deny or attempt to erase the past but to demand that institutions that perpetuate legacies of ways of knowing, of valuing that reproduce oppression, enact responsibility-taking moves. They demand that their university become a site of negotiating the undoing and reconstitutions needed to redress an epistemology that has exempted itself from accountability to those whose lives continue to be impacted by ways of knowing that Cecil Rhodes exemplifies.

Another clue in the puzzle of tracing reparations is found in its constellation of synonyms: *Expiate, atone, restitution* and *recompense*. In the world of recovery and addiction, becoming sober requires making amends as distinct from apology. One cannot achieve a state of sobriety without this step. This cluster of terms and concepts reveals that reparation holds a collective dimension, that its active realization relied upon a collective negotiation or social engagement. When the bundle of concepts connected to reparation is unraveled, it exposes the complex ways of knowing needed to engage in reparative activity. This unraveling shows the necessity of reparations operating at the epistemic and ontological level; one cannot make amends, which seeks to undo the patterns of how an individual has behaved in relationships. To make amends in addiction recovery necessitates an awareness of the harm that has been caused, of the behaviors that continue harming and harmful relationships, and of the steps necessary to take responsibility for it. To make amends necessitates reconstituting oneself in relation to a person or community your actions have damaged. It requires an undoing of what one believed about their responsibility to the impacted person.

Reparation, as undoing necessary for amending, requires one to know *how* present conditions are in relation to, a present signal of, past trauma. The relationality asked for necessitates a kind of critical memory—an orientation that the dominant narrative of what occurred and its modes of memorializing are inaccurate because the reporter or the archive has been revealed as biased or in the service of maintaining oppression. It requires an ability to discern how social institutions, such as universities, carry suppressions and exclusions wrought by an epistemic system that valued racial domination, Europe, imperialism, and colonialism. The residue of such an epistemic relation is detectable when those who have historically been excluded are "included" as a gesture of recompense. But herein lies a second problem that the trace of epistemic reparation leads us toward: the invitation to be included, viewed by the institution as a mode of repair, does not consider the epistemic problem inherent in inclusion. Such an approach, an extension of an invitation by those already in possession of power, assumes and does not ask, draws in but does not shift or alter itself, extends to grasp the other, extracts but does not walk with or be changed by. Such an invitation is an assimilative force, habituated by decades of colonial habits to civilize, indoctrinate, and homogenize difference. That is, the invention of the invitation must spring from the relation to the traumatic past and its activation in the present, the result of which is unknowable prior. Exclusionary and oppressive logics cannot create conditions of inclusion, the conditions of what is to be valued now; they can only abandon what they cling to, hope to reform, and ask, what must remain? Power is only then redistributed and concomitantly given. But our universities do not function from processes of collective truth negotiations with those whose histories they have attempted to erase and exclude or from those who are presently pushed to the margins. They arise prior to, set the conditions for what and who is determined as legitimate participants and knowledge creators, so the character of reparation becomes, as Ahmed directs, "a memory of what is no longer, a memory that if it was kept alive would just leave us exhausted" (Ahmed 2012, 164). The exhaustion is already present for those affected by delinking. The past is ever-present for many, and the perpetual readjustments to epistemic systems that lack accountability to it are always exhausting. Making amends to one's epistemic order, taking responsibility for the impact of beliefs, values, archetypes, and systems that have facilitated the need for such knowledge-amending, is ensnared in poor epistemic habits. Delinking and amending cause and require fundamental shifts in epistemic order, in the social imaginaries we call upon to make sense of things.

Recasting Imaginaries: Third-Order
Epistemic Changes

In her 2014 article, "Conceptualizing Epistemic Oppression,"
Kristie Dotson employs a familiar social imaginary of Eurocentric philosophy in order to illustrate that the alleviation of
epistemic oppression requires shifts in the schemas that organize our truth systems; a process of delinking that the prisoner
in the cave must undergo which Plato describes as dangerous,
improbable, and unclear. She employs the scope-of-change
perspective offered by Jean Bartunek and Michael Moch in
their work on three distinct shifts that occur in organizations to
bring about changes in thinking (Bartunek and Moch 1987).
Importantly for this discussion, Bartunek and Moch identify
those who are able to alter a flawed epistemic system or their
own epistemic resilience as change agents who must manage
the affective dimension of such shifts. These individuals "must
be responsive to managing a number of very difficult feelings,
such as anger, a strong sense of loss, anxiety or hopelessness"
(Bartunek and Moch 1994, 28). So for the purposes of this discussion, epistemic oppression is significant because it helps illuminate where and how undoing and amending knowledge
systems might get stuck or why someone, or a group, may be
resistant to taking responsibility for the impact of beliefs that
nothing in the present is "owed" or that their present knowledge
systems have little connection to enslavement or settler colonialism. Dotson applies their argument of three distinct epistemic shifts needed to alleviate epistemic oppression. She
identifies the first and second as reducible, meaning that the
sources of the oppression can be attributed to social or political structures, and thus the shifts can be made through these
structures. According to Alison Bailey, first-order learning de-
tects and monitors biases, while second-order learning realizes

that there are insufficiencies to address these biases in our shared epistemic resources (Bailey 2014). For instance, in the case of the #RhodesMustFall movement, students identify that to uphold Rhodes is an expression of the value of apartheid (first order); to take the statue down articulates it as an insufficient source of history (second order). The third-order change needed to alleviate third-order epistemic oppression, what Dotson understands as the "deepest and most resilient form of epistemic exclusion" (Bailey 2014, 65) is manifested in the antagonism and anger expressed by students at the inability of the institution to decolonize or transform. The anger and antagonism are a hallmark of the change agent experiencing the third-order epistemic change, the one that feels that the endless correction or repair of monuments or curriculum is only tinkering within a larger framework that refuses to undo, sever, or discard those fundamental habits responsible for the reproduction of oppression. The third-order change is where the most challenging aspects of epistemic reparation may be found. Unraveling one's beliefs requires a "changing of one's mind" because one has seen the harm potential, taken responsibility for it through an epistemic shift toward altering not only the belief but also the processes by which that belief was created. During such moments, distrust of community or institutions that have upheld, produced, and reassured those beliefs arises, and profound alienation can occur, as can a breakdown of accepted communicative behaviors. If we return to Dotson's use of the allegory of the cave, it is the moment where the prisoner returns and attempts to communicate what she has come to see, only to be met with a threat of death.

Dotson describes third-order epistemic change as irreducible because first- and second-order exclusions are insufficient to explain the subterrain that maintains the resiliency of epistemic oppression; it is irreducible because the resources we have to rely on in order to alter or correct an unjust system of knowledge are inadequate to explain how to go about such work. Plato's prisoner scenario raises some persistent questions: How does the one prisoner extricate herself and look beyond the shadows? What occurs in that moment where a profound epistemic shift enables her to perceive that the shadows are not truth? How do we explain to others who see our anger from within the value-laden frame of rationality that the "irrational" marginal voice might be a source of authority? This question of the irreducibility of the third-order change highlights why amending social imaginaries or epistemic resources is so fraught; such shifts fundamentally destabilize one's sense of reality and can elicit anger, shame, and fear. A third-order change requires one to transcend foundations of how one knows the world, how one makes sense of existence. Dotson points to the challenge of understanding how this arises and how we may facilitate the third-order changes to our truth schemas. Cultural imaginaries—how our values of the past get communicated to us through exemplars, family history, monuments, such as statues of Cecil Rhodes—are used by institutions in order to reproduce, wittingly or unwittingly, epistemologies negotiated through collectives that legitimated racial, socioeconomic, ethnic and gender-based exclusions. How we engage in epistemic reparation is connected to the desire to undo cultural expressions of the social imaginary, such as monuments. However, its deepest challenge to undoing racism is to shift the epistemic structures that value, uphold and create cultural expressions such as monuments. This is the work of the third-order change that Dotson points us toward; it is the work of invention, new ways of untethered knowing and communications across breakdowns. This kind of change risks the collapse of social systems that we have come to believe as status quo or inviolable. The anger and antagonism of protesting students reveals the dissatisfaction with symbolic undoing that, while necessary, is not sufficient for ending the flow of the epistemologies that attempt to evade systemic accountability. What the students in #ConcernedStudent1950 revealed was not only the failure of a president and an institution to "do something" in the face of ongoing racist acts toward Black students, but also the institution's failure to understand how to alter a persistent way of knowing the world as anti-Black and take responsibility for what this knowledge does in the academy.

The epistemic shifts that Dotson describes reveal the gaps, the fractures, that emerge between the realization that one's truth systems have reproduced oppression or allowed one to be oppressed, the difficulty of having adequate epistemic resources to take responsibility for the impact of those beliefs and that the process of amending or undoing those flawed beliefs to account for unjust or racist practices is driven by the affective domain. It is in the gap that reparative knowledge is helpful to make sense of how to adjust to a truth system that has identified the sites and substrata of oppressive knowledge creation.

Dotson builds from Miranda Fricker's 2007 work on epistemic injustice through locating epistemic oppression as responsible for producing epistemic resources that perpetuate injustice. For example, a person who is a member of a subordinate or oppressed community describes what happens to them, such as in the case of racist police violence, and their truth claim is doubted (epistemic injustice is exerted) because of their identity category. As this manner of injustice occurs regularly over time, the doubt ascribed to the identity category leads to an epistemic exclusion (Dotson 2014): it contributes to the social imaginary that enables society to believe, despite the evidence, that, for instance, Black people lie about police violence or bring the violence upon themselves even when the victim, as in the case of Tamir Rice, is a twelve-year-old child. It excludes the knowledge produced by the communities that experience racist police violence as part of the schemas that surround the accepted imaginaries about police. Police cannot be racist because the truth produced from Black people's experience cannot be trusted. This is epistemic oppression at work and evidence of the first and second types of exclusions that Dotson outlines. A movement of reparative activity, a third-order change, acknowledges that a condition or system has arisen from a particular set of epistemic habits reproduced through a social imaginary and works toward undoing that form of knowing to alter the way of knowing, the belief system. Such activity allows epistemic reparation—a way of knowing that sets the individual or community free-falling away from the comfort of poor epistemic habits. It allows the individual who could previously see the police only from a single vantage point, a single story if you will, to unravel the entanglements of a dominant view. To delink from the colonial matrix of power, to decolonize in the everyday, is connected to the ascription of truth to those bodies historically denied as producers of truth and to become accountable for forms of knowledge responsible for the reproduction of racism and work to amend them. This activity, as Bartunek and Moch describe, elicits anger and antagonism; the struggle of undoing, delinking, is, necessarily, a volatile process.

Edouard Glissant's prophetic vision of the past, an idea he worked through in many of his texts, is a helpful concept in an effort to further illuminate the epistemic resources needed to facilitate the third-order epistemic change. This prophetic vision of the past seeks not only to fundamentally reconstitute social imaginaries used as shared epistemic resources but also to offer a way of thinking about how to create perceptions, visions, and values from reparative activity. Like Dotson's retelling of

Plato's prisoner and the students in the protest movements, the prophecy that Glissant describes occurs because the prophet or the poet has encountered their maladjusted system and has set off in search of a relation, a collective negotiation that communicates the truth about the maladjusted epistemic system. Errantry, what Glissant describes as "a sacred quest" (Glissant 1997) requires letting go, and wandering away from the shadows mistaken for truth. One might say that the protesting students experienced the fractures of delinking as they erred from dominant and accepted social imaginaries in order to clear the field for reinvention through the demand for amends. One might also say that their clamoring was not to change the systems, undo them, but be included in them. All student protest movements are not homogenous in their desires, nor are all of them interested in decolonial moves, as Robin Kelly points out in his 2018 essay, "Black Study, Black Struggle." In this, students act prophetically in the sense that something is unsettled; a third-order epistemic change is detectable though not guaranteed.

Glissant maintains that relation is that which opens the world for creolization, and the prophetic vision of the past is one of its behaviors. John Drabinski writes, "A prophetic vision of the past hearkens towards decolonization, towards decoupling historical experience and historical reading from the imperative to site and cite authority" (Drabinski 2015, 3). For Glissant, the Caribbean is characterized by the experience of the archipelago; to be Antillean is to be fragmented, rhizomatic, and errant and without a filial root. When held up against Eurocentric epistemic values (he identified linear origins, citation, and wholeness) such an ontology is seen as erratic, irrational, and without foundation. Relinquishing the desire for engaging in practices that revive lost traditions or piecing together mythological histories is essential to Glissant's approach to reconstituting the epistemic wounds of enslavement and colonization; the way through, for Glissant, is from the use of poetics to recast the subject matter at hand, the history and the present, creating new epistemic structures, new substrata of knowledge. Glissant writes, "For those whose history has been reduced by others to darkness and despair, the recovery of the near or distant past is imperative. To renew acquaintance with one's history, obscured or obliterated by others, is to relish fully the present, for the experience of the present stripped of its roots in time, yields only hollow delights. This is a poetic endeavor" (Glissant 2005, 15). Glissant was keenly attuned to the struggle with history and how poetics, as a way of knowing, could serve as a mechanism to diminish the ontological insecurity that can arise when one perceives the processes and institutions that have functioned to obliterate and obscure.

The colonized person or person struggling to be heard in the maladjusted epistemic frameworks comes to feel its weight, see clearly that while their knowing has been amended, the system of knowing has not been. They can be detected as prophets because they speak against rulers and cause friction with the accepted epistemic system. To recast the past is to retell a story woven into our social imaginary in a new way, from a vantage point or experience not yet put in relation, not yet taken responsibility for. It is through the retelling, through errancy, that the connection to one's obscured or suppressed history finds a way to amend poor or maladjusted epistemic beliefs.

How Is the University Like a Light Switch?

For a moment let me engage in an imaginative activity with you. Think about the university as a light switch—and not in the traditional sense as a place that illuminates, permits the individual to move from the uncivilized darkness of ignorance into the light of truth. For a moment let's put enlightenment and truth metaphors of education aside and turn, instead, to thermodynamics and Einstein's First Law. The Law of Conservation of Energy states that energy can neither be created nor destroyed; energy can only be transferred or changed from one form to another. For example, turning on a light would seem to produce energy; however, it is electrical energy that is converted.

What if we imagine universities as if they were light switches, like apparatuses that enable the transformation of energy from one form to another through the collective work of amending and redress? We are told to go to college, to study not only to get a job but also to encounter truth, to partake in a grand historical tradition that opens our eyes, enlightens us, and pushes us toward seeing the world through the lenses of truth and justice. But what if universities were sites to activate undoing and responsibility-taking? Not in the sense of coming only to study the grand ideas of human history but also to contend with the harms caused by said grand ideas and to engage in responsibility-taking? When students take their first classes on slavery and colonialism—classes specifically designed to study these topics—they are often destabilized, and universities offer little emotional support for this kind of encounter with the truth. Then universities get frustrated or angry when students agitate or organize to hold their institutions accountable for the truths revealed—when they turn the colonial logics of patrol upon the faculty member, the institution, or the topic.

I would like to pretend for a moment that universities, with their students, their faculty, staff, disciplines, museums, archives, sports, and libraries, are locations that draw and disperse energy. The heat and work that occur within a university help to uphold, reflect, and shape the social world. I often think about how the heat and work that occur within a university setting can serve as an apparatus to transform it into reparative energy; at the core of this is truth-telling about disciplines, about history, about the logics of societies. Where do we turn to heal? Where do we turn with the heat and the work that arise from truth encounters? Although likely a crude analogy, I find it helpful in transitioning my thinking of reparations from conceiving of it as a discrete object, such as a sum of money, to a curative life-giving energy, a human activity that can open space for the release of new forms. Currently universities engage in reparation not as a life activity, as a transformation of energy, but rather as discrete gestures such as apologies, plaques, or financial recompense. While these are potential interventions to shift our perception regime and alter our understanding of history, how it penetrates, shifts systems into new forms, and restructures to make discrimination or erasure an impossibility is the work of life activity.

Institutions of higher education, like the current debate around the removal of public monuments as reparation for slavery, have been engaged in their own processes of acknowledgment and apology for their role in perpetuating slavery (yet notably, not broadly for the occupation of Indigenous lands). The recent proliferation of diversity and inclusion-related jobs in higher education combined with efforts to study the linkages between institutional survival (at Rutgers, Harvard, Brown among many other universities) and the buying and selling of human beings may be read as another instantiation of a social world attempting to "repair" its legacy of perpetuating slavery and colonialism.

Let us return to Sara Ahmed's warning around repair—that it can engage the impulse toward making racism, inequality, and injustice more comfortable and more bearable to the dominant privileged in higher education. The recompense that Georgetown University gave in the form of "free" education to the descendants of people sold by the institution serves to make institutional history more bearable, as if through such an acknowledgment, something is fixed and ended. It reveals the limited nature of reparation as repair, as a move not to mobilize the undoing of present colonial procedures but rather to attempt to use the same mechanisms of oppression to quell, dam up, or annex out a moment that the institutions believe to be over. I agree with Ahmed in this regard. Such actions of repair reveal the epistemic schema of institutional perspectives that view the act of selling humans as a thin attenuated line, a frayed strand in its history that may, through acts of apology, be forever severed from its identity. Such acts stumble toward making amends, but they fall short because the epistemic system that produces the solutions—the acts of apology—have not engaged in third-order epistemic changes. The participation in the slave trade by Georgetown University and so many other institutions of higher education reveals that higher education is rooted in anti-Blackness and a willingness to place profits needed for institutional survival above human life. Providing free tuition, while a single spike on the reparative mace, does little to alter these values and behaviors of which we see creolized versions in the form of entrenched Eurocentric core curriculums, overwhelmingly white faculty, and a growing willingness to place institutional survival over providing living stable wages to adjunct labor. Therefore, while Ahmed is correct in her suspicion about repair, we may begin to understand reparative activity as something related yet distinct. The attempts of universities such as Georgetown, Rutgers, Columbia, Brown, and Harvard, among others, to contend with their dependence upon the slave trade for survival, while revelatory of a movement toward reparative knowing, shows a profound entanglement in and responsibility for systemic oppression. If they were to engage in epistemic reparation, putting themselves in relation with the trauma of the past and its present character, they would see that their continued survival in their present character is an impossibility. Taking a reparative turn characterized by relation, touching, encountering the events of injustice and seeing their creolized manifestations in the present would require fundamental institutional change. It could, I believe, recast the aims of the endeavor of higher education and lead to the reinvention of the university as a reparative instrument in society.

Recent student protests reveal that many students, who are drawn into universities as diversity commodities, sense the emptiness of the inclusion rhetoric: What are we willing to exclude for the sake of prestige? What epistemic shifts are needed in the beliefs, values and attitudes of higher education to assume responsibility for ongoing inequality? Two recent protests illuminate the impact of student pressure on universities and the challenge of taking up epistemic responsibility that potentially tilts universities in the direction of epistemic reparation.

From #FeesMustFall

Where can we look for evidence that delinking, part of the topography of epistemic reparation, is an affective endeavor, one directed toward the institution? Where can we look for evidence that the curriculum, policies, and behaviors of universities can provoke students into realizing that the system of learning is entangled with legacies of injustice and oppression that persist into the present? Student protest movements have been, since at least the early 1950s in the United States, connected to the daily function of higher education. The university has been a site of contestation and negotiation of truth by those who are allowed entry. In the last few years, campus protests have reemerged with renewed intensity at universities around the world. Many of these protest movements are organized by students whose identities remain persistently underrepresented and for whom the rising cost of higher education is becoming a barrier to access. Some of these protest movements are organized by graduate students and adjunct faculty whom higher education increasingly exploits through precarious and low-wage working conditions, such as the ongoing series of graduate student strikes organized at the University of Chicago in 2019, at the University of Michigan in 2020, and at Columbia University in 2021. These movements, I argue, expose the antagonism and anger felt toward a system that is perceived as reproducing—creolizing, if you will—ways of knowing and valuing developed through colonialism and enslavement and reproduced anew through the logics of neoliberalism and neocolonialism. These movements articulate themselves in the interstices, middle places between feeling outside the university; outside the dominant values of a system on which society relies for jobs and economic security as well as for power, yet also desiring to be included within these sites of power. While not all people involved in these protest movements are unanimous in their desired outcomes, they reveal overwhelmingly that the epistemic contestation of higher education is well underway. Importantly, activism within higher education by faculty, students, or staff is an act of rupture that opens space for reparative activity to potentially flow. Like Walter Mignolo's description of decoloniality, such ruptures can signal a direction for reparative activity, for turning into the undoing. Such protests are not, in and of themselves, reparative; rather, they are signals of reparative work to come.

Universities have always been bastions of power and resource hoarding by elite classes as evidenced in the long tradition of legacy admissions and maintenance of class position illustrated by social mobility indexes such as the one created by Raj Chetty. Many of these protest movements are, I believe, struggling toward reparative activity at the epistemic level, sought within and from their antagonism and anger at the failure of institutions of higher education to enact processes of decolonization and antiracism that move beyond what Ahmed describes as the "non-performative,"* or the way institutions can make statements that support diversity yet do nothing to activate these commitments into systemic overhauling (Ahmed 2012). Yet, as I have tried to explore in the first part of this book, diversity is inclined, within its use by neoliberalism, toward the nonperformative. For the purposes of this inquiry, I will focus, as an outsider to them, on two protest movements from 2015 that have been widely studied by scholars such as Roderick Ferguson, Rekgotsofetse Chikane, Kehinde Andrews, Judith Bessant, Analica Mejia Mesinas and Sarah Pickard interested in student protests in higher education.

The year 2015 saw many protests by students and precarious faculty across a range of geographies. They often happened within months of one another and were almost always led by

---

*Although I prefer Ahmed's more nuanced and accurate definition, *performative* has come to be used synonymously with virtue signaling or stating commitments without actualizing them in systems, policies, or procedures. So, in social movements, *performative* often means *nonperformative*.

racialized populations who have historically been marginalized and excluded from the institutions that now seek to include them. They are almost always led by populations, Black and Indigenous in these cases, who have long been the object of study by white academia but whose epistemologies, cultural productions, history, land, and bodies have been devalued and exploited by higher education. The two protest movements I will use to illuminate my attempt to trace epistemic reparation within the site of universities are #FeesMustFall begun in 2015 at the University of the Witwatersrand in Johannesburg, South Africa, and #ConcernedStudent1950, begun in late 2015 at the University of Missouri, in Columbia, in the United States.

On March 9, 2015, students at the University of Cape Town in Cape Town, South Africa, organized a protest to remove the statue of Cecil Rhodes from the campus. The movement, Rhodes Must Fall, describes itself as "a collective movement of students and staff members mobilising for direct action against the reality of institutional racism at the University of Cape Town" (Pather 2015). It called not only for the removal of the statue but also for the institution to redress the legacies of colonial anti-Black violence still present in the institution. The movement demanded an Afrocentric and Afro-Indigenous curriculum, worker rights, and the hiring of a greater number Black academics. Throughout the protest movement, which eventually led to the removal of the statue of Cecil Rhodes, student leaders called for the decolonization of the university. "From the time that it was colonised there was never an attempt to decolonise the university. The university culture is still very white, it's very elitist, patriarchal, and it's very heteronormative," Kealeboga Ramaru, student organizer involved in Fees Must Fall, said (Pather 2015).

Soon after the Rhodes Must Fall movement succeeded in the removal of the statue through occupying buildings and maintaining the protest over a few months, #FeesMustFall began in order to organize students around the proposed increases in tuition at the University of the Witwatersrand in Johannesburg. The fees movement spread across South African universities, drawing international attention to the student-led resistance that demanded free tuition, an accessible education as well as a decolonization process to occur across the university. The latter included revising curriculums, hiring practices, staffing, and pay scales to acknowledge what the protesters described as persistent anti-Blackness. The protest maintained that the fee hike was an attempt to disenfranchise Black students from being able to access higher education, the majority of whom, post-apartheid, are low-income (Mbembe 2015). Those involved in the protest also identified the fee hike as symptomatic of the lack of social transformation in South Africa after apartheid—that broader racialized socioeconomic and social inequality persisted and that the university, they argued, continued to reproduce these inequities by preventing access through fee increases. The protesters, at least those who were speaking to the press and through social media, understood the university as a social organism, one that embodies, reflects, and reproduces ways of knowing through its daily function. Their antagonism, particularly the demand for the removal of statues of individuals once believed honorable and the redress of the curriculum, is evidence of the workings of a reparative epistemology—a way of knowing that reveals the presence of the past and the iterative, reproductive character of oppression through institutional policies and values. It articulates a reparative epistemology through the expression of a desire for undoing and amending, for acts of

altering or adding on, in order to unleash an infinite procedure toward responsibility-taking measures.

#ConcernedStudent1950

Across the planet, only a few weeks prior to the start of the
#FeesMustFall movement in November 2015 several Black
students, including Peyton Head, the president of student
government at the University of Missouri (Mizzou) experienced acts of racial harassment, hate speech, and intimidation
on campus. These events came after a number of years of persistent anti-Black sentiments and racist acts, one of which, the
dropping of cotton balls in front of the Gaines/Oldham Black
Culture Center on campus, resulted in the arrest and suspension
of two students, Zachary Tucker and Sean Fitzgerald. Though
the two were arrested under suspicion of a hate crime and sus-
pended from the institution, they were ultimately charged with
littering and given community service, contributing to the perception that racist acts on campus had, ultimately, little consequences (Heavin 2010). In late September of 2015, a graduate
student, Jonathan Butler, began a hunger strike to demand the
resignation of the university's president, Tom Wolfe. Other
students joined, and over several weeks, they endured and re-
sisted attempts by the administration to end the protest. An
additional tactic they employed was to organize a mock college
tour during which impacted students recounted the various
racist incidents that had occurred on campus over a number
of years. The university's football team subsequently began a
boycott, refusing to play until the president resigned. The
protest of the football team garnered greater attention than
the hunger strike or other efforts by the students due, many
surmised, to the amount of money that the football team gar-
ners for the university. The protest ended with the resignation
of President Tom Wolfe on November 9. In the years following

the protest, Mizzou experienced a 35 percent drop in first-year students enrolling in the university (Hartocollis 2017).

The students identified, as did their peers in South Africa, the persistence of history in their movement and the significance of operating as antagonists to a social organism responsible for shaping a social imaginary that they came to understand as responsible for the atrocities committed against their ancestors and for cultivating present conditions of oppression. #ConcernedStudent1950 commemorated the year the first Black student was admitted to Mizzou. What the name communicates, to me, is an attentiveness not to the essentialization of Black experience at the university but to the persistence of anti-Blackness within the behaviors and functioning of the university due to an absence of systemic redress. The protest reveals the emptiness of inclusion efforts that do not seek or are not empowered to undo oppressive systems or policies within institutions with significant legacies of racism. In *Black Study, Black Struggle,* Robin D. G. Kelley is critical of this and other student protest movements, arguing that they often collapse into reformist demands and focus too much on attempts to make universities more welcoming or supportive to Black students (Kelly 2016). While I do not disagree with this characterization of student protest, having been intimately involved with many student protests since 2015 that often call for mandated diversity training as the solution, I have found that students are also, though not necessarily unanimous, pushing against the epistemic underpinnings of the university. That is to say, their ruptures and struggle point toward anti-Blackness as a fundamental way of knowing and existing embedded within higher education that can't be addressed through reform; they turn to this because, I believe, there is a lack of imagination of what possibilities might exist within education beyond reforms. Mariame Kaba often describes groups that push for reform not as less than or deficient, but struggling under a limited imaginative framework. This limit is a product of epistemic oppression. Framing their commitment this way reveals how the past moves and persists in the present. It communicates to the present that the legacy of marginalization and discrimination that the first Black student encountered persists through institutional logics. It speaks of how admission and inclusion efforts are insufficient in the face of persistent anti-Blackness and that it is against all of this that the weapons of reparation must be unleashed.

In 2016 Field of Vision released a short documentary, "Concerned Student 1950" created by three undergraduate Mizzou students, Adam Dietrich, Varun Bajaj, and Kellan Marvin. The short film, shot from within the Mizzou protest movement, exposes the level of trauma and stress that the students were enduring, both from being driven to strike and protest an institution that failed to adequately respond and from the weight of the legacy. It exposes, to someone like me who knows very well the kinds of discussions that were likely happening among senior administrators, that this psychological toll would never be redressed. It reveals that their wakefulness, brought on the heels of the murder of Mike Brown in nearby Ferguson, is located within the body and that they make their bodies antagonists against a social organism, the university, accustomed to shaping the discourse about them and deciding how history will be remembered through its management tactics. Their protest reveals an opening for activating reparative epistemology in that the movement expresses that present thinking must amend the way the university undertakes responsibility; the protesters see the locations and persistence of anti-Blackness and believe it to be not just an unfortunate history but rather the control and dictate of Blackness, a fundamental logic woven into higher education and perpetuated through diversity work that upholds colonial beliefs about difference and its place. The protest movement reveals that for identities historically excluded, the university can be experienced as fracture or control; it is offered conditionally through clear terms of participation for how diversity can identify, participate and be viewed.

These examples speak to the tension that people endure who attempt to delink from institutions that have occupied authority. They speak of the affective domain of reparative epistemology and of whether it is possible for the individual and the institution to engage in reparative action as a process of collective amending. They speak of the perils of diversity work undertaken in the absence of critical understanding of the university as a neocolonial structure and of how the diversity worker may inadvertently become an agent in its epistemology of difference.

As individuals engaged in the process of education, we need to ask: If the history of higher education in the United States has relied on creating policies and practices to uphold the self-interest of the university, which historically has been linked to the self-interest of the wealthy, then singular expressions of sorrow or apology are insufficient as they do not operate at the level of episteme. Such acts run the risk of working as transactions, exchanges of assets between buyers and sellers; the university is the seller of a repaired, inclusive educational space to the buyer that is the student. Thus, allowing the actors to believe that participation in the "fixed" space constitutes a shift in their modes of acting—that because, as Ahmed points out, "diversity, equity and inclusion," is uttered, epistemic shifts must be occurring. At the foundation of the university is its predication on learning as a unit of exclusive exchange and its dependence on the commodification of humans, creativity, and the drive to manage the chaos of life. This exclusive exchange is an asset to be protected at all costs.

The Harvard University (or insert another Ivy League or Big 10 institution here) commodity is to always be distinguished from the community college commodity, and its moves to distinguish itself are dependent upon the marginalization of community colleges and other institutions. While these universities attempt to find a means of correcting historical injustices through recognition and apology, without accounting for how traumatic injustices are not isolated in a past moment but have built the present culture, values, and operations of the institutions themselves, a reparative society or more inclusive institutions will be relegated to the nonperformative.

Placing the university in *relation* to its traumatic, unjust histories, to the paradox of its character, opens higher education to its potential to engage in epistemic reparation, to redress where and how those injustices live today, and what shared collective responsibility social institutions and their actors, such as universities and their workers, hold. This activity is what permits us to understand where, how, and what unraveling has to be made to the institutional structures, values, and norms that persist in creolized versions of past inequities and traumas. This is not work for the faint-hearted. Rather, such epistemic reparation requires wandering away from tradition and relinquishing or seizing power. It poses the risk that the familiar and the elite might need to be razed in order to clear space for the reinvention of education that performs and activates a new future. Such reparative activity is, as Glissant directs us, a poetic endeavor.

Afterthoughts

Reparation asks the individual born in this moment to attend to how she meets the flow of history, what it means to step into it, take it up, and benefit or suffer through its aftermath. This measure of selflessness—the ability to comprehend that one's life is because of what has come before it and that something is owed, something asks of redress and responsibility—is rarely found in contemporary society. The most common response given in discussions of reparative activities, particularly its economic forms, is Why should I pay for someone else's sins? As Justice Lewis Powell said of Allan Bakke, "he should not have to bear a grievance not of his making." Yet the United States' social imaginary bears little evidence of awareness of the inverse of this sentiment: to the bearing of privilege not of one's making.

This epistemic framing of society's relationship to history is where universities may take up the responsibility not only for engaging in reparative activities but also to instruct in reparative ways of knowing and being. How we struggle against persistent forgetting and cultivate critical memory is of critical concern to educational institutions, understanding that it will likely lead to the certain demise of many aspects of what we consider higher education to be and what we have relied on diversity work to accomplish.

"Reparation" as a concept, though it traces its origins back to late Latin and fourteenth-century French, entered into the English language with the abolition of slavery in Europe and in the colonies (Nehusi 1993). It is a word used more and more widely in our society due to the persistence of small committed groups in a range of regions and countries that have suffered extraordinary abuse and that continue to fight for financial recompense and for the truth telling that must come along with it. Reparation has been applied in many different countries for causes other than slavery and settler colonialism. Germany, as one example, was required to pay reparations to European countries damaged by World War II and to survivors of the Holocaust; the United States paid reparations for Japanese internment. Yet, still today, Haiti pays recompense to France for the "sin" of its liberation, and the British royal family takes no responsibility for the crimes of residential schools in Canada. These latter examples are offered as a way to emphasize that reparative activities have dimensions as yet to be unraveled for the harms committed and continued against Black and Indigenous people.

Higher education has a role to play in how generations are socialized into responsibility-taking moves. I have focused narrowly on a few key historical events that, among many others, hold significant implications for higher education's engagement with reparative knowledge and actions. Since the Civil War in the United States and the abolition of slavery, there have been calls to administer reparations to formerly enslaved people and their descendants. When legislation was passed in the United States as well as in the United Kingdom, reparations were paid not to the people enslaved but to the slave owners for the loss of capital. In the United States, it was called the District of Columbia Emancipation Act, signed into law by President Lincoln on April 16, 1862. This first movement of reparations reveals something of how societies evolved to conceptualize redress as moves to protect and uphold racial capital. From the outset of the formal abolition of slavery, arguments have been made that financial recompense as well as redress for the loss of language, traditions, knowledge, and humanity was necessary to repair the deep wound of racism. Outside of higher education in the United States this work has begun, most recently exemplified by the creation of the Legacy Museum and the National Memorial for Peace and Justice in Montgomery, Alabama.

Reconciliation efforts for Indigenous loss of life, ways of existence, land, and treaty honoring have also been ongoing. We have few examples of material reparations granted to Black and Indigenous people that move beyond discrete financial sums, formal apologies, and commissions that study the need and methods of remedying harm for decades of discrimination, violence, and exclusion. Recently, we have begun to witness more moves toward reparation by individuals and institutions, such as Cornell University and the Coming to the Table Project.* Reparative activity is, I believe, unfolding in various ways, but whether and how higher education will engage or decide to manage it remain to be seen.

Where to begin such processes and who bears the responsibility are questions that arise over and over in discussions about remedying. From the earliest writings on Reconstruction to affirmative action and financial recompense today, we witness a fundamental epistemic problem: the problem of persistent racial injustice is connected to what W. E. B. Du Bois described as a willful amnesia. Du Bois emphasizes that legal, social, and other efforts to ensure racial equality (and I extend this to Indigenous rights movements) are and will be futile if memory suppression persists. This memory work—work on how our social imaginary has suppressed how we

---

* Coming to the Table is a project of personal reparations. See comingtothetable .org.

come to know ourselves in the wake of slavery and settler colonialism—is not simply a matter of education, of knowing more about people who are racially or socioeconomically different from ourselves. It is a matter of reflecting on what higher education's self-interests are and why it is so frequently unwilling to give up power to those whose ancestors sacrificed their lives and legacies to enable existence and why so many believe that they hold no responsibility despite their participation and benefits derived from institutions that profit from present and historical exploitation. This is, I believe, far different from inclusion efforts. Reparative activity does not seek to be included in what exists; it seeks to undo ways of knowing and being, to transform and unravel.

Education is bound to the work of reparation if we believe education to be, as so many institutions describe themselves, engines of equality, democracy, and social justice. The work of reparation by those who desire transformation in higher education requires self-determined action on the part of those communities that have been excluded, that incur oppressive amounts of indebtedness to participate, and for whom higher education has accumulated for its own benefit while unengaged in systemic antiracist or decolonizing change. The history of education in North America in particular is intertwined with the history of continually setting the conditions of participation in education for Black and Indigenous people, and uncritical or decolonized diversity work is a helpful companion in this endeavor. But how, then, can institutions and institutional workers concerned with transformation practically engage in reparative activity? In the next part of this book, I aim to provide readers with insight into the "what now and how" questions that have likely arisen throughout the first two parts. The constellation of reparation has financial, symbolic, and affective dimensions. I will engage with how reparative activity might map onto present functional areas of higher education, offering examples and thought experiments where the micro-locations of undoing, unsettling, might be (or already are) undertaken. I will work to explain how poetics, place and, space are central to efforts to unsettle diversity work and unleash reparative energies.

PART III

Reparative Endeavors

This endeavor to unsettle diversity through coming to terms with its links to colonial epistemologies of difference has been undertaken both as an offering, a grounding in reparative activity, and as evidence of my own epistemic reparation. I have had to unravel diversity in order to more clearly see its logics and to more accurately define efforts to unsettle higher education from oppressive practices. This endeavor may leave DEI practitioners, those most caught within the snare of diversity, frustrated and asking what then: how do you propose commitments to transforming education into institutions that center equity, decolonization, redress, or antiracism? What actions, one might justifiably ask, can institutional workers engage in that do not reinscribe behaviors such as accumulation and patrol but unleash transformative reparative activities? What does the practice of reparative activity, as distinct from diversity within institutions, look like in practice? I do not seek to offer a formula of steps to follow in this next part, much less a comprehensive set of directives. What I will offer is a perspective on ways that I have endeavored, failed, and succeeded at unsettling institutional oppressive ways of knowing. What I offer are practices that have helped guide me through Gloria Anzaldúa's *intersticios*. In the following part of the book I will offer a few narratives and ideas drawn from my own experiences as a diversity worker, in an effort to share several focal points and practices for reparative activities, ones that work to unsettle how institutions function and understand themselves. I offer poetics as a critical partner, one often overlooked in favor of quantitative methods, in reparative institutional endeavors.

The first chapter will explore place-based approaches and efforts to unravel and amend beliefs, attitudes, and behaviors that frequently reinscribe colonial practices of expansion and patrol that knowledge is elsewhere from where one studies. Next, I examine the occupation/reinvention of space as a tactic to unsettle and instruct, through imaginative activity, how institutions may function otherwise. I offer counterspace, a mechanism that has a long history in Black, Puerto Rican, and Indigenous social movements, as a tactic for reparative efforts. The third chapter examines the symbolic, aesthetic choices of higher education campuses, in particular the use of gates, as a method of spatial politics representative of the epistemic frameworks of higher education's reliance on gatekeeping behaviors, values, and attitudes. Finally, I offer co-creation and co-ownership models as methods that are essential to undoing power hierarchies entrenched in higher education and that offer significant pathways for decolonial institutional possibility.

Thread 1

Why Poetics?

In efforts to "transform" higher education into locations of possibility and equity, aesthetics or aisthesis is rarely invoked as a method for change.* Recently, however, large foundations such as the Andrew Mellon Foundation and the W. K. Kellogg Foundation have been driving forward projects that connect repair and racial healing work to monuments and narrative change. These interventions, fueled by the foundations' significant resources, ask people to reconsider how the past and present are communicated or formed in US society and among institutions of higher education, particularly through aesthetic modes.† More often, work to undo epistemic frameworks is

---

* Aisthesis is defined here as distinct from pure conceptual thought. It is knowledge derived from immediacy, from sense and emotion. Jacques Rancière explores aisthesis in his canonical work *Aisthesis: Scenes from the Aesthetic Regime of Art*. In this work Rancière identifies the regime of perception, defining it as the sensible fabric of experience within which the work of art or culture may be interpreted. He defines this sensible fabric as exhibition spaces, modes of production and consumption as well as thought patterns, values, and emotions that circumscribe visions of the social world. The university, as a type of sensible fabric, shapes feelings and visions of society, a dimension of aisthesis that yields poetic communications. I am interested in poetics in the sense not only of the literary form of expression but as a lived enactment that arises from a relationship to experience that is expressed through narrative, design, artfulness. I engage with poetics through Edouard Glissant's *Poetics of Relation,* where the text undertakes to expose poetics as a transformative mode of history (political and aesthetic), capable of enunciating creolized modes of existence.

† The Mellon Foundation's monuments project "is an unprecedented $250 million commitment by the Mellon Foundation to transform the nation's commemorative landscape by supporting public projects that more completely and accurately represent the multiplicity and complexity of American stories.

dominated by reliance on measurement tools that encourage the counting of bodies and identities as a way to prove that difference matters. This approach to difference, as I have sought to show, reinscribes colonial epistemologies that seek to control, patrol, and limit the transformative power that differences unleash. The presence of diverse identities does not mean that transformation of oppressive structures has been attained; representational equity is insufficient for decolonial transformation. This jumble of nothingness cleverly circumvents the work of ending and undoing systems, behaviors, and policies that permit the continuation of white supremacy and settler colonialist legacies. It, strangely, uses such representational values to legitimize admitting low-income Black, Latinx, and Indigenous people on the condition that they assume crushing indebtedness. This indebtedness is the price of admission charged by the census takers, the individuals who count and report where difference is placed. Such accumulation, indebtedness, and counting processes closely track capital accumulation, or the means through which institutions and systems acquire assets that increase their value. Black and Indigenous people in particular have always been assets for North American higher education, whether in the form of selling them and their children for "survival" or stealing land or sacred objects to study and house in their archives and museums. The latest practices of increasing numbers of "students of color" in the absence of inclusion efforts that alter the culture and the way

---

Launched in 2020, the Monuments Project builds on our efforts to express, elevate, and preserve the stories of those who have often been denied historical recognition, and explores how we might foster a more complete telling of who we are as a nation." https://mellon.org/initiatives/monuments/.

The W.K. Kellogg Truth, Racial Healing and Transformation campus centers ask higher education institutions to engage narrative change as part of this work. Kellogg defines narrative change as critical to undoing hierarchies of human value and the need to undo and shape perspectives that generate how we value racialized experience.

that the institution functions are little more than another form of this capital accumulation. The behaviors of acquisition, recruitment, and admission, and the expectation that students take on debt for the privilege of accessing what their communities have historically been excluded from, are often, though not always, predatory. This is the fault not only of institutions but also of governmental policies that have, since the late 1970s, defunded financial aid for low- or middle-income students such as the Pell Grants. In the institutional work of DEI, racial identity—particularly Black identity—has been consistently valued as a form of capital whose possession does not benefit the community or the individual but rather augments institutional worth as a diverse institution—not necessarily one engaged in social responsibility-taking or transformation. How the ways of knowing that facilitate these behaviors can be undone, is, I believe, connected to poetic interventions, the kind that engage a transformative relation to history, self, and place.

Organizations and companies that place "Black Lives Matter" slogans on their websites do so not because they are doing much to increase wages, benefits, or redistribute assets to their Black workers but rather to engage in the long-standing practice of racial capitalism. They use the slogan to project that they care for equity-seeking groups while doing little to amend, correct, or repair the systemic harm that they have caused through predatory hiring, resource extraction, pillaging black communities, and underpaying workers. Many institutions of higher education should not seek to claim that they are any different. As the number of chief diversity officer positions in higher education has increased, the racial disparities in student debt have grown exponentially. By 2016, two-thirds of higher education institutions had created a CDO position, with thirty more added in the past five years, mostly among the top-ranked institutions (Wilson 2013). During this same period, we have witnessed students of color, Black women in particular, become increasingly burdened by unmanageable debt. In 2014, before the economic free-fall caused by the COVID-19 pandemic, Black students, even when controlling for family wealth and income, held substantially more debt by age 25 than their white counterparts. Higher education continues to perpetuate predatory inclusion, practices that open a market not to correct or atone for exclusionary histories but rather to exploit a particular group, contributing to continued social inequality (Goldrick-Rab, Houle, and Klechen 2014).

Keeanga-Yamahtta Taylor analyzes the concept of predatory inclusion in *Race for Profit*, revealing that redlining gave way to practices that found ways to earn tremendous profits from exploitative rates that strictly controlled how Black and Latinx communities could participate. Their existence was predetermined, a hallmark of colonial subjugation. This is not dissimilar to the way that higher education presently includes low- or middle-income Black and Latinx people. They are permitted to apply to any institution of higher education they desire. But as access has increased, so has the cost. Many students have had to acquire punishing amounts of debt to participate in a system that had actively excluded their ancestors or used them for survival. These active exclusions, which, for many, prevented generational economic mobility that education can otherwise provide, are now replaced by crippling debt, the cost of access for historically excluded groups. Enacting a commitment to equity is not only a question of data, of showing the generational economic repercussions of discrimination. It is also a question of how we shift the ways we think and learn about collective responsibility for past harm. It is also a question of perceiving that these harms are continued in the present in the form of debt, de facto quotas, and legacy admissions. The aesthetic/aisthetic, particularly embodied decolonial poetics, offers a powerful modality for shifting social imaginaries to perceive, believe, and value that the cultivation of responsibility is the work of education. Those committed to higher education (in whatever forms are to come) need spaces for imagining beyond the gates, storytelling and envisioning possibilities.

While quantitative methods have important uses for illuminating inequality, they have also served as a means of controlling, ordering, and defining existence for racialized people. Poetic orientations, the expression of the particular and the intimate through storytelling, enactment, affective embodiment, and symbolism, can often bridge knowledge gaps between those who sense acutely that undoing and amending is needed if we are to be able to imagine otherwise and those who believe the present is disconnected from past injustice. To enact such embodied amending, we need spaces and places within which we may exercise and learn to practice the self-determined existence that can facilitate reparation.

As a social system, higher education engages in the accumulation of racialized groups to increase its image as a socially just institution. Yet many of our most esteemed institutions participate in iterations of predation and exploitation of the descendants of groups used for the construction, survival, and knowledge production of higher education institutions. Importantly, this does not mean we should seek to abolish higher education altogether, nor should we be so naive as to believe that the abandonment of citadels of power and resources will bring social transformation. Rather, we should understand that universities are a site of revolutionary contestation, of counter-spatial poetic practices that can instruct, if institutional agents and actors have courage and community, in the undeniable force of self-determination. This is the curriculum, the new requirements, and the pedagogy. We should seek to support all the ways that higher education can be a healing, transformative, and equitable social force. Many people's engagement with the full horror of what slavery and settler colonialism wrought, what neoliberalism continues to exert, is limited because everything has been constructed to prevent us from grappling with what those who came before us perpetrated and what their victims endured. Everything has conspired to create mirages of rights, of individuality, of bootstrap imagining that cultivates scant responsibility to the past or reveals that our relative comfort rests on a foundation that came from the exertion of harm. The Manichean world is expert at its partitioning, and those of us who are on the bright side—the side of marble staircases, expansive green courtyards, secure houses, and abundant food—glimpse the other side with disdain, dismay, pity, or disbelief.

There is real difficulty in imagining ways of educating and participating in institutions through practices that heal and invent new forms of relation, ones that take responsibility for exploitation. What is higher education conceived apart from neoliberal and capitalist strangleholds? Can it, through poetic endeavors, be wrested from these forces? It is difficult to imagine that higher education can assume a function in our societies that provides a model of social responsibility that takes seriously its participation in the perpetuation of inequality and racism, particularly for those who have become cynical, jaded, and even nihilistic about the future of higher education. As la paperson brilliantly argues in *A Third University Is Possible*, institutional agents must hot-wire the power and resources toward locations where decolonial possibility can be ignited; this, frequently, is outside the institution. This poetic description, an image of the reconfiguration of institutional systems to ignite change, is the kind of epistemic resource helpful in processes of institutional unsettlement.

Elite institutions establish criteria to carefully select BIPOC and low-income people, paying little attention to the "house" that they have been finally permitted into; a house that has actively nourished white supremacy for generations through ensuring that European thought and cultural production constituted the intellectual center of what it means to be an educated person. The legitimacy of the canon is such an enduring and tired debate that I can scarcely bear to rehash it here. I am not interested in offering yet another argument for why a curriculum dominated by European thought is problematic. A beautiful house, one with gates and gardens, churchlike libraries, and land for contemplation as far as the eye can see, all in an effort to realize the success of the enlightened individual who is never asked what their responsibility is for benefiting from the resources and wealth gained through the exertion of harm: what a beautiful dream the most elite of higher education has been, what a beautiful predatory beast.

My critics will think this too harsh and cynical—that my analysis should be more nuanced because, after all, we have to protect and defend these institutions, particularly during a time where intellectuals, science, and free speech are under attack. But as the struggle against such sacred things intensifies, what aspects of all of this are worth protecting? Higher education, particularly the more elite institutions, has been an incredibly comfortable life for several generations of mostly white men, with some white women included as well. What does it mean for them to have benefited so profoundly from the exploitation, oppression, and harm of Black, Indigenous, and people of color? More precisely, who are we protecting and why? As diversity officers in particular, or as individuals within these institutions committed to social justice and transformation, what do we work to defend while saying we are transforming it or "undercommoning" it, or hot-wiring it? Poetics, a component of aesthetic/aisthetic experience, reveals a dimension of human experience that can open us to empathy and spiritual movement that quantification cannot. But how do we create counter-space and actions poetically? How do we inhabit a vernacular of reparation in an effort to bring such a world forth? I wonder this as I read so many beautiful writings, inspiring visions of futures that have yet to be birthed. But I want to know and see the space of this, the place and home of vernaculars of reparation. These poetic endeavors are what place and space-making can reveal. Feeling, touching, and hearing the story, imagining the possible beyond violence, is what aesthetics allows. Poetics can be the language of outsiders, of marginal perspectives because it is often that communication against, under or in opposition to the dominant is often the only way we are able to express. How does one get someone to see that the shadows on the wall they took for truth were in fact a distorted perception? Poetics, that branch of aesthetics that can enact what is not yet, that can highlight the distortion or the absence, is a powerful but underused tool for shifting higher education toward a broader purpose of teaching for undoing, redress, and atonement. To define poetics, its colonial and decolonial forms, has consumed entire books, lifetimes of effort. For the purposes of this discussion, I work with poetics in its sense beyond the written or spoken text, as an enacted expression that employs drama, narratives, or structure and safeguards the particular (Glissant 1997). The expression of the particular in the web of relations between human, nonhuman, nature, is the realm of poetics. Poetic expression, as I have come to understand it, is detected as an interruption in the dominant visual, spatial, or communicative vernacular. Poetics intervenes as difference that exceeds boundaries, startling us, awakening us, to attend to the forms of utterances wrought through the relation of distinctiveness to common boundaries. Poetics captures and communicates dimensions of knowing and existence that the literal cannot. As I attempt to define poetics, through the analytical, it reveals itself as already challenging such encapsulation. Poetics opens us to the irreducible aspects of existence, the mystical and the transformative. Transformation arising from undoing, repair, and amends, as a constellative experience, carries within it irreducible dimensions.

As discussed in part II of this book, the challenge to reparation is that, for transformative activation, it requires an existential shift that unsettles socially conditioned core beliefs about responsibility to historical events, the meaning of a social contract, and interdependency. Jean Bartunek and Michael Moch (1994) argue that human experiences that unsettle socially accepted truths are difficult to transcend through "rational" arguments, meaning that we cannot rely exclusively on data, changes in law or policy, or civilized conversation to resolve racism and the legacies of its continued harm.

Poetics, as a means and a method, may help transcend the epistemic resistance that arises from unsettlement.

Breathtaking Landscapes

Place-Based Interventions

In 2016, at the beginning of Donald J. Trump's presidency, I took a job at a small liberal arts college in upstate New York as its inaugural chief diversity officer. Trump's presidency helped ignite awareness among many people of the tactics and procedures of anti-Black racism; it also stoked the simmering resentment at play within white communities with regard to diversity-related efforts. Yet it also revealed the powder keg of the social imaginary regarding the persistent past of racism in the United States. The hatred and violence that accompanied attempts to remove monuments to the confederacy, such as the statue of Robert E. Lee in Charlottesville, Virginia, peeled back fragile layers that had, for a time, made appearing publicly as a neo-Nazi or white supremacist a rare event in the United States. The images from the Unite the Right rally (which turned into a violent riot) could have been from the marches against Black people and their rights that occurred throughout the four decades spanning the 1930s to the 1960s, when Nazi armbands were regularly worn at marches protesting desegregation.

The face of white supremacy in the United States, changed after the civil rights movement, as did the lives of white people in the increasingly deindustrialized areas of the United States. The consistent activation of the impacts of unresolved racism in the country changed, resulting in the acceleration of the prison industrial complex, the militarization of police, the defunding of public education, and ongoing practices of discrimination such as redlining. For me, a child of the early 1980s, it seemed for a time that many people (white, Latinx, and Black) were convinced that racism was a vague historical phenomenon that had been resolved by the civil rights movement and the social protests of the 1960s. When in the early 2000s institutions such as Brown University began to inquire into their relationship to slavery, Indigenous dispossession, and genocide, it felt, for many involved, like a bombshell, as if the main function of white supremacy was to drop a veil, a spell of concealment, over the privileges of the present and what they meant in relation to the violence and harms of the past. The point of this vignette is that the need for concrete strategies for those seeking to intervene in the systems of white supremacy, to whom I direct this book, is critical.

Many institutions, like the one that I worked for in 2016, believed that they had no history of slavery or that the history was incidental to the present, like a footnote or a side comment, much like the remark made by one of my undergraduate professors to ignore what Immanuel Kant says about Black people—to chalk it up to a "product of the time." It had, he explained, no relevance to Kant's philosophical theory. At the time I remember thinking how strange this was, how uncomfortable I felt yet lacked the language to articulate why. When educators behave this way, when they believe that such statements of racism have not infected the epistemic framework that the work has yielded—a hierarchy of human value presented clearly on the page defined by race and geography—it instructs in the continuance not only of racism but also of the belief that knowledge production can somehow be exempted from privilege, vantage point, oppression, or life circumstance. It is strange to believe that intellectual products, such as books, are not the material of a social imaginary and evidence of how epistemic frameworks become reproduced. But this is reflected in the manner in which many institutions relate to the environment where they are located. Their geographic location, with notably few exceptions, is incidental to academic study; knowledge is an elsewhere activity, and students from all over the world are temporarily dropped into a place whose history and present have little bearing on their ivory tower engagement. Until fairly recently in the history of higher education, most institutional workers behaved like my undergraduate philosophy professor, maintaining that "products of the time" were discrete, incidental, and finished rather than created from a system still running under the same protocols, ones that saw the landscape as a backdrop that had little significance to the values, attitudes, and beliefs being encouraged.

Place instructs in another form of value hierarchy, one most tangibly experienced through the environmental abuse wrought from perceptions that the land, the trees, the water, the animals, the histories, and the local people are not nearly as significant as the ideas of elsewhere. With the work of people interested in engagement, in land and place-based pedagogies and experiential learning, there are critical locations looking to shift this habit of institutional life. But my experience, as someone tasked with doing diversity work, was that such place-based attentiveness was met with confusion and even hostility.

While place-based approaches in DEI efforts are being increasingly discussed, they began in the United States in the early 1990s through the work of educators such as Laurie Lane-Zucker, John Elder, and David Sobel. Briefly, place-based education has links to early service-learning models in higher education characterized by community service to individuals where institutions were located. As an educational philosophy it maintains that the "local community" is a primary resource for learning (Sobel 2017) What is local—the environment, the culture, language, landscape of the student or institution—within place-based approaches, becomes objects of the curriculum.

The approach was critiqued early on by scholars such as David Greenwood who argued for a critical pedagogy of place that located the individual, the student, within a particular community to develop an awareness and understanding of social oppression and their role in its alleviation (Greenwood 2008). Critical pedagogy of place moved discussions of place-based education into urban environments and began to emphasize that work with the local environment was, in the face of unchanged ways of knowing places and land, particularly that its approaches did not unsettle colonial epistemologies of domination, appropriation, and control of land, people and animals. Land-based pedagogy centers Indigenous relationships to land, distinguishing itself from other models of environmental education by emphasizing tribal ways of knowing land as the foundation for instruction (Simpson 2017). Land-based approaches assert that reconnection to land and land-based Indigenous practices are essential for undoing the harms inflicted by colonization. Decolonizing work places Indigenous communities and scholars as the leaders and necessary experts in approaches to place (Tuck et al. 2014). The writings of Indigenous scholars such as Eve Tuck, Glenn Coulthard, Leanne Betsamoke Simpson, Marcia MacKenzie, Kate McCoy, and Delores Calderon are essential texts for institutional practitioners committed to decolonization. Land-based approaches offer important pathways for institutional workers, like myself, concerned with unraveling forms of relation to places that continue Manifest Destiny and settlement-and-savior behaviors in places where students are newcomers.

Decolonizing commitments articulated within and by universities that hold investments in land purchases that do not respect Indigenous rights, participate in water holdings that threaten human rights to water, continue to view land as an asset for the accumulation of capital support the continued squeezing of southern Black farmers off their land, as well as supporting, through their retirement investments, land-grabbing practices in Brazil,* are empty statements. While institutions may wave the banner of social justice, antiracism, or environmental justice, the heart of the matter is the use of land, assets, and capital. Unraveling the persistent ways of knowing that result in these kinds of investments while hiring vice presidents for DEI reveals that undoing oppression, in the absence of epistemic shifts, is nothing more than decoration for perpetuating violence elsewhere in order to sustain the continued growth of multibillion dollar endowments.

Critical pedagogies of place and land-based pedagogies offer supportive methodologies to institutional workers committed to understanding how to unravel the logics of dispossession, domination, and extraction that still characterize institutional decision-making. How to intervene in these institutional practices is located not only in the framing of curriculum but also in the institutional policies, asset investments, real estate plans of an institution and even in the act of exposure, as Kat Taylor chose to do when she resigned as overseer of Harvard's endowment.†

---

* A 2019 cover story by Vann Newkirk in *The Atlantic* magazine titled "The Great Land Robbery" chronicles decades of practices that defrauded Black farmers from their land in the Mississippi Delta through the denial of loans and federal funding. Newkirk connects the current practices of Wall Street, notably the retirement fund most widely used by US academic institutions, TIAA-CREF. He writes, "In just a few years, a single company [TIAA] has accumulated a portfolio in the Delta almost equal to the remaining holdings of the African Americans who have lived on and shaped this land for centuries" (Newkirk 2019).

† In 2018 Kat Taylor, an overseer (I note the irony of this title as an indicator of the persistence of plantation logics) of Harvard's investments funds resigned, expressing grave concern about the use of portions of the university's multibillion dollar endowment in "fossil fuel reserves we can never afford to burn, land

What this means is that administrators, people running institutions either as diversity workers, presidents, trustees, or vice presidents of operations, should orient themselves toward these theories. These are also critical pain points for institutional actors committed to activism for change. Transforming institutional logics that contribute to environmental degradation, community displacement, and the ongoing oppression of tribal groups is located in the operations of higher education and can be alleviated by the work of practitioners who understand these approaches and take them seriously in running institutions. So long as powerful institutions like Harvard or TIAA-CREF conduct themselves opaquely, what changes will truly come for commitments to redress, justice, equity, or decolonization? Critical place- and land-based approaches have the potential to shift the logics of higher education from institutions that believe they are separate, particularly in terms of knowledge production to places in which the needs, culture, and ways of knowing where they are shape the teaching and learning of responsibility to land. It is a model of higher education that is responsive, interested in co-creation and responsibility-taking with the places in which these institutions are located. Such approaches have the capacity to transform the way that institutions view investments in land and their ties to the ongoing dispossession of Indigenous land and epistemologies. These approaches offer hope should institutional actors, particularly at the levels of leadership, engage seriously with what they instruct in. So while institutions have begun to undertake project such as those outlined in the essential anthology *Slavery and the University,* more

---

purchases that may not respect indigenous rights, water holdings that threaten the human right to water, and investments at odds with the safety of children and first responders. But we don't know what we don't know, especially now that so much of the endowment is held in opaque funds. And not knowing what endowment investments might be supporting will never be an excuse" (Taylor 2018).

is to be done in locating and narrating the story of each institution's entanglements, through its operations, in continued colonial practices.

Place-based approaches, rooted in archives and history as a kind of "place," helped inform the maneuvers that I undertook while navigating a new inaugural diversity role. The college I was working for had recently acquired Montgomery Place, an estate owned by Janet Livingston. A member of the Livingston family was a signer of the Constitution; another founded Kings College (now Columbia University), but a significant portion of the family's wealth derived from buying and selling human beings in the transatlantic slave trade. Craig Wilder in *Ebony and Ivy* explores the extent to which the Livingston family's wealth fueled the development of particular higher education institutions. Bard College, which had purchased Montgomery Place, had not previously acknowledged that its history of slavery, Indigenous dispossession, or indentured servitude was relevant to institutional remembering and its present functioning. That historical significance was "elsewhere" to the institution. Until the acquisition of the neighboring estate, Bard had not seemed to imagine that the land on which the college had been constructed and the structures built prior to 1868 (of which there are a few) had been made by anyone worth remembering, through literal breath-taking of humans. Such remembrances were not seen as relevant to the narrative that the institution told about itself or to the future-oriented project of educating progressively minded students. What did place matter to an institution concerned, like so many, with knowledge and life elsewhere?

The college's website describes Montgomery Place and the landscape that it overlooks as "a designated National Historic Landmark set amid rolling lawns, woodlands, and gardens, against the spectacular backdrop of the Catskill Mountains. Renowned architects, landscape designers, and horticultur-

ists worked to create an elegant and inspiring country estate
consisting of a mansion, farm, orchards, farmhouse, and other
smaller buildings." There is no mention of the enslaved people
who contributed to the creation and maintenance of the landscape of leisure, the spectacular home overlooking a breath-
taking landscape. That Janet Livingston owned slaves or that
slave labor had been regularly used at Montgomery Place was
known and documented both by the historical society, Historic Hudson Valley (the organization that had sold the property to the college) and by several faculty, notably history professor Myra Armstead, a scholar of northern slavery particularly
in the Hudson Valley and the northeast. It was largely because
of her efforts to create a class titled Window on Montgomery
Place that an institutional inquiry into the history of slavery
was undertaken. It was not that the history was previously unknown; rather, it was that, save a select few, the institution did
not seem to understand or know why it should matter to the
present beyond a historical footnote. It is noteworthy that this
college, for which, as a graduate and former employee, I have a
great deal of affection, focuses much of its attention globally in
diverse geographies from Hungary to Palestine; its core identity is education as an "elsewhere" project though, increasingly,
it focuses its work in the local community. For students and for
several faculty and staff, the acquisition of Montgomery Place
provoked the question of what was to be done by the institution to recognize and amend how the institution took responsibility for the truth of slavery on the property and whether it
understood how its way of knowing such history might be
linked to the campus's persistent anti-Blackness. What space
was being made for these truths to be part of how the institution remembered itself and how it produced knowledge about
place? What responsibility did the institution have in relation
to these truths? These questions—how the institution was to

practically go about acknowledging its narrative, taking responsibility for the slavery and dispossession that had occurred on
its land, through its buildings and its legacy and undoing the
modes of knowing that had contributed to its concealment—
became central to unsettling the institution and to an attempt
to cultivate an ethical institutional imagination.

At the center of the unsettling work that arose during my
time at this institution was Alexander Gilson and his legacy. His
life instructed in the significance of place-based approaches to
institutional reparative work and poetic imaginings. Gilson
was born to Ruth and John Gilson, who were enslaved on the
grounds of Montgomery Place, Annandale on Hudson, on
the banks of the Mahhicantuck River, somewhere around 1823,
only a few years before the New York legislature abolished slavery in the state effective July 4, 1827. Gilson grew up on the
grounds of Montgomery Place and became the head gardener.
He became a renowned botanist, creating well-regarded strains
of begonias and achyranthes. How Gilson developed into a botanist and renowned gardener of one of the most sought-after
landscapes is something that may never be known. We know
that his father was enslaved as part of the livery staff and his
mother was enslaved as a housekeeper. For the Black and Latinx
students encountering Gilson in the scraps of the archive that
survived, important lessons for epistemic reparation and the role
of place-based efforts in institutional transformation are found.

Bard's Black and Latinx students had long agitated for a
space on campus dedicated to centering the concerns and
needs of racially underrepresented students. There had been,
as in many colleges and universities, a reluctance to creating
this kind of space on the grounds that it was "exclusive" and
would be unwelcoming to white students. This sentiment is
so frequently expressed by white people that it inspired Beverly Tatum to dedicate an entire book to the topic, *Why Are*

All the Black Kids Sitting Together in the Cafeteria? When non-white students congregate in groups, it is viewed, through the lens provided to us by whiteness, as a problem. This sentiment, in spite of all the good people with kind intentions, created insecurity and doubt within the college; the idea of ceding space, space whose use would be determined by BIPOC students made the administration deeply uncomfortable, though never articulated directly to the students. The institution eventually established a multicultural lounge, much like the ones found in most institutions particularly in the 1990s. These spaces, designated and shaped by administrators, are fairly ubiquitous on university campuses. Some make clear that the space is for racially and ethnically underrepresented people to feel a sense of relief from the white-majority campus. These are rarer than spaces that state that their mission is to develop cultural competencies and engage in social justice and intergroup conversations. While these are of course important missions, they dilute the centering of space for racialized groups to retreat from what is often the relentless experience of overwhelming whiteness. When these spaces are asserted or self-determined by students as for them, they are rapidly managed by university administrators. As recently as 2020, a student at the University of Virginia asserted on video, "Frankly, there are just too many white people in here, and this is a space for people of color, so just be really cognizant of the space that you're taking up, because it does make some of us POCs uncomfortable when we see too many white people in here. . . . There's the whole university for a lot of y'all to be at, and there's very few spaces for us, so keep that in mind" (Burke 2020). The university, after the video was posted on social media by a conservative group called Young Americas Foundation, issued a statement which asserted that the Multicultural Student Center was open to all in spite of the student's assertion that the space was for POC. Such institutional assertions, which move quickly to ensure that white students are not alienated or made to feel unwelcome, seek to manage and control student self-determining actions.

Often institutions want to develop such spaces without the population they are intended to support having control over the mission, the function, or the services offered. Fundamentally, I believe, institutional administrators are afraid that students will create counter-spaces that work against the notion that the institution is a place that welcomes all and provide a space where students, if they choose, function in opposition to the institution. If universities, particularly predominantly white institutions were spaces of belonging for Blackness and/or Latinidad, then why is there a persistent need for spaces of relief, for microclimates in which anti-Blackness is not the norm?

Alexander Gilson, his life and particularly the decisions he made after he was manumitted to move his entire greenhouse off the Montgomery Place property and onto a plot of land he owned in a neighboring town, was compelling for the students, faculty, and staff involved in the project because it was an act to mark his right to self-determine. The student place that ultimately emerged at Bard College from the first iterations of a multicultural lounge was ignited by the narrative of Gilson, a campus movement of Black students in response to the University of Missouri protests and the efforts of a number of administrators and faculty to hold back the institutional attempts to prevent this activist group of BIPOC students and employees from having control over the project to create a space where Black identity could be centered, upheld the dominant narrative of Blackness as outside the history of the campus. Gilson's narrative, his labor as an enslaved person in a breathtaking landscape—a landscape that literally took breath—yet is still described as a "pleasure ground," ignited students to imagine that, in spite of the image of the institution as persistently white and European, Black identity and history had always been part of the narrative. Professor Armstead's research describing Gilson's move from "property to property owner" (Armstead 2019) seemed to resonate with a number of the undergraduate students who felt little ownership or control over what and how they were learning. The decision to name the place after Gilson was, in spite of a number of white staff members' objections, not only because he was notable, Black, and had been enslaved at Montgomery Place but also because his life seemed to speak to the sense of a number of BIPOC students who felt that their accumulation into higher education did not mean they "owned it" or "belonged." It meant that their creative energy, much like Gilson's creativity and brilliance with plants, was a way to enact a poetics of home-making, to undo the narrative that race had no place in the institution.

The creative enactments of self-determined existence through spatial resistance activities cannot be engineered or prescribed by university managers or earnest diversity workers. The best that I was able to do in the case of Gilson Place was to provide cover for the project against institutional attempts to wrest self-determination from the students. In the end, while Gilson Place still exists, I remain unsure whether the students continue to hold it as a center for their own self-determined action against and within a historically white institution. A fundamental part of this uncertainty is the absence and continuation of political education in the significance of counterspace to self-determination within an institutional setting or even the clarification of what self-determination or decolonizing acts are. However, another lesson in the creation of counterspaces that I learned is that they are probably mutable. Their mutability is an intervention against the lie of fixity, against the mirage that institutions are fixed regimes. They perhaps should not have a type of permanence, though this is something that is likely best decided by those engaged in the counterspace activities. This is not offered as an argument for how universities might be reorganized to permit or provide an area in which counterspace may be practiced. This examination of how these groups, all working in what Frantz Fanon would describe as a vernacular of the oppressed, is intended to highlight the contestation of space through poetic and political action as a crucial tactic for institutional transformation or toppling. University managers or administrators should, if they care about the realization of equity and justice or decolonization in the world, resist the need to manage such activities, control them, or even institutionalize them. The best approach is to participate in them and learn the lessons being offered so that the microclimate of decolonization or resistance might unsettle the status quo of how universities function sufficiently to undo their oppressive systems.

Participate, don't manage, offer resources, don't call university police and fundamentally listen, learn, and change. Epistemic reparation is best taught aesthetically, spatially, through the structures of our daily lived engagements. These projects offer a glimpse of how institutions might be otherwise; the otherwise is waiting and for university administrators, it is only through risk to your career, your salary, to the stability of the institution that you can learn what is being offered. We who can afford the risks rarely take them and far too frequently place the interests of the institution (protection of the trustees, the president, or wealthy or vocal alums) above the work of justice. How reparation is unleashed is linked to the control and use of space and its liberative potential.

Counter-Space as the Dramatization
of a Poetics of Refusal

Spaces become places through aesthetic actions, among other activities. A table signifies little until it is put into a particular room or building and used for a purpose. Things become what they are to us through how they are used. The thing is only "thinged" or becomes what we understand it to be through what we repeatedly do with it.* This is why Marcel Duchamp's infamous urinal (1917) was provocative and thought-provoking at the time of its exhibition. It provoked us to think that art (and a urinal) could be used in a manner other than its original intent and that the meaning of things is heavily dependent on our decision to use them as we have been told to use them. The interaction of the table and the room builds a story, and our subsequent participation builds layers of sediment, signaling that this has become a place, a place for study, a place for discussion or for listening. Space, in this context, precedes or creates a condition for places to be made. A space, a territory, for instance, or a field of study becomes defined by participation and use. Refusing to use something, to participate in the way we are expected, upends and unsettles. As Sara Ahmed argues in *What's the Use?*, previously excluded difference queers the way that universities were intended to function. When students and employees refuse to use the university in the way

---

* See Sara Ahmed's 2019 book, *What's the Use?* In the book she follows use to reveal the challenges and possibilities of diversity work and complaint as she dismantles the sexist and racist structures of the modern university.

that they are socialized or instructed to, it creates a disturbance within the institution. As an administrator, I have witnessed many instances of what happens when students refuse: refuse to incur debt, refuse to "listen" to what the messaging wants them to hear, refuse to continue to work for free, and refuse to use spaces, such as offices or classrooms or designated student lounges, in the way they are expected. When students and employees refuse the institution, they create a fundamental disturbance, as one of the purposes of higher education is to socialize, assimilate, into the proper way to use systems. Few students understand the significance of even seemingly small refusals in unsettling higher education, as they are not in the rooms to hear the anger directed toward their inability to "figure out" how to use the institution. More students, faculty, and staff should begin to enact refusal toward institutional practices that facilitate ongoing oppression. This chapter examines the creation of counter-space, space that illuminates how institutions are *not* working for equity-seeking groups because it creates a generative space, space that does precisely enact what it *could* be and does this through what I am calling a poetics of refusal.

I remember the chairs in my undergraduate classroom. They were wooden with large flat arms that had, over many generations of students, been inscribed with words or doodles in dark pen. There was the feeling that this chair, this room, had a sacredness, an ineffability that I couldn't fully capture. It was a feeling of participation in something that everyone else already knew and that I was just joining. The room and the chairs signaled, as many spaces on campuses can, that something particular was happening, something connected to a greater purpose beyond myself—something that I never felt as if I belonged in for a whole range of reasons. I never determined or decided that sitting in a chair was the best way to learn; it was provided to me and I complied: I participated.

Ownership is often communicated through a self-determined activity that shows you know how to participate, to act, or to behave in accordance with a set of criteria. It is to have, as we often like to say in higher education, environmental mastery over the behaviors, values, and attitudes of a particular environment. It is Michel Foucault's cultural capital. "Fake it until you make it" or "walk in like you own the place" are often heard in environments where people are outsiders, where people who have been excluded are now attempting to be included. We are rarely told to refuse to participate in the way we are expected to. This interplay of space and self-determination has powerful implications for belonging, ownership, and power. It is why the wealthy put their names on buildings of the universities they attended: as a reminder to subsequent generations that this space belongs to them and that they have made it their place.

Home, when we use that term, is one of the most significant ways we understand the feeling that we belong in a place. Even a work environment can be "familiar" or "homey" when we feel comfortable or powerful there. Whether that memory, that backward-dreaming of the place that cultivated you, served as the lighthouse for what intimacy meant, was supportive, abusive, or neither, or if there was not a home in the traditional sense of the word and that was what you always sought, home shapes a sense of belonging and not belonging. The drape of a curtain, the stain on a table, or the creak of a floorboard; the way we cultivate a place for ourselves, our family, or community is a marker of human existence, and when it is denied or taken from us, when we are not given permission to homemake, or when places do not bear any familiar markers, we can feel adrift or as strangers. We do not feel at home.

Throughout my career in higher education, the students who have most powerfully expressed a lack of feeling at home or sense of belonging in higher education have been BIPOC and low-income students despite the concerted efforts of administrators to create "welcoming environments." They are not the students from elite private preparatory high schools or the children of people who easily inhabit these spaces effortlessly because generations of their people made those spaces or attended them. Often the spatial experience in universities is a constant reminder of not-belonging, of aesthetics derived from a distant place of wealth and power. I remember how deeply it signaled to me my smallness, my family history of poverty and immigration. It was intended to instill awe, and that awe reinforced the presumption that white men were the root of and the path to enlightenment. It was intended to make me want to work to become part of that environment because no other option was presented as safe. It was impossible to imagine any other reality that didn't lead back into poverty. There was no way to refuse this world because it was unimaginable that there could be another. Universities today are startled to find that they have essentially been constructed around celebrating white male European accomplishments; they have been dedicated to the elevation of the supremacy of Europe and its intellectual production. Now this is not a new argument in the least. It is one that has been actively discussed since the mid-1960s, when groups of BIPOC people in the United States began agitating for ethnic studies and contesting the canon as exclusionary and narrow in its focus on the greatness of the West. These contestations have engaged curricula through the occupation of physical space, providing us with an important clue: reparative activities must include spatial enactments of possibilities. Universities, as locations of how countries socialize students into cultural norms and essential shared sets of knowledge, are opportunities to exercise possible other decolonized worlds; they are locations where refusal might be practiced. Through the creation of spaces and places of reparative knowing, we may begin to practice existence that is amended from the traumatic legacies of rapacious racial capital.

Higher education, particularly elite private higher education in the United States, bears the imprints of exclusion within its walls, within the very materiality of what it is. The first communications that students, staff, or faculty often receive is the names of buildings, recorded in the plaques that line walkways commemorating, in perpetuity, the donors of the college. Sometimes those names connect to current students who are legacy admits. The names rarely if ever signify a place where anyone but those who were very wealthy mattered. This is, of course, undergoing changes on university campuses recently, as buildings that were named for slave owners are renamed, and monuments celebrating those who sought to uphold slavery are toppled. Yet the place remains laden with residue, its practices and behaviors fundamentally unchanged by the presence of those who were excluded, whose knowledge and cultures were suppressed and used as objects of fascination. It is not only that the decor remains unaltered, that in many universities you can still feel as if you are walking through the doors of a castle or a cathedral, the names of innumerable white men towering above you etched onto the facades of the libraries. It is also that the way space is used in universities and who gets to decide how, why, and for what it is used remains relatively unchanged. Whether it is possible to enact within universities refusal processes that ignite collective imagining for the practice of other kinds of worlds remains an open question.

Often when we walk onto a college or university campus, we know where we are. Stepping through the gates of venerable institutions, ones that have tradition and extensive histories, can feel awe-inspiring, particularly for those of us who are experiencing such environments for the first time. The most elite of these campuses feel like kingdoms, as if they are a version of royal access. Of course, as settler colonial–derived institutions, they are designed to invoke the same sense for which European castles and royal estates were designed. The gates are tall and ornate, the buildings Gothic with stained glass, and sometimes there are vast expanses of land, breathtaking in their views. There are exceptions to this, particularly for public state universities that struggle and have to find creative ways to identify afford-able locations to hold classes in places such as underutilized malls in suburban areas. But for the most part, the feeling of the space of learning signals its intent clearly. Its aesthetics is fre-quently offered through a remarkably consistent vernacular, a regime that dominates with a singular voice. Princeton feels like Harvard, which feels like Rutgers, which feels like Yale, and so on. Many new institutions attempt to claim legitimacy through such architectural signifiers: faux Gothic architecture interwoven with contemporary futurist structures. The shape of learning dictates how we know and what learned, intellec-tual, and successful existence looks like. It means, sometimes, vast collections of other people's cultural property; it means gates and doors and desks. It means communal spaces for eat-ing, for living, and for learning. It means hierarchies, debt, and exclusions.

Counter-space is an effort to interrupt and refuse this domi-nance, to offer living and learning otherwise, to show how the places of higher education have not been home and to ask whether they hold potential for being used otherwise. It is the creation of this imaginative space, this counter-space that is real-ized through enactments that harness image, slogan, and occu-pation and redesign where higher education's static moldiness can be unsettled. The unsettling of space through place-making activities by those who have never felt at home, who, through such efforts, refuse to use the institution as it has been prescribed, is a powerful pedagogy for instructing how to exercise liberation while straddling the tensions that participation in universities presents.

Spatial Lessons from Social Movements

Willard Straight Hall

On April 18, 1969, members of Cornell University's Afro-American Society (AAS) occupied the university's student union—Willard Straight Hall—to protest the university's persistent racism and its slow progress in establishing a Black studies program. A few days earlier, a cross had been burned on the front lawn of Wari House, a new cooperative residence for Black women students. Wari House had been created after a protracted struggle for the university to recognize that it was a hostile environment for Black students and that they needed spaces free from the daily experiences of racial aggression. The slowness, a management technique, of the university to enact modes of redress for the persistent anti-Blackness manifested through a range of exclusionary practices, incited the enactment of occupation. This enactment of occupation, I argue, is a reparative move; it is a movement that communicated that amends had not been made and that redress was something that the students had to demand—redress for exclusions and redress for persistent harms.

The act could be interpreted as a claim for a place, a place that could be made to feel like home for Black students, for amending what the university had continually failed to do. Wari House was created to counter the dominant overwhelming white habitus of Cornell. It was met with terrorizing acts such as the burning of a cross on their lawn; a potent reminder of the techniques and persistence of the Ku Klux Klan that Blackness was to have no place, even at an elite Ivy League university. Students gathered to occupy Willard Straight Hall in an effort to protest the slow pace of the university toward reparative measures such as Black studies. The students' action sought to highlight that, though the university had admitted them, it had not done enough to repair the legacies of their exclusions.

In response to the occupation, a group of white fraternity brothers entered the Straight (as it was known) and attempted to remove the Black students from the building themselves and end the protest through physical violence. In a 2009 article in the *Cornell Chronicle* that looked back at the event on its anniversary, the author wrote: "At 9:40 a.m., in an attempt to take the building back, white Delta Upsilon fraternity brothers entered the Straight and fought with AAS students in the Ivy Room before being ejected. Fearing further attacks, the Black students brought guns into the Straight to defend themselves."

The building where the Black students were staging their protest was the student union, so it is important to note that language used in this article highlights the contestation of space in universities as belonging, primarily and mostly, to white-identifying people. The author writes that the white students attempted to "take the building back," implying, even in 2009, that the Black students did not have a rightful place, that the building was not theirs to occupy. It was described in the national media, as a "takeover." The AAS students armed themselves for protection, and upon the end of the event, the image of several Black students carrying guns as they exited the building, was taken and made into a *Newsweek* cover titled "Universities under the Gun." The images of the cross burning and the violence perpetrated by white students against Black students were not as prominently featured as the image of the students carrying guns out of Willard Straight Hall. Upon writing this book, without access to in-person archives due to the global pandemic, I was not able to find images of the white students involved in the archives of the Willard Straight Hall available in Cornell's libraries. I was also not able to locate mention of what repercussions were exerted on the white students who burned the cross on the lawn of Wari House and attacked the students in Willard Straight Hall. The most famous images of the event were of the Black students and their guns. This communicates to something of how our social imagination works—what we are socialized to value, believe, and perceive. It reminds us to interrogate not only what universities do about anti-Blackness but how the topic is even framed.

How a narrative is framed through what remains, or what is and is not perceived as important to preserve, tells us a story about the mechanisms of erasure and concealment. Why the records of sale for people enslaved by universities such as Georgetown, Princeton, Rutgers, and other institutions long remained unnoticed communicates that we have been socialized not to notice certain kinds of harm; the attempts at erasure exist within how we know, how we learn, and how we are socialized into existence. Why images of the white students' actions in the course of the protests (if they were captured at all) were not broadcast across national media, but images of armed Black students are important to unpack for the purpose of this discussion about counter-space. The Pulitzer Prize–winning photograph taken by Steve Starr that captured the moment when armed Black students were exiting Willard Straight Hall could be interpreted in a range of ways depending on viewer bias.

For some, the image is heroic. It reveals that Black students, Black people, in the United States have always defended themselves, enacted resistance, and demanded amends for the violence of white supremacy. To others, the image communicates that Black people are a problem, have criminal tendencies, and are dangerous to established order. The latter perception, particularly in the absence of images of what ignited this action, are all too common reactions in the United States. Images of Black people with guns are only palatable in Hollywood, not as assertions of existence but rather as entertainment to reinforce beliefs of Black pain and Black criminality. To choose to distribute an image of Black students armed in a takeover without extensive mention or images of the white students' violence (or even of the cross burned on the lawn of Wari House) is a tactic to maintain white innocence; whiteness often conceals how it incites the need for self-defense that can be read as "violence." It points out the aftermath, the reaction to the violence with little account of its role or of its responsibility.

The events that occurred within Willard Straight Hall are described as a "takeover" rather than the Willard Hall resistance or defense or the Willard Hall "claiming." The white students are described as attempting "to take the building back." This communicates perceptions of who the places of the university, like Willard Straight Hall, belong to or are controlled by. It is evocative of the recent rallying cry of the red hats to "Make America Great Again," if only they could "take back" the country. A takeover, though common parlance now in the world of business and finance, connotes property, its root coming from conquest. It means controlling or taking property or land by force. In this case it signals clearly that the students involved in the protest were not members of the university who had control over the space; the place became theirs because they asserted that they could dictate its use. They asserted, by picking up guns, to the white students that it belonged to them. Their enactment of resistance and demand for amends for the violence, exclusions, and terror that were perpetrated against Black members of the Cornell community created a counterspace, one which reveals that the regular functioning of the university, its use of spaces and places, was not intended to ever be controlled by Black people. Rather, they were always to be guests. The white students who attempted to "take it back" and who burned the cross on the lawn of Wari House were operating under the belief that Black people could not have places where they enacted what they believed necessary or needed for healing. The Black students who occupied Willard Straight Hall enacted a possibility that countered the dominant belief, attitudes, and values of the time: that Black people were capable, at any moment, of seizing methods of power to demand transformative and swift change. Their occupation highlighted that the university did not view them as belonging, as integral to the identity of the place or recognize that significant amends by the university were necessary to counter the persistent anti-Blackness and terror that had been exerted. The use of counter-space, of momentarily transforming a place into one that was controlled and "owned" by Black students was an essential tactic for demanding amends for the continued harmful behavior of the university.

Comedores Sociales at the University of Puerto Rico

The creation of the Comedores Sociales, communal kitchens, at the University of Puerto Rico is a current example of how a poetics of refusal and decolonization can be practiced through spatial contestation, enacted within or against a university setting. The Comedores Sociales, originally formulated as donation-based food stands to feed university students engaged in strikes, evolved into a key political project for enacting decolonial possibility and the blossoming of Centro Apoyos Murales after the 2017 hurricanes. The Comedores Sociales provide an example of how the radical and oppressed spatial tactics used by the Black Panther Party (BPP), the Young Lords Party (YLP), and the American Indian Movement (AIM) can be powerfully implemented to unsettle universities and provide a pedagogy for self-determined healing from coloniality.

In 2013 students at the University of Puerto Rico began organizing against the austerity measures that had been increasingly exerted on the island by the United States. Underfunding of the public university system, declining employment, privatization of public infrastructure, and overall economic stagnation due to the ongoing colonial condition of Puerto Rico resulted in a series of student-led strikes. These strikes must be understood as part of a larger sustained campaign for Puerto Rican self-determination that included struggles to free political prisoners held by the United States, to reclaim Vieques from the United States military occupation, and to reestablish food sovereignty for the island. The organizers of the initial Comedores Sociales, notably Paola Aponte, Giovanni Roberto, and the members of the Center for Political, Educational and Cultural Development (CDPEC), link the movement to the larger anti-capitalist and anti-colonial political struggles happening within Puerto Rico and the diaspora. They describe the project of the Comedores as a project about more than just food. Kique Cubero, a member of CDPEC and the mutual aid centers that developed in the wake of Hurricane Maria and Hurricane Irma, describes the project as a "way to visualize hunger in the university." The effort, in the tradition of the spatial politics enacted by the YLP and the BPP, seeks to generate experiences of social change as a way to overcome fear of an inability to survive without the support of the colonizer; it enacts a mutual aid that instructs in self-determination and community care (Roberto 2019, 2). Puerto Rican colonization has been engineered to foster dependency and a devaluing of anything autochthonous or indigenous to the island. Ricardo Alegría, notable Boricua intellectual and co-founder of the Institute for Puerto Rican Studies, described the colonial project of the United States in Puerto Rico in his explanation of the reason the institute was needed as an attempt "to counteract decades of harmful influences, which at times were openly contradictory to our cultural values, with an effort to promote those values. There was an urgent need to struggle against a psychological conditioning which had become deeply rooted in our colonial society, and which led many Puerto Ricans to systematically diminish anything autochthonous or anything that seemed autochthonous, while disproportionately valuing everything that was foreign, or that seemed foreign" (Alegría 1978). Up until this point, even the educational institutions of Puerto Rico scarcely taught much about the critical colonial project and the decades of resistance to it. There were scarcely mentions of the history of the indigenous group, the Taínos, as more than the story of extinction. The Comedores Sociales and the work of the individuals nourishing these projects, are efforts to feed the people and visualize that the university does not care for the students, but they are also political projects that are seeking to unsettle the dominant narrative that dependence on the United States is essential for survival. Their efforts are permitting the experience, the enactment of what self-determined existence could be alongside revealing what the university is not yet. Giovanni Roberto explains that the project of the food tables became a political project as they met resistance from university administrators and the private food service company contracted to serve food on the campus. At one point, the food tables were blocked by security officers, as the university attempted to curb the students from accessing them. Food on university campuses is provided through expensive contracts with private food-service companies that hold exclusive rights to control food prices and vendors. Often campus food options are part of the expensive financial aid packages and debt students that take on to get an education. At the University of

Puerto Rico, the food tables began because many students could not afford the options made available and were attending school hungry. The censure revealed that the claiming of space to practice the construction of "another social, political and economic system that would be different from capitalism and all its extractive ways" (Roberto 2019, 3) directly threatened the university. It revealed that students did not have to depend on the system of food distribution and access as determined by private companies and university management. In turn, it instructed in the challenges surrounding Puerto Rico's food sovereignty and the potential of Puerto Ricans to regain control of localized food production. Presently in Puerto Rico, a fertile and tropical climate where crops can grow year-round, 80 percent of food is imported. This dependency has a deep history in how, during the early years of the United States colonial occupation, campaigns were launched to convince farmers to leave their land and work in factories; the narrative of dispossession and degradation of agricultural life and the freedom from dependency that comes from it was successfully waged. Projects such as the Comedores Sociales are instructing a new generation of Puerto Ricans in the politics of unsettlement. The self-determination practiced through the *Comedores Sociales* highlights the space of universities as locations for instructing in reparative activity: the amends and recompense needed to recover from decades of colonial conditioning. Solidarity around the topics of food sovereignty, anticapitalist and anti-imperialist resistance is practiced through the co-creation of a place to counter/reinvent the hegemonic practices of universities and enact self-determined existence.

Thread 4

Gates/Gatekeeping

The economist Raj Chetty's 2017 analysis of the income distribution of families at the top 200 colleges and universities in the United States shows that the needle has moved only slightly over the prior decade and since the creation of programs to increase access of low-income students, such as the Pell Grant in 1972; these institutions still serve the top 1 percent of earners. The institutions, known as "Ivy Plus," are recruitment pools for industries offering high wages and power; they enroll more students from the top 1 percent of earners than from the entire bottom half. These institutions spend close to eight times more per student than the least selective ones. That elite higher education institutions function as locations that serve and ensure the power of the rich should come as no surprise to anyone who pays close attention to higher education research. This fact was brought into public view with the 2019 college admissions bribery scandal, known as Varsity Blues. The families, who collectively paid an estimated $25 million to ensure their children's admission into top schools, were CEOs, actors, and vineyard owners; they were families that sat comfortably within the top 1 percent of earners (Gluckman 2019). But their children, despite having access to considerable financial resources, were not necessarily academically competitive for regular entrance into elite colleges, and even those who were knew that didn't guarantee admission to schools in which the vast majority of applicants are academically talented. Though these families were prosecuted for bribery, the power of the ruling classes to ensure entrance to elite institutions has long been guaranteed through birth into families that have historically attended these institutions, make large financial donations, and have access to private boarding preparatory schools known for being feeders into Ivy League admission. Legacy status, which offers preferential admission to the descendants of alumni, means that the odds of admission increase nearly 4 percent (Hurwitz 2011) and according to a 2020 study by the American Talent Initiative, legacy spots can comprise up to 20 percent of an incoming class at a top college or university. Though certainly not bribery, the similarity in efforts to ensure admission startle those who are not insiders to the workings of wealth in higher education.

In late 2021 some institutions, such as Amherst College, moved to eliminate legacy admissions permanently. Johns Hopkins University, under the presidency of Ronald J. Daniels, had done so seven years earlier. The movement to eliminate legacy status has increased in momentum. Nonetheless, Catherine Hill, head of the research group Ithaka SR and former president of Vassar College, argued in an October 2021 *Chronicle of Higher Education* essay titled "Ending Legacy Admissions Won't End Inequity" that discarding legacy admissions would not lead to significant changes in socioeconomic diversity at the top US colleges and universities. The entrenchment of class hierarchies, beginning in early childhood education, paves the way for economically sorted higher education institutions; the most elite are where one finds the children of the wealthiest, and the most under-resourced community colleges are where the vast majority of low-income students start their education. Hill points to the solution as connected to greater public investment in public institutions and the need for wealthy institutions to spend far more on student financial aid than they presently do. The fix, Hill points out, is located in unraveling a system in which rich institutions are more highly valued by funding sources (government, foundations, private donors, endowment investments) than public, less prestigiously ranked ones. These practices highlight the way that higher education is structured for exclusions, for hierarchies based on socioeconomics, inheritance, and insider knowledge that fundamentally privileges the wealthy and powerful. The spatial politics of higher education can be understood through how gates and gatekeeping function to dictate the terms and qualifications for participation.

Anthony Carnevale began highlighting such divisions in the late 1990s, revealing that institutions of higher education, in spite of their claims of serving democratic ideals of egalitarianism, were far from realizing them. His most recent book, *The Merit Myth: How Our Colleges Favor the Rich and Divide America,* exposes the persistence of wealth and privilege, rather than academic promise, in gaining advantage through admissions practices. These institutions were and continue to be not institutions that provide universal access for low-income students who are bright and talented; rather they are insurance policies that the wealthy use to maintain their chokehold on power and that the wealthiest institutions use to remain wealthy and prestigious. In the United States this does not always mean that white people are the only identities found in these institutions. The ruling class of the world, though overwhelmingly white, does include a percentage of wealthy cosmopolitan people of color. Statistically, if you are Black or Indigenous or Latinx in the United States, you are more likely to come from a low-income background, but there are plenty of people of color who are part of the wealthiest groups vying for their children to gain admission to prestigious institutions.

This contest for access to the resources that the most elite institutions of higher education possess, resources that are not simply classes or faculty but pathways to levers of social power, must be understood also through an analysis of how gatekeeping is used to cement power within ways of knowing descended from colonialism. These institutions of higher education, encircled by walls, their entrances defined by elaborate gates, are reminiscent of palaces. Requirements to enter are vetted according to criteria of value. Students are judged as more or less valuable as candidates through logics of prestige, merit myths, and diversity benefit to the college. These are the colonial spaces of Frantz Fanon's "Manichean delirium"; they are meant to evoke the sense of a distinct society, an ascent from what is narrow or poor to what is luminous and luxurious through admittance through the gates. Many people enjoy this sorted elitism. It serves a self-interested story that, I believe, makes people feel as if they matter, and confirms that the most powerful and wealthy are, indeed, the tiny gods needed to continue social progress.

Within these gates are the luxurious reflection and creation that is focused time in a residential college, a place of leisure where your basic needs, such as food and clean spaces, are serviced by those who can only observe and hope to participate, to cross the divide. The most elite institutions of higher education do not only confer power; they delineate it and teach us how it looks, feels, and behaves—the hierarchies that power relies on, the oppressions ever present. The space of elite higher education, the institutions that most others have modeled themselves after, defines itself through the creation of exclusive, conditional space where the individual is anointed to be the power broker of the future. Within these spaces are other, even more internal chambers of power maintenance that are impossible to see from outside. The innermost chambers, where boards of trustees make decisions, are the innermost gate, protected by layers of protocols and top administrators.

To be included within the circles that hold decision-making power over our everyday lives, a requirement is having access or being admitted to these "territories" or places. Those who have attended these institutions, determine, on a regular basis, what happens in the vast majority of people's daily lives. The right to self-determination for the very privileged comes with the territory. For those colonized subjects, or those descended from enslaved people or those who suffer under the generational strain of engineered poverty, the right to determine your existence, your life, has always been met with conditions. As Fanon writes, the "colonial subject is almost always predetermined from without" (Fanon 1982). Many exist, suffering under those conditions, without question, believing that the requirements— passage through the gates by taking on indebtedness, leaving behind familiar communities and cultural practices—are necessary for access to privilege and into locations needed to transform and determine a better existence for ourselves, our families, or our communities. Acceptance into the world behind the gates occupies the dreams of many. One of the profound lies that must be unraveled in higher education is that the gate must be widened, reformed, or renovated rather than abolished. The many gates and gatekeepers must be undone, the gates unlocked and discarded, the enclosure opened. This is not an argument for an abandonment of expertise, of research, but rather an effort to show that the spaces of knowledge production have closed out, deliberately through gatekeeping procedures, the wide expanse of human experience that is necessary for social transformation. Difference, which wanders beyond the gates, may be the signal of where and how enclosures are dismantled, when they are no longer needed, or when gatekeepers see themselves clearly for their function as a tool of exclusions rather than as guides co-navigating the young, the curious, or the adult into territories as yet unknown. This is why self-determination is integral to reparations: the remedy for harm inflicted or harms suffered must be determined by those harmed. To throw off the yoke of coloniality, colonized thinking, self-determined existence must be practiced and learned, for there are a thousand ways every single day that autonomy over daily existence is denied. Education is a site where self-determination may be practiced, where its yoke may be disrupted, and where the contestation of the mechanisms for its denial to the under-resourced and marginalized, who are permitted a trickle of participation, must endeavor.

The struggle to be included, to be admitted to the curriculum, to the institution, or to share one's knowledge production with those beyond the enclosures of campuses, journal paywalls, or conferences is met with gatekeeping criteria and literal gates. Academia is predicated on the enclosure,* and reparative activity, in this sense, is the undoing of enclosures, the dismantling of gates in all its forms. Reparative activity attempts to undo the gates of enclosures, unraveling the boundaries that

---

* The enclosure movement, about which there are many books written, is defined by the Community Environmental Legal Defense Fund as "a push in the 18th and 19th centuries to take land that had formerly been owned in common by all members of a village, or at least available to the public for grazing animals and growing food, and change it to privately owned land, usually with walls, fences or hedges around it." This moved society from practices of commoning, areas of land that were used communally for hunting, fishing, collecting firewood, or grazing animals. Commoning was a practice found in many Indigenous societies, including those in Europe. The enclosure movement, exported through colonial settlement in the Americas, is an epistemic framework, a social imaginary, that extended to the creation of the plantation and its current iterations. Karl Marx believed that the enclosure movement was, in some senses, the start of modern capitalism. The practice of enclosure continues to operate through neoliberalism's success in using public funds for private investment. Dis-enclosure efforts, or efforts to return to commoning or reimagine the commons are exemplified by the work of the Zapatistas, Standing Rock, the women of Via Campesino and the anti-globalization protests of the 1990s. These efforts are examined in Peter Linegard's 2019 book, *Red Round Globe Hot Burning*.

control commoning. Access to education for Black, Latinx, and Indigenous people in the United States has been a history of struggle, resistance, and demands for space to think, to contemplate, and to create, even to be together. Enclosures of place, claiming territory and land, are at the core of settler colonialism's violence and a key tool of universities mired in this legacy. Few institutions of higher education think about their real estate acquisitions and expansion into surrounding communities with an awareness of these as descendants of enclosure practices, reverberations of the colonial practices brought from Europe that caused, and continue to cause, separation and segmentation—that foster hierarchies of human and nonhuman value. If there is awareness of the impact of these behaviors beyond the gates, there is no indication of it mattering beyond statements or acknowledgments that do little materially; there is no offer to share the assets or power, or open enclosures for common use in a material way.

For example, Columbia University, where I received my PhD, has settled throughout Harlem, expropriating land, enclosing it for the purposes of the university. The 1968 struggle to prevent Columbia from constructing a gym on neighboring public park land with segregated entrances for Columbia University members and "community" members in Morningside Park is only one example of the persistent practice of land grabbing, enclosure, and gatekeeping that universities perpetrate. In this particular struggle, residents of Harlem objected to the use of public land to construct a private gym that would mostly benefit members of the university. They identified that the university was seeking, as enclosure movements do, to take an area designated for all, for use by anyone, restrict its access, and designate its use. Significant to this discussion of gates/gatekeeping and enclosures is that Columbia, when planning the gym, designed it with a separate entrance for community members. This ignited the critique of the initiative as a "Gym Crow" effort as expressed in the flyers and articles published in the *Columbia Spectator* in the 1960s. The organizers of the protest understood that the behavior of the university, in spite of its attempt to "include" the community, communicated colonial and racist ways of relating to the surrounding community through the disregard for a common, public space as well as the attempt to dictate, control the entrances, the gates of participation.

The community groups, students, faculty, and staff that joined in this protest ultimately won; they succeeded in stopping the construction of the gym. They did not, however, succeed in unraveling the ways of knowing that the university exemplified in this project. The behaviors, beliefs, perspectives, and attitudes of private use of public space, gated access, and separations between the community and the university persist, legitimated by university philanthropic giving to community-based organizations in Harlem, community programming, an extensive government relations office, and a newly announced fourth purpose of scholarly activity, extending the traditional three composed of teaching, service, and research. In a February 2021 letter to the university, Columbia's president, Lee Bollinger, wrote, "I proposed that it was time the University embrace and foster what we have called the Fourth Purpose of institutions like ours—namely, the advancement of human welfare through the complex process of merging scholarly knowledge and our distinctive intellectual capacities with groups and institutions beyond the academy that respect what we do, possess the skills and power to bring about change, and are dedicated to doing that work in partnership with us."

The fourth purpose outlines a self-described bold realism, one that seeks to direct the resources of the university toward collaboration outside the academy on complex human challenges. The guiding documents offer a hopeful tone, one crafted in collaboration with groups outside the realm of academics. Whether such bold realism will seek to unravel ways of knowing that have subjected communities to short-term, unsustained support or solutions created for them, rather than through their participation, remains to be seen. As an optimist, it is my hope that such a new direction for a university with the vast resources of Columbia can chart a new direction, one that opens the idea of academic research to participation by the many, that sees expertise as located in relationship and unravels the long history, exemplified by Gym Crow, of expropriation of public space and gatekeeping enclosure strategies because it finally connects behaviors as having a negative effect on "human welfare."

I cannot engage in a discussion of gates/gatekeeping practices of higher education without discussing the practices of higher education admissions explicitly. The most obvious form of reparative action in admissions work is to identify communities that have historically and deliberately been excluded from admission, whose communities (as the Land-Grab Universities project shows) have been dispossessed for the financial gain of the institution and, as affirmative action attempted, build classes through these commitments to redress: to admitting students whose communities have been plundered and exploited for the purposes of institutional gain. This can come in many forms: debt-free attendance for those who have a clear need; specialized programs, such as the Higher Education Opportunity Program in New York State, which offers admission through recognition of the systemic underfunding of public schools in the United States that serve low-income students who, disproportionately, are Black, Indigenous, or Latinx; through local scholarships for members of groups that have historically worked in the institution or been displaced by its expansions; as well as consistent supportive pathways for transfer students coming from community colleges. College and universities are enacting many of these ideas but infrequently use the language of reparation and redress to describe them.

Unraveling the complexity of admissions requirements to top college and universities seemed, prior to the COVID-19 pandemic, an effort in incremental movements on the part of dedicated admissions officers working with tiny amounts of available slots, to usher in promising students who were low-income, Black, Latinx, or Indigenous and to make the admissions process far more transparent and tangible for first-generation students. These efforts have been undertaken by many admissions officers across the United States, most exemplified in the work of the National Association of College Admissions Counselors, which now integrates an anti-racist institution in an effort to undo the biases and exclusions that exist in the admissions process. With the pandemic, higher education witnessed the fall of one of the most significant gates to access, one that seemed sacrosanct for institutions that still accepted it: the SAT. The pandemic ushered in several admissions seasons during which universities and colleges waived the SAT requirement, a standardized test long proved to privilege wealthier and historically college-bound families. It was, up until 2020, viewed as critical to attaining admission to top schools, although, increasingly, many colleges have made it optional. College admissions in the United States has not been exempt from the Black Lives Matter movement and anti-racist efforts, contributing to the abandonment of the SAT as well as to a growing number of admissions counselors committed to pushing their institutions to fully fund students, decrease indebtedness, and advocate, nationally, for the elimination of notoriously difficult and opaque forms such as the Free Application for Federal Student Aid (FAFSA) as well as difficult-to-interpret financial aid award letters. These efforts are all significant in eliminating the many micro-barriers that privilege wealthier, predominantly white peers in the process of admissions to college in the United States.

But from my perspective, the most radical undoing of the exclusions and hierarchies, the gates and gatekeepers, reinforced by higher education is to unravel private and exclusionary higher education, the institutions, and the associated practices of private libraries, journals, and so on, and opening them, dismantling fences, redistributing resources more equitably so as to unleash reparative energies that may move them toward greater co-creation and liberative modes of teaching, learning and research. What story do we need to write about the future of education beyond the gates? What does it look like? If the undoing throws wide open the plantation, the enclosure of the university, what can we look to for guidance into such uncertainty?

Unraveling Patrol

Patrol, as I discussed in part I of this book, is connected to a need to monitor and dictate how difference participates in a dominant environment, defining where it is allowed to enter or be included. Who is permitted on campuses is enforced by checkpoints, IDs, security, or police officers. How difference is expressed, or how the difference that enters an institution seeks to make a difference, is more heavily patrolled by growing policing practices on university campuses today than it was when modern campus police forces were formed in response to the Vietnam War protests on university campuses in the 1960s. When protests erupt against institutional policies or practices, campus security forces are the first responders.

University police departments now have access not only to guns but even to pepper spray, tasers, drones, and body cameras, their technology keeping pace with that of public police departments in spite of their limited transparency and lack of public accountability. Students, from the moment they apply, are monitored and patrolled in how they participate in the life of the institution. This is not done with malicious intent; rather, it should be understood as an ingrained behavior of higher education: to grant access, to monitor, and to require behavioral compliance. (One of the first documents students sign upon enrollment in higher education is often a code of conduct or honor code.) Even after their enrollment, students, particularly Black students on predominantly white campuses, are monitored, surveilled, and frequently assumed to be trespassers, as evidenced in far too many high-profile cases such as those at Smith College and Colorado State University in 2018 and at Barnard College in 2019. These incidents, representing only a fraction of the widespread racial profiling that Black, Indigenous, and Latinx students are subjected to during their higher education experience, speak volumes about who is perceived to belong on higher education campuses; the calls to campus security from faculty, staff, and students alleging trespass are evidence of a climate of patrol that goes beyond sworn officers.

Patrol within higher education is not simply about harm reduction, crime deterrence, or physical and psychological safety; it is also about territory and property: who has the "rights" to access it and who is hired to enforce access. Campus security, one manifestation of higher education's value of patrol, is receiving increased attention in the attempts to abolish or defund policing in the United States. It is a part of higher education, deeply integral to its identity, that, if the institution is committed to equity or decolonization or social justice, must be interrogated for what its presence instructs and what might be imagined or practiced in its place. Reparative activity in this area of an institution constitutes working to unsettle and unravel how patrol, security, and surveillance shape educational environments and to reimagine what safety means and how it is carried out.

The earliest documented campus police department was established in 1894 at Yale University. The university hired two local police officers to patrol its grounds, later transitioning the officers to become employees of the university and establishing a campus police department. The early watchmen style of patrol was used by campuses primarily to protect university property from theft, fire, or other damage. This style of security evolved, particularly after the Vietnam War protests, into a system based on modern law enforcement practices and the full campus police departments that are typical of large universities today (Sloan 1992). College and university administrators who previously dealt with students' disciplinary, behavioral, or other types of unrest have increasingly turned over this responsibility to campus police or security departments. At most of the institutions I have been part of (with the exception of Bard College, whose campus remains a rare open space without checkpoints or gates), a security or police officer is the first person to greet you at the gates to the institution. It is a feeling not dissimilar to crossing a border; one must, through a checkpoint, prove one's right to exist in this territory by producing the appropriate credential.

The lynching of George Floyd on May 25, 2020, in Minneapolis, Minnesota, by police officers moved the work of defunding the police and prison abolition into mainstream conversation. Prior to this event, the vast majority of people in the United States had not heard of nor considered the possibility of defunding or abolishing the police; they were, like the monuments to Robert E. Lee, an unquestioned part of the fabric of daily experience. After the Ferguson, Missouri, protests of 2014 and the images of police with tanks patrolling and abusing protesters were broadcast around the world, people began to wonder about the funding of local police departments. Social movements such as Black Lives Matter and the organizing to abolish the prison industrial complex and defund police departments began to dovetail with efforts to abolish or defund campus police departments; it has gained critical momentum since the University of Missouri campus protests of 2015 and the increased visibility that social media has provided for campus police engaging in racial profiling, excessive force, and failure to adequately respond to requests for protection from domestic violence on campus. The police abolition movement has come to university and college campuses at a moment when there is a marked increase in student and staff protests. The takedown of Silent Sam on the University of North Carolina's Chapel Hill campus, the 2021 campus protests for the abolition of Greek life on the campuses of the University of Massachusetts, Wake Forest and Columbia University, tougher measures against sexual violence on campuses, and the 2021 graduate student strikes at Columbia University and Harvard University are recent examples of protest movements in North American institutions. Since 2015 the numbers of student-led campus protests, frequently harnessing social media to organize and amplify activism, have increased and, many believe, reflect a climate in higher education similar to that of the civil rights movement and the protests of the Vietnam War—a period when campus police began to be more heavily funded and relied upon to keep what was described as civility and order.

In 2019 Ronald J. Daniels, the president of Johns Hopkins University in Baltimore, proposed to state lawmakers establishing an armed private campus police force due to what he described as the unrelenting violence of the city that surrounds the campus. His proposal, in a city still reeling from the 2015 murder of Freddie Gray Jr. by the Baltimore police, was met with a firestorm of criticism from local organizers seeking to reduce police violence. In 2020, President Daniels announced that the university would suspend its plan for an armed campus police. As of 2015, more than 44 states authorize institutions of higher education to form police forces (Nelson 2015, Harvard Law Review 2016, 1167). It would seem that policing on campuses is increasing, even as movements for its abolition gain traction. Yet students feel more unsafe than ever on campuses as they return to places and people changed by the COVID-19 pandemic and protest what they perceive as the complicity of institutions in perpetuating sexual violence, racism, and environmental degradation. All of these actions, I believe, are expressions of people who do not feel safe or cared for by the system within which they find themselves. They are expressions of a profound lack of confidence that institutions genuinely care for the people who participate in its structures. Though campus police departments practice a harm-reduction model of crime control, they are increasingly heavily armed. The increase in the use of technology and the percentage growth in armed police on campuses that has occurred over the last decade now outpace student enrollment. This is according to the findings of the 2011-2012 survey of Campus Law Enforcement Agencies, the US Justice Department's first statistical analysis since 2004 of the activities and characteristics of university security and police activity. Such practices reflect an undeniable culture of violence and militarized surveillance in the United States. Educational institutions are profound socializing mechanisms for the behaviors of society; order, control, and compliance have long characterized educational systems. What higher education, its administrators in particular, must face today is the question of what such practices are socializing students for? What do we mean when we say "safety," and how is that sense of safety inculcated, reproduced, and carried out as an aspect of the curriculum in a university? The way that students, faculty, and staff are treated, how they learn to relate to one another and the community that surrounds the institution, instructs in this meaning of safety.* Safety from what,

---

* According to Mia Mingus, "Transformative Justice (TJ) is a political framework and approach for responding to violence, harm and abuse. At its most basic, it seeks to respond to violence without creating more violence and/or engaging in harm reduction to lessen the violence. TJ can be thought of as a way of 'making things right,' getting in 'right relation,' or creating justice together. Transformative justice responses and interventions (1) do not rely on the state (e.g. police, prisons, the criminal legal system, I.C.E., foster care system (though some TJ responses do rely on or

from whom, and by what means are questions critical to un-raveling the strictures of security protocols intended for control and assimilation rather than for communal responsibility and reciprocal care.

In this last tactical area for consideration for reparative activity I am interested in encouraging practices that seek to make counter-spaces for imagining and practicing what safety beyond campus police departments might mean and look like, and how to reduce our dependence on a system of punishment through incarceration that has only increased violence. In 2017 the Vera Institute for Justice published a public policy brief, *The Prison Paradox*, showing that "increased incarceration has a marginal-to-zero impact on crime. In some cases, increased incarceration can lead to an increase in crime" (Stemen 2017). The study reveals the tension that persists in the United States between a society dependent upon patrol and punishment in spite of evidence that such systems, given the inability to enact alternative possibilities, are causing more violence. Learning how to be otherwise when habituated to a society that values punishment necessitates the kind of epistemic reparation, third-order epistemic shifts, that I discussed in part II. These drastic shifts are not simply habits but rather reconstitutions of how a collective relates to harm. Far too often in my career I have encountered students who, despite studying police abolition and transformative justice, ask for punishment and police intervention when harm occurs; they are un-willing or unable to enact other modes of repair. They, as well

incorporate social services like counseling); (2) do not reinforce or perpetuate violence such as oppressive norms or vigilantism; and most importantly, (3) actively cultivate the things we know prevent violence such as healing, accountability, resilience, and safety for all involved." This definition was developed through the collaborative efforts of transformative justice practitioners Ejeris Dixon, Mariame Kaba, Andi Gentile, and Javiera Torres. See TransformHarm.org.

as faculty and staff, exist on campuses frightened by the real possibility of being the next site of a mass shooting or experiencing the reality of sexual assault. How campuses might carve out small spaces, microclimates, to practice the difficult work of moving away from armed police as the answer for what safety means, away from instruction in discipline and punish, may come through the creation of community safety teams, mutual aid, and transformative justice practices. However, liability, insurance, and legal mandates to have safety and security departments are real considerations that must be part of any efforts to defund, abolish, or dismantle campus police forces. Who a person on a college campus calls when they are threatened or under duress, who is responsible for such support, is undeniably a question that must be answered. There are a number of examples that courageous university employees and students can look to in efforts to reimagine and co-create the ways safety is enacted.

A few examples found on university campuses already exist in the form of peer escorts, walking buddies, peer listening hotlines as well as ensuring that trained mental health professionals, not armed campus police, respond to mental health concerns on campus. One notable example of efforts to unsettle the reliance on institutional systems such as Title IX, which governs the procedures for campus sexual misconduct, and policing responses to harm in higher education, is the Brown University Transformative Justice pilot project begun in 2020. The pilot project, housed within Brown University's Community Dialogue Project, is the first of its kind on a university campus: an institutionally supported effort to develop transformative justice practitioners through a year-long apprenticeship training, mentoring, and participatory action research experience for twelve undergraduates. In addition to the practitioner program, the Transformative Justice Initiative at Brown offers a number of supports to build capacity to respond to harm in nonpunitive and transformative ways (Brown University 2020). The initiative offers workshops for student organizations, designs transformative justice and accountability processes for harm within the university, and serves as a hub for education and training in transformative justice. The initiative is staffed by a full-time coordinator. Given that it is a recent attempt to enact reparative activity within institutional safety practices, the results and challenges of engaging transformative justice within a university setting remain to be seen. However, in efforts to unravel and unsettle practices and systems of oppression, "success" is multilayered, encompassing psychological safety, accountability, and transformation. How such spaces can dwell within universities, pressing against traditional categories of study while providing an opportunity to learn and fumble through the possibilities of new modes of relating to one another outside of patrol, surveillance, and punishment is an open question.

From Rank to Rhizome

For part of my career, I had the humbling privilege to work alongside some of the most dedicated educators I have encountered in higher education. Justice and equity were not catchphrases designed to increase the institutional profile and rank; they were lived principles in a collective effort to unravel the lack of support, under-resourcing, and sorting mechanisms of higher education for low-income students. In 2012, I joined the faculty of what was then called the New Community College of the City University of New York. This was an experiment on the part of CUNY to create a college that intervened in the abysmal retention numbers of students enrolled in community colleges. At the time, the three-year graduation rate of students attending a CUNY community college hovered at around 20 percent; community colleges offering the Accelerated Study in Associates Program (ASAP) had higher graduation rates. The New Community College (now named Gutmann Community College) was influenced by the best practices of ASAP, a comprehensive support program that offers continuous advisement and support for purchasing books, obtaining mental health services, and even buying metrocards. These supports are essential in a system in which at least 70 percent of students come from families with incomes under $30,000 per year and that is one of the most racially diverse higher education systems in the world. CUNY serves as an example for how resources and rank are frequently, if not always, unaligned with racial and socioeconomic diversity and equality of access. CUNY, with significant economic limitations, provides an incredible education to low-income and first-generation students while maintaining a comparatively low tuition rate. Faculty, many with administrative knowledge or expertise, were hired to help in the design of the college's structure as well as the curriculum. It was innovative and saddled with controversy; some alleged that it was a charter school version of higher education. I offer this example not to provide a comprehensive analysis of that endeavor, which requires an entire other book, but rather to highlight that the work of unraveling social inequities, of driving social mobility, is happening in places that are viewed as less valuable, peripheral to the power and prestige that transfix so many.

In the hierarchy of higher education, community colleges are ranked way at the bottom; they are not viewed as prestigious, rigorous, or staffed by promising research faculty. The sentiment expressed to me when I left the place that I had been working to take the position at CUNY was "you won't ever get a prestigious tenure-track position anywhere after this." The work was incredibly hard and incredibly rewarding; ultimately I left because the teaching load was crushing, and I felt that I could not teach well under such conditions. My subsequent roles led me to the most elite private institution I had been part of since getting my PhD: Barnard College, an amazing place yet one that confirmed the obsession with rank, distinctiveness, and the lack of connection to the community colleges that, only a few miles away, truly drive social equity. Institutions such as Barnard define themselves based on who is excluded and how different they are from other universities.

The obsession with rankings, building a brand, and making oneself distinctive has, from my perspective, been a driver of inequity in US higher education. Families and students pursue brands, believing that a given institution will dramatically change their life outcomes. It is true that institutions that are Ivy-plus allow students to rub elbows with wealth and power, leveraging their degrees into these worlds. It is true that their faculty are leading scholars and cutting-edge researchers and that they have access to high-tech facilities that drive what they are able to do. But I remain unconvinced that these places deserve to be enclaves. The focus on rank and prestige in colleges and universities, as social institutions that uphold and socialize hierarchies of human value, should come as no surprise. Yet this is one very concrete area that institutional workers or those concerned with opening higher education can focus on: moving how higher education is structured. The question that should be asked is, should we care about this anymore? Has it resulted in more social harm than benefit? Can the mission of these institutions be broadened, as one institution I worked for, Bard College, has attempted to do in focusing on the public good? Is there another form, rather than discrete, competitive enclosures, that higher educational institutions can shape together? This shift from viewing the local community college or other college not as a competitor but rather as a supportive, nourishing additional partner, or the significance of redistributing vast wealth to lesser-funded institutions that serve a majority of low-income students of color as beneficial to the health of a system, of a society is slowly emerging. But it means unleashing a reparative energy that dismantles and opens the modes of isolation within which higher education has operated. This is an epistemic and ontological endeavor.

Lately, I have been learning, at the direction of Edouard Glissant, from mangroves. Living through a time of pandemics, climate change, racial reckonings, and an unprecedented upheaval in higher education (which I understand to be entangled with one another), I have sought out new forms, epistemic resources, for comfort as I have undergone phases of epistemic reparation unsettling and undoing of how I understood the relationship of diversity, equity and inclusion to higher education. I have looked for confirmation that there are many ways to exist other than through the enclosures of curiosity cabinets, check boxes, and gated communities that are presented as desirable territories. The many-rootedness of rhizomatic plants like mangroves offers, if we pay attention, a pattern of existence that higher education may learn from.

Mangroves are able to live in conditions that no other kind of tree can withstand: salty coastal waters and the interminable ebb and flow of the tide. They protect the lands closest to them from extreme weather events such as tsunamis. Mangrove forests sequester and store more "blue carbon" per unit area—than terrestrial forests, and they are increasingly recognized as powerful agents in the struggle to mitigate climate change. Importantly, mangroves are an organism that does all this while growing in multiple directions. Glissant, as do Gilles Deleuze and Félix Guattari, sees rhizomatic forms as interruptions in the vertical singularity of treelike forms in which the plant arises from a single point, a seed. This offers higher education a way that could make discrete institutions part of a connected, sharing, and open system. It could be small movements, like wealthy institutions sharing their endowments and other resources with local community colleges; it could be large movements, like a group of universities in a region committing to becoming a kind of *rhizaphora,* a system of visible carrying roots, distinct yet supportive of one another.* Yet

---

* See the beautiful essay by Ana Deumert titled *The Mangrove; or, Moving with and beyond the Rhizome.* She writes, "The Latin name for mangrove is rhizaphora. It is derived from the Greek words for 'root' (*rhiza*) and 'to carry' (*phoros*). It

such a rhizaphora overwhelms patrol, that entrenched behavior of institutions evidenced in security and policing practices. The rhizome, as an open, multidirectional system upends and tricks attempts at surveillance.

translates as 'carrying roots'". https://www.diggitmagazine.com/column/mangrove-or-moving-and-beyond-rhizome.

Diversity work, like many methods of the neoliberal university, is an effort that often seeks to enact singular prescriptions for the sickness of racism. It is work that is, to state the obvious, a hallmark of historically white settler institutions' varied attempts to use difference, to tell it where it can reside, how it can participate, and where it is permitted. Throughout this book I did not engage with tribal colleges or historically Black colleges and universities; what they have to offer in efforts to understand how higher education might transform, decolonize, or enact racial justice warrants an entire book dedicated to the topic. It is also important that an analysis of these institutions is not to see what they can do for holistic workplace inclusion, but rather what they are as institutions that exist without needing to be in use by or in service to the project of undoing coloniality.

One of the most obvious points of a work concerned with reparation in higher education needs little rhetorical ornamentation; institutions that benefited from dispossession and genocide of Native people owe tribal colleges materially through land-back processes and material recompense. It is the morally good thing to do. Most elite higher education institutions with vast resources have done little or nothing to redress their roles in Indigenous dispossession beyond placing plaques in visible locations that acknowledge whose land it was, creating Indigenous studies departments, and funding scholarships for Indigenous youth to attend white settler institutions. This is inclusion work, not redress. The Land-Grab Universities project, as one example, lays out the total costs owed to tribes who lost land under the Morrill Acts. At the time of writing this book, Cornell University was the only elite private university to begin to address the expropriation of land through the Morrill Acts. Colleges and universities whose wealth was gained from participation in the slave trade would do well to think hard and act upon redistributing their sizable endowments to the many struggling historically black colleges and institutions, such as community colleges, that educate large numbers of students of color. Self-determination—collective decisions on what to do materially with resources that have been deliberately denied—cannot come in the form of feeble inclusion attempts that offer access to a miniscule percentage of the world. The critique that I offer of diversity work is not, importantly, aimed at the people hired to do this work, who labor under inadequate staffing, incommensurable aims, and constant pressures to manage their institutions' brand and reputation rather than make bold moves to unravel oppressive systems. The problem is a collective one, one that reinscribes diversity as an epistemic framework useful to maintaining race and class hierarchies.

Bias and antioppression workshops, which examine white identity and its persistence, are offered as the solution for higher education's continued reproduction as spaces that cannot let go of a social imaginary that is in love with its mythologies: mythologies of meritocracy rather than the reality of pay to play, pipelines of wealth and privilege; mythologies of the best and the brightest rather than the wealthiest maintaining their control of the gatekeeping and socialization mechanisms of economic power: mythologies of who can make claims to expertise; mythologies of exclusivity as a positive social value.

Diversity has been positioned as a social good, a valued mythology, without interrogation of whether the forms of knowing and existence that it facilitates can move systems toward greater racial justice, antiracism, decolonization, or economic justice. There have been plenty of studies and statements on the failures of diversity training, but these critiques do not account for the epistemic and ontological frameworks of diversity. The problem isn't that diversity doesn't "work"; it is that diversity is conceptually misaligned with aims of racial justice, decolonization, and economic justice. Epistemic habits of taxonomy, exclusion, patrol, extraction, and accumulation as I have worked to explore in part I, are difficult to separate conceptually from diversity. This matters because the words that we use to explain phenomena of existence reflect our existence. Diversity can only be allowed, to quote Nick Mitchell, if it makes no difference. Higher education is riddled with mythologies of origins, mythologies of truth, and mythologies of hierarchies into which many universities socialize generations of students. Diversity work has been and will continue to be used as a tool to support these mythologies, to reproduce them through the assimilative forces of inclusion into locations of wealth and power in exchange for a lifetime of indebtedness. Diversity efforts will be simultaneously dismissed as stereotyping and marginalizing white peopleand pressured to center viewpoint diversity above the need for systems to change in order to truly enact racial equity or even put into practice the ethical imperative to frame all racism as a moral wrong.*

---

* Although President Trump's Executive Order on Race and Sex Stereotyping was reversed by President Biden, the executive order made clear, at the highest levels of government, that diversity, equity, and inclusion trainings are under scrutiny and increasingly being viewed by conservatives as "anti-American" and works to chill efforts to dismantle systemic racism. On the heels of this executive order has come an attack on culturally relevant pedagogy and teaching about race and inequality in K–12 schools. Misconstrued as "critical race theory," these efforts have been gaining

The challenge facing diversity work lies in many corners but fundamentally when antiracism or decolonization efforts attempt to move outside of prescribed boxes or expectations, when difference attempts to carve out space, take resources, or truth-tell, it is met with a backlash that reasserts the superiority of free expression and multiple viewpoints. The line between diversity training that reinscribes the whitewashing of history and seeks to expose the present perpetuation of systemic racism is a perilous one. It is precisely because some diversity workers have attempted to push beyond the confines of the collector's cabinet into systems change work that, I believe, the accusations of divisiveness and stifling multiple viewpoints have increasingly arisen. Hiding behind the claim to "many sides" or "both sides" on the topic of racism, discrimination, or oppression is a way that whiteness and coloniality works; it is an old maneuver that refuses, as W. E. B. Du Bois explains, to cede ownership to all things, especially the epistemic frameworks that govern social relations.

If people today, in particular white people with wealth and power, are asked to be accountable for past and present harm, the refusal arrives in ways it always has—as a claim to territory. The territory of beliefs, values, and social order, of how we come to know anything, has always been patrolled through dominance that, over five hundred years of colonization, disciplined difference and told it what was truth and what was not. Contestations of truths are abundant in the present day, an information quicksand pulling people into tailspins of fake news, conspiracy theories, and intractable polar opposites. It is not that everything has become relative; rather, it is that the redress of racism and oppression threatens the self-interested

---

momentum, exemplified by Texas passing a law (House Bill 3979) to regulate how race-related topics are taught, instructing an opposing view to always be offered even when teaching topics such as the Holocaust.

dominance that has been enjoyed by a small group of people for many generations. Diversity work, as it presently is enacted through well-intentioned workshops that are framed by opponents as indoctrination or as one-sided, won't get the burdens of the past taken up in present social transformation. Reparative activity, as an educative force of unraveling will, and it cannot be neutral or apolitical. It is a set of commitments to a way of knowing and being; it is a vision of existence that can be learned and accepted. But to wrest power, to unravel epistemic frameworks of dominance is, as Jean Bartunek and Michael Moch warn, a perilous endeavor.

Reparation, in this work, is presented as an active force that holds potential to self-determine through processes of unraveling. Reparative knowing and existence necessarily move beyond recognition because their activation unsettles, redistributes, and reorders knowing and existence. Reparation causes shifts and should not be reduced to thin acts of apology or recompense; its activation must account for how to end the logics that continue oppressive and harmful forms of life. This is why we must look to the formal, to the poetic, if we are interested in actions that push universities beyond decorative diversity work. Reparation offers potential to unleash a weapon that undoes the mythologizing of settler colonialism institutions by revealing that continued forms of oppression and violence have been disguised through beautiful campuses, orderly disciplines, justifications for high costs and debt, and glittering high-profile jobs. To be a high-level administrator or tenured faculty member in the most elite of these institutions is to live like members of a royal court. We have yet to abolish our royalty. Diversity workers in many of these spaces, though attempting to enact justice and transformative efforts, are constantly hemmed in by the very logics of diversity, by its inability as a conceptual category to include self-determination. Colonized or underrepresented identities are always wrought through being in opposition to, in struggle against; existence remains defined by positions in relation to oppression. Poetics, the invention of counterspace, the unleashing of reparative epistemology and ontology, no longer waits for the perpetrator to recognize the forms of harm; it intervenes to create forms of life it needs to open space for grieving, for nourishment, for liberation, and for an experience of the present that goes beyond the limit of opposition. Edouard Glissant writes, "For more than two centuries whole populations have had to assert their identity in opposition to the processes of identification or annihilation triggered by these invaders. Whereas the Western nation is first of all an 'opposite,' for colonized peoples identity will be primarily 'opposed to'—that is, a limitation from the beginning. Decolonization will have done its real work when it goes beyond this limit" (Glissant 2010). The experience of bodies of culture within historically white spaces has, through diversity work, been positioned in opposition. The promise of poetic interventions refuses this opposition and enacts a vision of self-determined existence in joy and in love for their communities.

While reparation is conceived as something administered by those who have committed harm as recompense, what I have tried to do in this book is show that reparation, when it functions at the level of knowledge and existence, does not have to wait for administrative edicts; it is administered through refusal, invention, creation, and resistance by those communities that are subjected to continued logics of settler colonialism, afterlives of slavery, coloniality, and racial injustice. Self-determined existence, for many who have been socialized to accept that inclusion efforts will ever lead to racial justice or decolonization, is something to be learned through affective experience. Entrenched hierarchical systems, like universities, want to persist in nonperformative diversity efforts, while the redistribution of power and structures (such as exclusive admissions practices or the composition of boards of trustees) remains fundamentally unaltered. Such institutions struggle to ensure that diversity does not mean justice or decolonization in order for the work to remain predictable and manageable.

Poetics, as Glissant explains throughout *Poetics of Relation*, is never predictable and arises through the tensions between chaos and particularity. The chaos of poetics, as a tool for reparative activities, is desperately needed in any efforts to bring antiracism and decolonization to realization in the space of higher education. I have no prescription for this other than that poetics arises, as it always has for social movements such as the Zapatistas, Sem Terra, and so many others, through relation: the forms that arise through identity's particularity, locality, time, and culture. While these movements bear similarities, their manifested forms of life are distinct. As much as higher educational institutions have sought "brand" distinctiveness, so many of them are standardized, reproducing ways of knowing and being that are homogenizing for the benefit of capital. They often attempt to offer distinct programs, boast about their selectivity, or highlight their global presence as indications of how they are distinct but, with very few exceptions, most institutions are uniform in their effort to brand and make themselves into marketable and competitive products. These homogenizing tendencies have limited the material impact of institutional work to illuminate and identify modes of redress for participation and benefit from the slave trade. While the list of institutions participating in the recognition of this history is miniscule in number, administering forms of financial recompense has grown, and the projects are significant steps in antiracist institutional work, they have failed to activate reparation. They have failed to identify and redress the logics embedded within themselves that expose the ongoing afterlife of slavery and genocide—of the project of higher education that is dependent upon accumulating and extracting needed capital for survival from the human, from land, and from animals.

The example of this logic I return to over and over again is found in the collusion of higher education to produce a precarious disposable labor force in the form of adjuncts, graduate students, and free undergraduate labor and the contribution to the creation of economic and psychological forms of indebted existence.* This will not be solved only through demands for better wages or by ending institutional practices that indoctrinate students into uncompensated time. It will be solved by exposing the truth that academic labor depends on an unending chain of exploitation and by ending the entrenched logics in higher education which posit that some life is more valuable than other life. It will be solved through the abolition of debt as a practice in higher education and through moves to make all higher education open access, a public asset that is supported through public funds. It is possible for higher educational institutions to be controlled by the community, by people not trustees, but we are very, very far from there. Ending social inequality will not be achieved without such structural transformations. In a transformative vision of the future of education, it is liberated from a transaction, a unit of financial exchange laden with indebtedness. While the work of examining and seeking to redress institutional histories of benefit and participation in the slave trade and Indigenous dispossession is essential, recognition without material and systemic shifts provides the persistent oppression with lovely decorative wrapping. These systemic and material shifts that reparation

---

* See the Debt Syllabus for numerous resources on the global project of indebtedness. https://debtsyllabus.com/.

can bring strike at the heart of higher education and its role in the reproduction of class domination.

Achille Mbembe's and Ramón Grosfoguel's work on the pluriversity as a decolonizing direction for higher education should not go unmentioned. While the notion of the pluriversity has influenced my thinking on possibilities of decolonizing higher education, my efforts in this book have attempted *not* to provide an answer for where the activation of reparation will take higher education. I feel ill equipped to prescribe what "the end" of reparative work looks like because I understand it as an emergent process, one that arises from attentiveness to space, history, time, and identity. While epistemic diversity is a hallmark of the pluriversity, and much of what I explore in epistemic reparation is opening to ways of knowing that have been devalued, erased, or suppressed, I feel that much more work is needed to grasp whether certain epistemic coexistences are possible. There are modes of knowing and being that must be abolished if we are to survive as a species. Holding all sides and all viewpoints removes from the human project of knowledge creation any moral imperative to reduce harm, to live in right relations, and to come to understand that some values and beliefs cannot coexist because they are predicated on the annihilation of the other. Whether epistemic reparation can lead to epistemic abolition is something that I am not yet clear on. However, what I have come to understand through extended practice is that it is possible to be socialized into epistemic frameworks such as anti-Blackness, racism, and logics of elimination yet learn to suspend their formative power in the behavior of an individual or set of policies. Universities, whether many believe this is a good thing or not, are a significant (though not singular) social organ for instituting and reinforcing modes and norms of human relations. As I have sought to explore in this book, higher education presents a possible location for socializing and normalizing reparative knowing and existence, but, as I have come to convince myself at least, this can be possible only through self-determined poetics. It can be possible only through institutional workers (faculty and staff) and students absorbing that the curriculum is not the content, the curriculum is the form of relation instituted, and time should also be spent on unsettling institutional space, language, and practices through playing with institutional forms, spaces, and policies. More mental health services, better antiracism training, or more formalized access to institutional resources will not open emergent spaces for tinkering with self-determined possibilities. Reparation unleashes a weapon of undoing against oppressive forms because it is through the form (the systems) that oppression and injustice have been enabled to thrive.

If my reader has gotten to the end of this test of ideas, I would like to tell them that my critique is not at all in the spirit of nihilism or to support the notion that there is no hope for higher education. I believe that attentiveness and truth telling are what allows for the existence of hope as a muscular activity. Hope springs from clarity about the mechanisms of harm and the belief that, as Mariame Kaba shares, fumbling toward repair is possible. Reparation remains sidelined within institutional work not only because of a lack of onto-epistemic resources or its devaluation as a legitimate transformative set of actions but also because, fundamentally, higher education has always been a tool for maintaining and ordering class hierarchies and dominance; it is an unapologetically neoliberal and capitalist project. Whether higher education, as it presently exists, can or should continue to exist is not something I can comment on. But the unleashing of reparative thinking and being inside and outside these institutions will, more than likely, hasten its demise. This hastening should not be viewed as a negative but rather as a hopeful opening to generate new kinds of spaces for knowledge production. Increasingly, thanks to big data projects such as Raj Chetty's research on which schools contribute to high social mobility, highly resourced institutions have been exposed as catering to small numbers of low-income students and not facilitating economic mobility in the way that institutions like the City University of New York do. These research projects, building off the work of Anthony Carnevale and many others who have argued for years that the top institutions were serving the wealthiest, expose a truth about higher education in settler colonial societies: they are socializing and sorting mechanisms to aid the elite in maintaining authority. The case for justice, decolonization, decoloniality, or antiracism cannot be realized without material commitments—commitments that include money, decision-making power, land, buildings, and assets. But, as I have attempted to show, greater inclusion or better financial aid packages will not matter if ways of knowing remain the same.

If higher education is to become a social force for the emergence of life that is decolonized, anticapitalist, and antiracist, it needs reparative actions—fundamental epistemic shifts in the social imaginary that unravel accepted values that uphold racism, inequality, and oppression. What new worlds can be built together through enactments of counter-spaces, within and outside existing institutions is what I am excited by. Diversity has never been the right container for such efforts because, as a concept, its intention is to contain difference, enclose it so as to make it into standing reserves for siphoning energy needed for institutional survival. But, within reparative constellations lies the spillage of hope, and its activation needs no administrative approval.

Acknowledgments

This book was written in the isolation of the COVID-19 pandemic, in the interstices of interruptions from online schooling for my six-year-old and endless Zoom calls while I worked remotely as a senior DEI administrator. It was also written in the isolation, the silence, within which many chief diversity officers toil, as academic freedom does not apply to at-will employees, who are privy to some of the most confidential topics that institutions handle. However, nothing is created in isolation. All that we endeavor to make, those of us interested in attempts at knowledge creation, arises from the threads that weave through time, making a strange and wonderful fabric. The seeds of this book were planted much earlier than I realized initially, going all the way back to a sixteen-year-old girl sitting in a high school English class asking why we never read literature from Latin America. She was told that we didn't read books in translation. Yet, she pointed out to the teacher, we read the Greek myths. So that girl, who was fortunate enough to be in the kind of school that allowed it, created her own class in which we read the likes of Pablo Neruda, Gabriel Garcia Marquez, Sandra Cisneros, and Jorge Luis Borges. I am grateful to that sixteen-year-old, who, for a time, lost her way but who was always listening to the lacuna.

The community of people, particularly Jason Wozniak, Samir Haddad, Penelope Ann Deutcher, and Jorge Medina, who encountered early iterations of this thinking through our project *Hacer Escuela / Inventing School: Rethinking the Pedagogy of Critical Theory*, a subproject of the Andrew W. Mellon Foundation grant Critical Theory in the Global South. I am grateful for a brief snowy night at Northwestern University, where the philosophy faculty were generous enough to listen and respond to my thoughts on epistemic reparation. I am thankful to the Latin American Philosophy of Education Society (LAPES) for allowing me to be an itinerant participant and for building a philosophical home where there was previously none; to Jennifer Rosales for quickly reading an early draft and providing much encouragement to keep going; and to Lanna Crucefix for being an abiding writing partner who enjoys 25-minute intervals as much as I do. Generations of students have helped me grow; they remind me of the reason for all of this.

I am particularly grateful and in admiration of Kyle Gipson, formerly assistant acquisitions editor at Johns Hopkins University Press, now associate editor at Basic Books, for his curiosity and willingness to see the potential in this work, to open the door to someone not on the tenure track, and to continue a relationship that started many years ago at Bard College. And to Greg Britton, Adriahna Conway, the team at Johns Hopkins, and the anonymous reviewers who took the time to read this manuscript during the height of the pandemic. The kindness and interest of strangers should never be underestimated.

Without the work of scholars such as Craig Wilder, Christina Sharpe, Sandy Grande, Myra Armstead, Leanne Betasamosake Simpson, Eve Tuck, Edouard Glissant, Frantz Fanon, K. W. Yang, Kristie Dotson, Papel Machete, Kique Cubero Garcia, Comedores Sociales, CDPEC, and the Centros de Apoyo Mutuales de Borinquen, to name only a few, I would not have been able to think the thoughts and do the work that fills these pages.

I hope I have, in some small way, contributed to the ecosystem and diversity of ideas that their works represent.

Finally, yet most importantly, I am grateful to my comrade in life and love, Jacob Leibovitch, without whose support I could not have written this. And to my Idahlia, who makes the world anew each day.

Bibliography

Act of July 2, 1862 (Morrill Act). Public Law 37-108, 12 Stat. 503.

Act of August 30, 1890 (Agricultural College Act of 1890). Public Law 51-841, 26 Stat. 417.

An Act Relating to the Social Studies Curriculum in Public Schools. Texas House Bill 3979, passed June 15, 2021, effective September 1, 2021, https://legiscan.com/TX/text/HB3979/2021.

AFT [American Federation of Teachers] Higher Education. 2010. *Promoting Racial and Ethnic Diversity in the Faculty: What Higher Education Unions Can Do*, https://www.aft.org/sites/default/files/facultydiversity0310.pdf.

Ahmed, Sara. 2012. *On Being Included: Racism and Diversity in Institutional Life*. Duke University Press.

———. 2019. *What's the Use? On the Uses of Use*. Duke University Press.

Alegría, Ricardo. 1978. "El Instituto de Cultura Puertorriqueña, 1955–1973: 18 años contribuyendo a fortalecer nuestra conciencia nacional." *Instituto de Cultura Puertorriqueña*, vol. 1.

Ambroise, Jason R., and Sabine Broeck, eds. 2015. *Black Knowledges / Black Struggles: Essays in Critical Epistemology*. Liverpool University Press.

Andrew W. Mellon Foundation. "The Monuments Project: Our Commemorative Landscape." https://mellon.org/initiatives/monuments/.

Anzaldúa, Gloria. 2012. *Borderlands: La Frontera—The New Mestiza*. 4th ed. Aunt Lute Books.

Bailey, Alison. 2014. "The Unlevel Knowing Field: An Engagement with Kristie Dotson's Third-Order Epistemic Oppression." In *Social Epistemology Review and Reply Collective* 3, no. 10, ed. James H. Collier, 62–68.

Bard College. *The Montgomery Place Campus at Bard College*. https://www.bard.edu/montgomeryplace/.

Bartunek, Jean M., and Michael K. Moch. 1987. "First-Order, Second-Order, and Third-Order Change and Organization Development Interventions: A Cognitive Approach." *Journal of Applied Behavioral Science* 23, no. 4: 483–500, https://doi.org/10.1177/002188638702300404.

Bartunek, Jean M., and Michael K. Moch. 1994. "Third-Order Organizational Change and the Western Mystical Tradition." *Journal of Organizational*

Change Management 7(1): 24-41, https://doi.org/10.1108
/09534819410050795.

Bhambra, Gurminder K., et al., eds. 2018. *Decolonising the University*. Pluto
Press, 2018.

Booysen, Susan, ed. 2016. *Fees Must Fall: Student Revolt, Decolonisation and
Governance in South Africa*. Wits University Press, https://doi.org/10.18772
/22016109858.

Brophy, Alfred. 2016. "Debating Slavery and Empire in the Washington
College Literary Societies." *Washington and Lee Journal of Civil Rights and
Social Justice* 22, no. 2: 273, https://scholarlycommons.law.wlu.edu/crsj
/vol22/iss2/3.

Brown, Sarah. 2019. "Building Diverse Campuses: Four Key Questions and
Four Case Studies." *Chronicle of Higher Education*, https://www.chronicle
.com/chronicle-intelligence/report/building-diverse-campuses-4-key
-questions-and-4-case-studies.

Brown University, Community Dialogue Project: "Transformative Justice,"
https://cdp.brown.edu/programs/transformative-justice.

Burke, Lilah. 2021. "Supporting Mental Well-Being for Students of Color."
Inside Higher Ed, June 17, 2021, https://www.insidehighered.com/news
/2021/06/17/new-report-looks-practical-ways-support-mental-health
-students-color.

Calderon, Dolores. 2014. "Speaking Back to Manifest Destinies: A Land
Education–Based Approach to Critical Curriculum Inquiry." *Environmental Education Research* 20, no. 1 (January): 24–36, https://doi.org/10.1080
/13504622.2013.865114.

Carnevale, Anthony Patrick, Jeff Strohl, and Peter Schmidt. 2020. *The Merit
Myth: How Our Colleges Favor the Rich and Divide America*. New Press.

Casas, Bartolomé de las. 1992. *In Defense of the Indians: The Defense of the Most
Reverend Lord, Don Fray Bartolomé de Las Casas, of the Order of Preachers,
Late Bishop of Chiapa, against the Persecutors and Slanderers of the Peoples of
the New World Discovered across the Seas*. Trans. Stafford Poole. Northern
Illinois University Press.

Castoriadis, Cornelius. 1998. *The Imaginary Institution of Society*. Polity Press.
———. 2011. *Cornelius Castoriadis*. Hatje Cantz.

Chetty, Raj, et al. 2020. "Race and Economic Opportunity in the United
States: An Intergenerational Perspective." *Quarterly Journal of Economics*
135, no. 2 (May): 711–93, https://doi.org/10.1093/qje/qjz042.

Coates, Ta-Nehisi. 2014. "The Case for Reparations." *The Atlantic*, June 2014,
https://www.theatlantic.com/magazine/archive/2014/06/the-case-for
-reparations/361631/.

Code, Lorraine. 1987. *Epistemic Responsibility*. University Press of New England.

———. 2006. *Ecological Thinking: The Politics of Epistemic Location*. Oxford University Press.

———. 2011. *Self, Subjectivity, and the Instituted Social Imaginary*. Oxford University Press.

———. 2015. "Care, Concern, and Advocacy: Is There a Place for Epistemic Responsibility?" *Feminist Philosophy Quarterly* 1, no. 1: 1–20. https://doi.org/10.5206/fpq/2015.1.1.

Conley, Dalton. 2001. Review of William A. Darity Jr. and Samuel L. Myers, *Persistent Disparity: Race and Economic Inequality in the United States since 1945* (Edward Elgar, 1998). *Social Service Review* 75, no. 1 (March): 171–73, https://doi.org/10.1086/591889.

Cornell University and Indigenous Dispossession Project. 2021. *Debts, Ethics, and Redress: Moving Land Grab University Work Forward.* October 1, https://blogs.cornell.edu/cornelluniversityindigenousdispossession/2021/10/01/debts-ethics-and-redress-moving-land-grab-university-work-forward/.

Cornell University Library. *Willard Straight Occupation Study Guide,* compiled by Eric Kofi Acree, https://guides.library.cornell.edu/wshtakeover/home.

Cornell University Library. *Willard Straight Takeover Documents—John Henrik Clarke Africana Library*. https://africana.library.cornell.edu/willard-straight-takeover-documents/.

Cornell University Library. 2012. *Willard Straight Hall Takeover and Student Protests.* https://media.library.cornell.edu/media/Willard+Straight+Hall+Takeover+and+Student+Protests/1_aiscnmpj.

Coulthard, Glen Sean. 2014. *Red Skin, White Masks: Rejecting the Colonial Politics of Recognition*. University of Minnesota Press.

Coulthard, Glen, and Leanne Betasamosake Simpson. 2016. "Grounded Normativity / Place-Based Solidarity." *American Quarterly* 68, no. 2: 249–55, https://doi.org/10.1353/aq.2016.0038.

Darity, William A., and A. Kirsten Mullen. 2020. *From Here to Equality: Reparations for Black Americans in the Twenty-First Century*. University of North Carolina Press.

Davis, Angela. 2018. "Excellence through Diversity." University of Virginia, March 27, 2018, https://engineering.virginia.edu/about/diversity-and-engagement/excellence-through-diversity-series.

Davis, Leslie, and Richard Fry. 2019. "College Faculty Have Become More Racially and Ethnically Diverse, but Remain Far Less So than Students." *Pew Research Center,* July 31, 2019, https://www.pewresearch.org/fact-tank/2019/07/31/us-college-faculty-student-diversity/.

Day, Mark R. 2016/2018. "'Still Exploiting Him': Remembering Ishi, the 'Last Wild Indian in California.'" *Indian Country Today*, March 25, 2016, updated

September 13, 2018, https://indiancountrytoday.com/archive/still
-exploiting-him-remembering-ishi-the-last-wild-indian-in-california.

De Greiff, Pablo, ed. 2006. *The Handbook of Reparations*. Oxford University
Press.

Delgado, L. Elena, et al. 2000. "Local Histories and Global Designs: An
Interview with Walter Mignolo." *Discourse* 22, no. 3: 7–33, https://doi.org
/10.1353/dis.2000.0004.

Desai, Saahil. 2019. "The First Reparations Attempt at an American College
Comes from Its Students." *The Atlantic*, April 18, 2019. https://www
.theatlantic.com/education/archive/2019/04/why-are-georgetown
-students-paying-reparations/587443/.

Deumert, Ann. 2019. "The Mangrove; or, Moving with and beyond the
Rhizome." *Diggit Magazine*, 27 Sept. 2019, https://www.diggitmagazine
.com/column/mangrove-or-moving-and-beyond-rhizome.

Dobbin, Frank, and Alexandra Kalev. 2016. "Why Diversity Programs Fail."
Harvard Business Review, July–August 2016, https://hbr.org/2016/07/why
-diversity-programs-fail.

———. 2018. "Why Diversity Training Doesn't Work: The Challenge for
Industry and Academia." *Anthropology Now* 10, no. 2: 48–55.

Dotson, Kristie. 2011. "Tracking Epistemic Violence, Tracking Practices of
Silencing." *Hypatia* 26, no. 2: 236–57, https://doi.org/10.1111/j.1527-2001.2011
.01177.x.

———. 2014. "Conceptualizing Epistemic Oppression." *Social Epistemology*
28, no. 2: 115–38, https://doi.org/10.1080/02691728.2013.782585.

Drabinski, John E., and Marisa Parham, eds. 2015. *Theorizing Glissant: Sites and
Citations*. Rowman & Littlefield.

Du Bois, W. E. B. 1903. *The Souls of Black Folk*. Bartleby Library

———. 1999. *Darkwater: Voices from within the Veil*. Dover.

Eizenstat, Stuart E. 2019. "What Holocaust Restitution Taught Me about Slavery
Reparations." *POLITICO Magazine*, October 27, 2019, https://politico
/343jnxB.

Escobar, Arturo. 2018. *Designs for the Pluriverse: Radical Interdependence,
Autonomy, and the Making of Worlds*. Duke University Press.

Executive Office of the President. 2020. Executive Order 13950: "Combating
Race and Sex Stereotyping." 85 *Federal Register* 60683–60687 (September 28,
2020). https://www.federalregister.gov/documents/2020/09/28/2020
-21534/combating-race-and-sex-stereotyping.

Fanon, Frantz. 1982. *Black Skin, White Masks*. Trans. Charles Lam Markmann.
Grove Press.

———. 2007. *A Dying Colonialism*. Trans. Haakon Chevalier. Grove Press

Ferguson, Roderick A. 2017. *We Demand: The University and Student Protests*.
University of California Press.

Fernández, Johanna. 2020. *The Young Lords: A Radical History*. University of North Carolina Press.

Fiolio, Karl. 2014. "Psychoanalysis, Reparation, and Historical Memory." *American Imago* 71, no. 4: 417–43, https://www.jstor.org/stable/26305101.

Fricker, Miranda. 2007. *Epistemic Injustice: Power and the Ethics of Knowing*. Oxford University Press.

Gegeo, David Welchman, and Karen Ann Watson-Gegeo. 2002. "Whose Knowledge? Epistemological Collisions in Solomon Islands Community Development." *The Contemporary Pacific* 14, no. 2: 377–409, https://doi .org/10.1353/cp.2002.0046.

Georgetown University. "Georgetown Reflects on Slavery, Memory, and Reconciliation." *Georgetown University*, https://www.georgetown.edu /slavery/.

Giovanni, Robert. 2019. "Solidarity, Education and Action! Comedores Sociales: An Emerging Movement in Puerto Rico." Why Hunger, https:// whyhunger.org/wp-content/uploads/2019/07/WhyHungerFoodJustice VoicesComedoresSocialesJune2019_ENGLISH.pdf

Glissant, Edouard. 1997. *Poetics of Relation*. Trans. Betsy Wing. University of Michigan Press.

———. 2005. *Monsieur Toussaint: A Play*. Trans. J. Michael Dash and Edouard Glissant. Boulder, CO: Lynne Rienner.

Gluckman, Nell. 2019. "How the Wealthy and Well Connected Have Learned to Game the Admissions Process." *Chronicle of Higher Education*, August 2, 2019.

Goldrick-Rab, Sara, Robert Kelchen, and Jason Houle. 2019. "The Color of Student Debt: Implications of Federal Loan Program Reforms for Black Students and Historically Black Colleges and Universities." Wisconsin Hope Center, https://hope4college.com/wp-content/uploads/2018/09 /Goldrick-Rab-Kelchen-Houle-2014.pdf.

Gonzales, Michael. 2019. "'Latin Power to Latin People': The Black Panther Party's Influence on the Revolutionary Politics of the Young Lords Organization." *Journal of African American Studies* 23, no. 4 (December): 335–51, https://doi.org/10.1007/s12111-019-09439-5.

Grande, Sandy. 2004. *Red Pedagogy: Native American Social and Political Thought*. Rowman & Littlefield.

———. 2018. "Refusing the University." In *Toward What Justice? Describing Diverse Dreams of Justice in Education*, ed. Eve Tuck and K. Wayne Yang, 47–65. Routledge.

Gratz v. Bollinger. 2003. 539 U.S. 244.

Greene, Maxine. 1993. "The Passions of Pluralism: Multiculturalism and the Expanding Community." *Educational Researcher* 22, no. 1: 13–18, https:// doi.org/10.2307/1177301.

———. 1995. "Art and Imagination: Reclaiming the Sense of Possibility."
The Phi Delta Kappan 76, no. 5: 378–82, https://www.jstor.org/stable
/20405345.

Greenwood, David A. 2008. "A Critical Pedagogy of Place: From Gridlock to
Parallax." *Environmental Education Research* 14, no. 3 (June): 336–48.
https://doi.org/10.1080/13504620802190743.

Grosfoguel, Ramón. 2012. "Decolonizing Western Uni-Versalisms: Decolonial
Pluri-Versalism from Aimé Césaire to the Zapatistas." *Transmodernity:
Journal of Peripheral Cultural Production of the Luso-Hispanic World* 1, no. 3
(Spring): 88–104, https://doi.org/10.5070/T413012884.

———, ed. 2016. *Decolonizing the Westernized University: Interventions in
Philosophy of Education from Within and Without*. Lexington Books, 2016.

Grutter v. Bollinger. 2003. 539 U.S. 306.

Haack, Susan. 1991. Review of Lorraine Code, *Epistemic Responsibility*.
Canadian Journal of Philosophy, 21, no. 1 (March): 91–107, https://www
.jstor.org/stable/40231735.

Hall, Kim F. 1996. *Things of Darkness: Economies of Race and Gender in Early
Modern England*. Cornell University Press.

Hamilton, Alexander. 1788. The Federalist Papers: no. 60: "Concerning the
Power of Congress to Regulate the Election of Members," February 26,
1788, https://avalon.law.yale.edu/18th_century/fed60.asp.

Harney, Stefano, and Fred Moten. 2013. *The Undercommons: Fugitive Planning
& Black Study*. Minor Compositions.

Harris, Leslie M., James T. Campbell, and Alfred Brody, eds. 2019. *Slavery and
the University: Histories and Legacies*. University of Georgia Press.

Hartman, Saidiya V. 2020. *Wayward Lives, Beautiful Experiments: Intimate
Histories of Riotous Black Girls, Troublesome Women, and Queer Radicals*.
W. W. Norton.

Hartman, Saidiya V., interviewed by Frank B. Wilderson. 2003. "The Position
of the Unthought." *Qui Parle* 13, no. 2 (Spring/Summer): 183–201, https://
www.jstor.org/stable/20686156.

Hartocollis, Anemona. 2017. "Long after Protests, Students Shun the University
of Missouri." *New York Times*, July 9, 2017, https://www.nytimes.com/2017
/07/09/us/university-of-missouri-enrollment-protests-fallout.html.

Harvard Law Review. 2021. Recent Cases: *Students for Fair Admissions, Inc. v.
President and Fellows of Harvard College*, 980 F.3d 157 (1st Cir., 2020),
https://harvardlawreview.org/2021/05/students-for-fair-admissions-inc-v
-president-and-fellows-of-harvard-college/.

Hefling, Kimberly, and Josh Gerstein. 2016. "Supreme Court Upholds College
Affirmative Action Program." *POLITICO*, June 23, 2016, https://politi.co
/2JEEbpo. Accessed 8 Dec. 2021.

Hurwitz, Michael. 2011. "The Impact of Legacy Status on Undergraduate
    Admissions at Elite Colleges and Universities." *Economics of Education
    Review*, 30, no. 3 (June): 480–92, https://doi.org/10.1016/j.econedurev
    .2010.12.002.

Irmscher, Christoph. 2013. *Louis Agassiz: Creator of American Science*.
    Houghton Mifflin Harcourt

Kaba, Mariame, Tamara K. Knopper, and Naomi Murakawa, 2021. *We Do This
    'Til We Free Us: Abolitionist Organizing and Transforming Justice*. Haymar-
    ket Books.

Kaiser, Cheryl, et al. 2021. "Diversity Initiatives and White Americans'
    Perceptions of Racial Victimhood." *Personality and Social Psychology
    Bulletin* 48 (6): 968-984, https://doi.org/10.1177/01461672211030391.

Kelley, Robin D. G. 2018. "Black Study, Black Struggle." *Ufahamu: A Journal
    of African Studies* 40, no. 2: 153–68, https://doi.org/10.5070/F7402040947.

Kendi, Ibram X. 2017. *Stamped from the Beginning: The Definitive History of
    Racist Ideas in America*. Bold Type Books.

———. 2018. *How to Be an Antiracist*. One World.

Khalid, Amna, and Jeffrey Snyder. "How to Fix Diversity and Equity:
    Ritualized Regimes of Political Expression Must Be Rejected." *Chronicle of
    Higher Education*, May 2021.

Klein, Melanie. 1984. *Love, Guilt and Reparation and Other Works, 1921–1945*. Free
    Press.

Knowing the Land. https://knowingtheland.edublogs.org/land-based-education
    -program/.

la paperson [K. Wayne Yang]. 2017. *A Third University Is Possible*. University of
    Minnesota Press.

Lee, John Michael, and Samaad Wes Keys. 2013. *Policy Brief: Land-Grant but
    Unequal: State One-to-One Match Funding for 1890 Land-Grant Universities*.
    Association of Public Land-Grant Universities, Office for Access and Success,
    https://www.aplu.org/library/land-grant-but-unequal-state-one-to-one
    -match-funding-for-1890-land-grant-universities. Accessed 8 Dec. 2021.

Lee, Robert, and Tristan Ahtone 2020. "Land-Grab University." *High Country
    News* 54, no. 2. March 30, 2020, https://www.landgrabu.org/.

Lee, Trymaine. 2019. "How America's Vast Racial Wealth Gap Grew: By
    Plunder." *New York Times*, August 14, 2019, https://www.nytimes.com
    /interactive/2019/08/14/magazine/racial-wealth-gap.html.

Leong, Nancy. 2013. "Racial Capitalism." *Harvard Law Review* 126, no. 8 (June):
    2153–2227.

Love, Heather. 2010. "Truth and Consequences: On Paranoid Reading and
    Reparative Reading." *Criticism* 52, no. 2: 235–41, https://www.jstor.org
    /stable/23131405.

Lowery, George. 2009. "A Campus Takeover That Symbolized an Era of Change." *Cornell Chronicle*, April 16, 2009, https://news.cornell.edu /stories/2009/04/campus-takeover-symbolized-era-change.

Maldonado-Torres, Nelson. 2016. *Outline of Ten Theses on Coloniality and Decoloniality*. Frantz Fanon Foundation.

Maloney, Catherine. 2016. "From Epistemic Responsibility to Ecological Thinking: The Importance of Advocacy for Epistemic Community." *Feminist Philosophy Quarterly* 2, no. 2: 1–13, https://doi.org/10.5206/fpq/2016.2.7.

Mangan, Katherine. 2021. "Arkansas College President Resigns After His Comments Anger Local Community." *Chronicle of Higher Education*, August 27, 2021, https://www.chronicle.com/article/arkansas-college -president-resigns-after-his-comments-anger-local-community.

Marks, Shula. 1991. Review of Robert I. Rotberg with Milton F. Shore, *The Founder: Cecil Rhodes and the Pursuit of Power* (Oxford University Press, 1988), *Africa* 61, no. 1 (January): 155–57, https://doi.org/10.2307/1160292.

Marshall, Virginia. 2019. "Removing the Veil from the 'Rights of Nature': The Dichotomy between First Nations Customary Rights and Environmental Legal Personhood." *Australian Feminist Law Journal* 45, no. 2 (July): 233–48, https://doi.org/10.1080/13200968.2019.1802154.

Mathijssen, Inge. 2018. Review of Sylvia Wynter: *On Being Human as Praxis* (Duke University Press, 2015), *PhiloSOPHIA* 8, no. 1 (Winter): 133–37, https://doi.org/10.1353/phi.2018.0007.

Mbembe, Achille. 2015. "Decolonizing Knowledge and the Question of the Archive," https://worldpece.org/content/mbembe-achille-2015 -%E2%80%9Cdecolonizing-knowledge-and-question-archive%E2%80%9D -africa-country.

———. 2016. "Decolonizing the University: New Directions." *Arts and Humanities in Higher Education* 15, no. 1 (February): 29–45, https://doi.org /10.1177/1474022215618513.

McCoy, Kate, Eve Tuck, and Marcia McKenzie, eds. 2016. *Land Education: Rethinking Pedagogies of Place from Indigenous, Postcolonial, and Decoloniz- ing Perspectives*. Routledge.

McDonnell, Jadie. 2014. "Challenging the Euro-Western Epistemological Dominance of Development through African Cosmovision" Chapter 5 of "Emerging Perspectives on 'African Development': Speaking Differently." *Counterpoints* 443: 98–116, https://www.jstor.org/stable/42982050.

Menakem, Resmaa. 2017. *My Grandmother's Hands: Racialized Trauma and the Pathway to Mending Our Hearts and Bodies*. Central Recovery Press.

Merelli, Annalisa. "The Jesuits' Plan to Compensate Their Slaves' Descen- dants Gets Reparation Wrong." *Quartz*, https://qz.com/2010943 /georgetown-and-the-jesuits-slavery-reparations-plan-falls-short/. Accessed 8 Dec. 2021.

Mignolo, Walter, and Catherine E. Walsh. 2018. *On Decoloniality: Concepts, Analytics, Praxis*. Duke University Press.

Mitchell, Nick. 2018. "Diversity." In *Keywords for African American Studies*, ed. Erica R. Edwards, Roderick A. Ferguson, and Jeffrey O. G. Ogbar, 68–74. New York University Press.

Morgan, Allison, et al. 2021. "*Socioeconomic Roots of Academic Faculty*." *SocArXiv Papers*, March 24 2021, https://doi.org/10.31235/osf.io/6wjxc.

Moten, Fred Charles. 2016. *The Poetics of the Undercommons*. Sputnik & Fizzle.

Nakamura, Brent K., and Lauren B. Edelman. 2018. "Diversity Structures as Symbolic Metrics in the Federal Courts." In *Metrics, Diversity, and Law: Papers and Proceedings of a Conference of the Research Group on Legal Diversity, May 5–6, 2016, Chicago, IL*, ed. Atinuke Adediran and Robert L. Nelson, 12–62. American Bar Foundation, https://www.americanbarfoundation.org/uploads/cms/documents/abf_metrics_diversity_and_law_volume_8_30_18.pdf.

National Science Foundation. 2018. *Doctorate Recipients from U.S. Universities 2018*, https://ncses.nsf.gov/pubs/nsf20301/data-tables#group2).

———. 2020. *Doctorate Recipients from U.S. Universities: 2020*, https://ncses.nsf.gov/pubs/nsf22300/data-tables.

Nehusi, Kimani. 2000. "The Meaning of Reparation." *Caribnet* no. 3: 31–39.

Newkirk, Pamela. 2019. *Diversity, Inc: The Failed Promise of a Billion-Dollar Business*. Bold Type Books.

Newkirk, Vann R., II. 2019. "The Great Land Robbery." *The Atlantic*, August 12, 2019, https://www.theatlantic.com/magazine/archive/2019/09/this-land-was-our-land/594742/.

Nunn, Kenneth. 2008. "Diversity as a Dead-End." *Pepperdine Law Review* 35, no. 3, https://digitalcommons.pepperdine.edu/plr/vol35/iss3/6.

Nuttall, Sarah. 2009. *Entanglement: Literary and Cultural Reflections on Post-Apartheid*. Wits University Press.

Nyamnjoh, Francis B. 2016. *#RhodesMustFall: Nibbling at Resilient Colonialism in South Africa*. Langaa RPCIG, https://doi.org/10.2307/j.ctvmd84n8.

Plato. 1979. *The Republic*. Ed. and trans. Raymond Larson. AHM.

Quijano, Aníbal. 2000. "Coloniality of Power and Eurocentrism in Latin America." *International Sociology* 15, no. 2 (June): 215–32, https://doi.org/10.1177/0268580900015002005.

———. 2014. *Aníbal Quijano: Textos de fundación*. Ed. Zulma Palermo and Pablo Quintero. Ediciones del Signo.

Ragland, David, 2019. "Reparations Are a Peace Treaty." *YES!*, August 8, https://www.yesmagazine.org/opinion/2019/08/08/slavery-reparations-peace-part1.

Rancière, Jacques. 2013. *Aisthesis: Scenes from the Aesthetic Regime of Art*. Verso Books.

Regents of the University of California v. Bakke. 1978. 438 U.S. 165.

Richardson, Troy. 2017. "Review of Decolonizing the Westernized University: Interventions in Philosophy of Education." *Philosophical Inquiry in Education* 24, no. 4: 419–24.

Robertson, Bruce. 2006. "Curiosity Cabinets, Museums, and Universities." In *Cabinet of Curiosities: Mark Dion and the University as Installation*, ed. Mark Dion and Colleen J. Sheehy, 43–54. University of Minnesota Press.

Robertson, Bruce, and Mark Meadow. 2000. "Microcosms: Objects of Knowledge." *AI and Society* 14: 223–229, https://www.academia.edu /47965989/Microcosms_Objects_of_knowledge.

Robinson, Cedric J., and Ruth Wilson Gilmore. 2019. *On Racial Capitalism, Black Internationalism, and Cultures of Resistance*, ed. H. L. T. Quan. Pluto Press.

Sedgwick, Eve Kosofsky, and Adam Frank. 2003. *Touching Feeling: Affect, Pedagogy, Performativity*. Duke University Press.

Seed, Patricia. 1995. *Ceremonies of Possession in Europe's Conquest of the New World, 1492–1640*. Cambridge University Press.

Sharpe, Christina Elizabeth. 2016. *In the Wake: On Blackness and Being*. Duke University Press.

Simpson, Leanne Betasamosake. 2017. *As We Have Always Done: Indigenous Freedom through Radical Resistance*. University of Minnesota Press.

Sloan, J. J. 1992. "Modern Campus Police: An Analysis of Their Evolution, Structure and Function." *American Journal of Police* 11, no. 2: 85–104.

Sobel, David. 2013. *Place-Based Education: Connecting Classrooms and Communities*. 2. ed, Orion Society.

Stemen, Don. 2017. *The Prison Paradox: More Incarceration Will Not Make Us Safer*. Vera Institute for Justice, July 2017, https://www.vera.org /downloads/publications/for-the-record-prison-paradox_02.pdf.

Stewart-Ambo, Theresa. 2021. "'We Can Do Better': University Leaders Speak to Tribal-University Relationships." *American Educational Research Journal* 58, no. 3 (June): 459–91, https://doi.org/10.3102/0002831220983583.

Students for Fair Admissions, Inc. v. President and Fellows of Harvard College. 2020. 980 F.3d 157. 1st Cir.

Svart, Maria. 2019. "Capitalism Isn't 'Broken'. It's Working All Too Well—and We're the Worse for It." *The Guardian*, June 12, 2019. https://www.theguardian .com/commentisfree/2019/jun/12/capitalism-isnt-broken-its-working-all -too-well-and-were-the-worse-for-it.

Swarns, Rachel L. 2019. "Is Georgetown's $400,000-a-Year Plan to Aid Slave Descendants Enough?" *New York Times*, October 30, 2019, https://www .nytimes.com/2019/10/30/us/georgetown-slavery-reparations.html.

Tatum, Beverly Daniel. 2017. *"Why Are All the Black Kids Sitting Together in the Cafeteria?": And Other Conversations about Race*. Basic Books.

Taylor, Kat. 2018. "A Message to My Fellow Overseers of Harvard." *Medium*, May 22, 2018, https://kat-taylor.medium.com/a-message-to-my-fellow -overseers-of-harvard-may-22-2018-12ea17d5d9ec.

Taylor, Keeanga-Yamahtta. 2019. *Race for Profit: How Banks and the Real Estate Industry Undermined Black Homeownership*. University of North Carolina Press.

Terrefe, Selamawit. 2016. "What Exceeds the Hold? An Interview with Christina Sharpe." *Rhizomes: Cultural Studies in Emerging Knowledge*, no. 29, https://doi.org/10.20415/rhiz/029.e06.

Tuck, Eve, and K. Wayne Yang. 2012. "Decolonization Is Not a Metaphor." *Decolonization: Indigeneity, Education, and Society 1*, no. 1: 1–40, https://jps .library.utoronto.ca/index.php/des/article/view/18630/15554

———. 2021. "La descolonización no es una metáfora," *Tabula Rasa,* no. 38: 61–111, https://doi.org/10.25058/20112742.n38.04.

Tuck, Eve, Marcia McKenzie, and Kate McCoy. 2014. Editorial: "Land Education: Indigenous, Post-Colonial, and Decolonizing Perspectives on Place and Environmental Education Research." *Environmental Education Research* 20, no. 1 (January): 1–23. https://doi.org/10.1080/13504622.2013 .877708.

United Nations, Office of the High Commissioner on Human Rights. 2005. *Basic Principles and Guidelines on the Right to a Remedy and Reparation for Victims of Gross Violations of International Human Rights Law and Serious Violations of International Humanitarian Law,* adopted as General Assembly Resolution 60–147 (December 15, 2005), https://www.ohchr.org/en /professionalinterest/pages/remedyandreparation.aspx.

US Department of Justice, Bureau of Justice Statistics 2011–12. *Campus Law Enforcement, 2011–12,* https://bjs.ojp.gov/library/publications/campus-law -enforcement-2011-12.

W. K. Kellogg Foundation. *Heal Our Communities,* https://healourcommunities .org.

Watson, R. L. 1992. Review of Robert Rotberg with Miles Shore, *The Founder: Cecil Rhodes and the Pursuit of Power* (Oxford University Press, 1988). *International Journal of African Historical Studies* 25, no. 2: 442–44, https://doi.org/10.2307/219416.

Whalen, Eamon. 2019. "A Lawsuit at Harvard Pries Open Debates about Science and Reparations." *The Nation,* November 28, 2019. https://www .thenation.com/article/archive/harvard-slavery-racism/.

Wilder, Craig Steven. 2014. *Ebony and Ivy: Race, Slavery, and the Troubled History of America's Universities*. Bloomsbury.

Wilderson, Frank B., III. 2013. *Reparations . . . Now. Vimeo,* https://vimeo.com /73991006.

Wilson, Jeffery L. 2013. "Emerging Trend: The Chief Diversity Officer Phenomenon within Higher Education." *Journal of Negro Education* 82, no. 4: 433–45. https://doi.org/10.7709/jnegroeducation.82.4.0433.

Wolfe, Patrick. 2006. "Settler Colonialism and the Elimination of the Native." *Journal of Genocide Research* 8, no. 4 (December): 387–409. https://doi .org/10.1080/14623520601056240.

Wynter, Sylvia. 1984. "The Ceremony Must Be Found: After Humanism." *Boundary* 2, 12, no. 3: 19–70, https://doi.org/10.2307/302808.

Zimmerman, Catherine. 2021. "Jesuits Pledge $100 Million in Reparations to Descendants of Enslaved People." *National Catholic Reporter*, March 17, 2021, https://www.ncronline.org/news/justice/jesuits-pledge-100-million -reparations-descendants-enslaved-people.

Index